EUROPE IN REVOLUTION

Books by John Scott

BEHIND THE URALS

DUEL FOR EUROPE

EUROPE IN REVOLUTION

EUROPE
IN
REVOLUTION

BY JOHN SCOTT

HOUGHTON MIFFLIN COMPANY · BOSTON

The Riverside Press

1945

The Riverside Press
CAMBRIDGE · MASSACHUSETTS
PRINTED IN THE U.S.A.

TO MY FATHER

Contents

Part Three
VICTORY IS NOT ENOUGH

Introduction

WORLD WAR II has cost some fifty million lives and destroyed incalculable wealth. Scores of millions of terrorized and brutalized survivors have learned to hate their enemies and suspect their friends. Many of Europe's greatest cities have been reduced to piles of rubble, under which warped, gnome-like civilians, living in pits, caves, and cellars, labored feverishly and interminably to make possible the destruction of other cities and other people. Boundaries and nations were shattered; populations uprooted, decimated, and dispersed. The structure of the Continent was shaken by a cataclysm from which no nation — even those which managed to maintain themselves in a precarious neutrality — has emerged without drastic modifications of the pattern of its existence.

Early in the history of World War II, it became apparent that this gigantic struggle of nations had become linked to a conflict of classes that became increasingly widespread and intense as the national war approached its climax. For centuries, relations between groups, classes, and even individuals, have, in Europe, been based on property. The Polish landlord's attitude toward his peasant tenant, the German businessman's attitude toward the Prussian *Junker* and the Bremen longshoreman, the French *rentier's* relations with the industrialist and the worker, were all determined by the poverty or wealth of these individuals. Property was, indeed, the rock on which the European social edifice has rested for generations. This foundation-stone was all but pulverized by the war, and, as a consequence, the social divisions erected upon it sagged and crumbled.

In occupied Europe, to the economic and social havoc brought about by the rigors of Nazi administration were added the devastation of bombings and the chaos and destruction caused by the movements of the vast armies. The systematic looting indulged in by the

Nazis, not only of private property but of whole industries and institutions, was carried on in such a manner as to make reconstruction of the original situation nearly impossible. As goods became increasingly scarce and the Nazi terror was applied with unsparing ferocity, the people were drawn closer together in a unity foisted on them by poverty and dictated to them by the law of self-preservation. Class lines were effaced among those who joined in partial or complete resistance against the invader, particularly since doing so usually involved the forfeiture of one's worldly goods. Those who did business with the conquerors and retained their property became marked off from the suffering impoverished masses. The collaborationists were the targets of a hatred that included their possessions as well as their traitorous conduct.

In Germany itself, for more than a decade, Nazi policy had forced large numbers of the petty bourgeoisie into the wage-earner's cage. The large landholders had been so severely taxed and regulated that their power as a class had been sharply curtailed. Even the big industrialists were not immune from the social ferment bubbling within the totalitarian state. Many of them were liquidated, and most of the remainder retained only the power they had acquired by becoming Nazi functionaries. Thus, within the Third Reich an irreversible loss of social and economic power took place through a process that was hastened rather than retarded by the approach of defeat.

The Allied air raids helped to complete the atomization of German society. In the air-raid shelters in Berlin, former landlords, government officials, laborers and professional men, all breathed the same musty air and lived through a common, intimate experience of panic and terror. Privileges and distinctions disappeared in the universal misfortune as vast numbers of Germans lost, not only their immovable property, but practically everything they owned. Nearly all suffered from the food shortage and were dressed in shabby, ill-fitting clothes. Those who still had apartments shared them with 'Hitler's guests,' arbitrarily chosen by the authorities.

Thus, Hitler and the war accomplished something which could hardly have been done in so short a time in any other way — destroyed, possibly permanently, the property basis for an economic and social system based on private enterprise and individual initiative. All of Europe that was under Nazi domination became not only the arena in which the Allied and Axis armies assailed each other with the lethal weapons of modern warfare, but an area of social change at an incredibly stepped-up velocity. In this way National Socialism rounded out its cycle and passed into history as one phase of the great collectivist revolution of the twentieth century.

In this revolution, which was touched off, so to speak, by the Russian Bolsheviks in 1917, National Socialism has played a perhaps negative, but, nevertheless, crucial rôle. An understanding of this revolution, its development and essence, is of fundamental importance. For, although it is difficult to determine the exact extent and direction of this revolution in the lingering haze of war, one thing seems absolutely certain: Europe cannot possibly go back to where it was in 1939 or at any time before that. A new Europe has emerged amid the shriek of bombs and the rumble of tanks: a tortured, twisted, harried Europe from which much fence-breaking and precedent-smashing are to be expected as it attempts to hack out a road to normal adjustment and stability.

Across this new Europe, from the east, falls the colossal shadow of the Soviet Union, a military power second to none, with a political ideology that inspires faith and hope in millions. The Russians know exactly what they want, and they go about getting it in a way that is systematic, efficient, and often brutally direct.

Across an ocean contracting daily with the achievements of modern science looms the United States, equally powerful and fabulously wealthy. But America is unsure of itself — divided and confused as to what it wants, and even more uncertain as to how to go about realizing its desires. The absence of a defined, workable policy toward Europe is certainly the fault of the President and the State Department, but it is also a consequence of the fact that the American people do not understand Europe, particularly the hungry, ardent, war-nurtured adolescent who is now crawling out from under the débris, and, therefore, have no idea of how to deal with it. In order to ensure a lasting peace, Americans must know what kind of Europe is practicable and what kind of Europe they prefer.

For fourteen months I have been working in Stockholm, meeting, as part of my journalistic duties, diplomats, newsmen, refugees, prompters, and renegades as well as normal people from some dozen countries on both sides. Every encounter in Sweden, every experience I had in the numerous trips I made to the neighboring countries, served to bring home to me the difficulties of communicating my impressions of the shape events were taking. In back of those events were historic occurrences and factors that have been almost completely neglected by the citizens of the country, which, for good or ill, must play a dominant rôle in the post-war world. In the following pages I have tried to make those occurrences and factors intelligible, give an account of the part of Europe I saw that stresses their relation to the present, and analyze our own position with regard to the future.

Victory has been won in Europe. But victory is not enough. Before World War II was well started, the outlines of World War III were being unmistakably traced on the chart of events and in the minds of millions of people. Ambitious leaders have attempted, more than once, to conquer and unify Europe. Every such attempt has been frustrated by a combination of powers, and in every case the victors have fallen out among themselves and new wars have ravaged the Continent. This time, a repetition of this unhappy pattern must be avoided, for the next war would be fought with weapons of such destructive power as might leave nothing of Western civilization but its ashes. The time to prevent World War III is now. The responsibility for doing so rests in great measure on the United States. The first prerequisite is an understanding of contemporary Europe.

PART
ONE

*The Revolution
of the Twentieth Century*

I

The Russian Revolution

IN THE EIGHTEENTH CENTURY, a series of revolutionary up-
heavals and changes freed western Europe from the last
shackles of feudalism and cleared the way for the age of individual
enterprise and an economy based on private profit and the hiring
of labor for wages. Government by absolute monarchs and hereditary castes yielded somewhat to the principles of democracy and
government by duly elected representatives of the people. The
theoretical right of every citizen to a share in determining by whom
he should be ruled was acknowledged as a complement to the basic
principle of equal opportunity for all.

However, in the age which had been ushered in by the slogan
of 'Liberty, Equality, and Fraternity,' new inequalities began to
show themselves as those who were most successful in amassing
wealth forged to the top and tended to monopolize positions of
prominence and power. As there had been theoreticians and
prophets who condemned the injustices and inadequacies of abso-
lutism and stimulated men to eradicate them, so in the nineteenth
century, numerous thinkers attacked the weaknesses of the reign-
ing political and economic systems and advocated various doctrines
that would eliminate them.

Foremost and most notable among them was Karl Marx, 'the
father of scientific socialism.' Submitting nineteenth-century institutions to an intense searching economic and social analysis, Marx
came to the conclusion that society would become ever more
sharply divided into two classes — the owners and the producers.
The former would become smaller in number, concentrate a steadily increasing amount of the world's wealth in their hands, and
wield greatly enlarged power over society. The latter would be-

come proportionately swollen and less and less able to control their own destiny. The differences between the two classes would be irreconcilable, the basic conflicts would become more acute, and would terminate only with the triumph of the producing class and the emergence of a society founded on the principle of the ownership of the sources of wealth by the people as a whole.

Various Socialist groups, each claiming to interpret the originator correctly, but differing from one another on many points, sprang into being and exercised a profound influence on political life the world over. Although, according to theory, Socialist revolutions were to occur first in the most highly industrialized nations, the first more or less stable embodiment of at least some of the Marxian principles took place, contrary to all expectations, in politically and economically backward Russia.

At the time of the 1917 Revolution, Russia was predominantly an agricultural country and its proletarian minority was overwhelmingly outnumbered by the peasant owners of small farms. The reasons for the occurrence of the Revolution in Russia were to be found in the stupidity, selfishness, and ineptitude of the Tsar and his administrative clique. The immediate cause of the revolutions (both in 1905 and 1917) was military defeat.

It was military defeat that weakened the authority of the Tsarist administration in 1904 and 1905 and precipitated the first revolutionary upsurge in Russia. The Government's loss of prestige was aggravated by the blundering tactics of Nicholas II and his lieutenants. An armed uprising was finally provoked by innumerable needless acts of cruelty that culminated in the wanton order to fire on the unarmed demonstration of January 9, 1905.

In 1914, an administration, ridden by corruption, favoritism, and incompetence, attempted to guide Russia through a war for which it was badly prepared economically and poorly organized. A succession of military defeats in 1916 and 1917 resulted in chaos and disorganization spreading through the civilian and military ranks. The prestige of the Government sank to a new low and insurrections broke out in the poorly supplied, ill-fed army. The failure of the Russian middle classes to produce a moderate group capable of hauling the country out of the quicksands of anarchy and chaos then made the October Revolution inevitable.

The October Revolution was a dramatic, drastic social operation that completely altered the very conditions of existence in a huge country and profoundly affected the future of the entire world. What was this revolution like? To what extent was the original theory modified in its first sustained encounter with the harsh realities of international politics and the practical difficulties of administration? How has it finally evolved and in what direction is it moving?

On October 24, 1917, over the cobbled square in front of the Winter Palace in Petrograd, charged an ill-assorted body of men — leather-coated workers, brawny Baltic sailors, and gaunt intellectuals, organized and led by a handful of Bolsheviks. They were armed with rifles, rusty sabers, and potato-masher hand grenades. They carried a red flag. Within a few hours they had accomplished their chief tasks. The telephone exchange, the railway station, the government buildings were captured. The leaders of the short-lived Provisional Government, instituted in March, 1917, fled or were arrested. Vladimir Ilyich Lenin, returned from a decade of exile, took his place at the head of the first Soviet Government.

Thus was inaugurated the era of collectivism, the most frightening, powerful, and misunderstood phenomenon of the twentieth century.

The Russian people wanted 'peace, bread, and land.' This was Lenin's immensely effective slogan. Within a few weeks the old institutions of Russia had melted away like mounds of snow beneath the blazing sun of a new ideology. Workers' committees (soviets) took over the administration of the largest country in the world. Millions of famished, lice-ridden, disillusioned Russian soldiers left the trenches and returned home — to seize the land. Workers took over the shops and factories.

The Russian Bolsheviks were Marxian Socialists. For years they had preached a doctrine in some ways reminiscent of the gospel of Jesus, a doctrine in the spirit of the Declaration of the Rights of Man. Imprisoned, exiled, feared, caricatured as bearded ogres with a bomb in either hand, they were the shock troops in the holy war against capitalism. Out of misery, naïveté, and intellectual sincerity they advocated a society in which classes and class antagonism would be banished and the State and its machinery of oppression would eventually wither away.

In this society everyone would contribute in labor according to his abilities and receive goods in accordance with his needs. Religion, 'the opium of the masses,' would vanish and money would have a place only in museums. Increasing numbers of children would be reared in institutions until the old 'bourgeois' family had disappeared. Most fundamental of all the changes, social ownership and operation of the means of production would replace private ownership.

With these as their aims, the Communists challenged the entire liberal-individualist creed of the nineteenth century. They denied the deeply rooted human traditions of respect for the home, belief in God, and the right to accumulate wealth through private initiative and buy and sell for profit. The Communists claimed to be working for a world in which no man would exploit another; where there would be freedom from want, brotherhood among men, and equality for all races and nationalities.

This program was originally designed to be put into effect on a world-wide scale, or, at least, in highly industrialized nations, the citizens of which had been trained in self-government by a long period of political democracy, nations in which the high productivity of labor would make the short working day and a high standard of living feasible for all. But insurrections in the rest of Europe were crushed. The revolution that Lenin hoped for in industrial Germany (pictured by Marx as the first Socialist country) failed to materialize. The Bolsheviks had seized power in feudal, illiterate, superstitious Russia — a country defeated in war, disorganized and rotten after decades of misrule by incompetent tsars and mad priests.

Lenin realized the incompatibility of Russia as it was and his program as it stood. He said: 'As long as Russia is a country of small, individual producers, capitalism has a firmer basis in this country than communism.' Unlike many of his successors, he realized the necessity for immediate compromise. Instead of nationalizing the land, the Soviet Government, under his leadership, socialized it, permitting the peasants to retain actual tenure. Money was not abolished and the State was not permitted to wither away. These deviations from the original plan aroused the ire of the old-school Bolsheviks, who wanted to go the whole way — to communism. Lenin denounced them for being sick with the 'disease of left infantilism.'

The new Government had barely grasped the reins of power when the Germans marched into Russia. Consternation gripped the leaders. Their choice was dire; either they had to make peace, however dishonorable or disadvantageous, or the German troops would march into Moscow and Petrograd, sweep away the Soviet régime, and crush the first workers' State. Lenin made another compromise. Overcoming the bitter opposition of virtually all his followers, he forced the Russian delegates to sign the Treaty of Brest-Litovsk. By its provisions Germany got the Ukraine and some of the richest lands in western Russia. Russia got peace.

For three years civil war raged in Russia as French, American, British, Polish, Japanese, and Czech expeditionary forces co-operated with Russian White armies in an attempt to destroy the régime whose revolutionary espousal of the abolition of class privilege and property rights earned it the enmity of all other governments. Nearly overwhelmed by internal difficulties and external attack, the new State was saved by several events. A Red Army was organized, poorly equipped, but with ten million zealous troops. Antagonism developed among the invading powers, particularly between America and Japan. The common people all over the world refused to aid in crushing the Soviet Government. French and American forces in Russia mutinied. English trade unions forced the Government to withdraw the British expeditionary forces under the threat of a general strike.

In 1921, when the smoke of battle had cleared, Russia was like a man beaten to within an inch of his life. Large portions of its territory had been torn away and vast numbers of its population killed. Factories were idle. Railroads had been destroyed. Famine and pestilence were widespread. In these circumstances, Lenin was compelled to make further compromises to speed up reconstruction. His New Economic Policy (Nep) permitted capitalist concessionaires to run some Soviet factories for profit. Peasants were encouraged to sell their products at high prices and to enlarge their farms. Money borrowed from the State Bank helped private manufacturers and merchants (Nepmen) to start in business.

Then Lenin died, leaving behind a nation of hungry workers and peasants, led by a few men with great ideas and little experience. Many of Russia's technicians, doctors, and administrators had fled or been killed. A historic mutation — a fish with scales that had turned to feathers before it had grown wings — Soviet Russia was dedicated to the principles of classless brotherhood, peace and plenty, but was still a nation of feudal-minded peasants, naked wild boys barely above savagery, grasping Nepmen and kulaks stung with the itching avarice of the *nouveau riche.*

Lenin's death in 1924 left Joseph Stalin and Leon Trotsky face to face as candidates for leadership. Trotsky was brilliant, magnetic, articulate, and insisted that world revolution was essential to the survival of Russia. Stalin, stolid, tenacious, and imperturbable, was skeptical about the possibility of world revolution and advocated building socialism in one country — Russia. The socialism of which he spoke differed from the communism of Marx and Lenin. Knowing the strength of human selfishness, he preached: 'From each according to his ability, to each according to his work.'

For several years the factions led by them were locked in a relentless struggle. Stalin was the more skillful politician and outmaneuvered Trotsky at every step. Moreover, the last great hope of the world revolutionists — the Canton Commune — collapsed in 1927. The same years witnessed the triumph of Stalin over Trotsky, and two years later, Trotsky's exile and the arrest and imprisonment of his disciples. Stalin proceeded to entrench himself as the unquestioned leader of the Communist Party and therefore of the Soviet Government. To achieve this end, he discredited and sometimes destroyed other potential leaders, in coalition with whom he had defeated Trotsky. When his position was consolidated, Stalin found himself at a historic crossroads.

A single formula had to be adapted to a multitude of foreign and domestic problems. The choices were limited. Stalin could pursue the policies of his eloquent, defeated rival and follow the star of world revolution, counting on the working classes of the capitalist countries to support Soviet Russia in an hour of need. Following the example of Napoleon, he could have himself crowned Joseph the First, re-establish private enterprise in Russia, and bid for recognition from the great powers of the world. Or else, rejecting both extremes, he could retain the basic economic elements of socialism (government ownership and the means of production) and, using world revolution only as an occasionally valuable attribute of Soviet foreign policy, concentrate on building up the economic and military might of the Soviet Union. To strengthen Russia, he would naturally not hestitate to retain or restore whatever attributes of the capitalist system served to increase the efficiency of farms, factories, and national institutions.

Stalin had passed more than three decades matching wits with Tiflis ecclesiasts, Tsarist police, and political rivals. He had learned patience, perseverance, and caution in an environment where a mistake entailed inescapable, dire penalties. The third alternative appealed to him most, since, in choosing it, he could arrange to be free for a change toward either of the others, to meet emergencies.

Stalin realized that the dynamism of his movement, its vital energy, came from the October Revolution — from the ideas of economic equality, freedom from want, national self-determination, and the goal of the resolution of class conflicts in a classless society of brothers. Like the leaders of the early Christian Church, he did not have to live up to his credo, but he was compelled to inscribe it on his banners. Like Napoleon, he did not have to practice liberty — equality — fraternity, but he was compelled to act in their name. In pursuing his middle-of-the-road policy, Stalin knew that he would face the accusing eyes of the old Bolsheviks as well as the hostility of other governments which did not realize that the Russian Revolution was becoming stabilized and restricted.

During the next twelve years, Stalin moved relentlessly forward on the road to 'socialism in one country.' Innumerable obstacles were hurdled and all internal opposition was crushed, to the enthusiastic plaudits of a few foreign onlookers and the bitter condemnation of millions. Painfully, Russia changed from a backward, agricultural country to one of the four most powerful industrial nations in the world. Small peasant holdings were welded into immense, efficient kolkhozes and sovkhozes, plowed by tractor and harvested with combines. Although thirty-five million peasants left the land to become workers, total crops increased. In the Urals and in Siberia entire new industrial districts were built. The Red Army matured from an informal body of brave fighters, led by elected officers, into an immense, mechanized monster staffed by an officer corps complete with gold braid, epaulettes, and sabers. Central bodies planned the economy of the country for years in advance.

In free state schools millions of technicians, scientists, and professional men and women were trained for their places in the Soviet economy. Socialized medicine, vacations with pay, equality of races and sexes became the rule. The ballet, the most extravagant manifestation of the dithyrambic Russian soul, flourished as never before. Soviet cinema directors, composers and writers, took their place among the best in the world.

Soviet society became stratified. The wage differential between the director of a factory and its janitor was twenty to one. Factory officials adopted piecework systems drawn up by Ford managers in Detroit, and did not hestitate to scrap old production techniques when new ones proved more efficient. Lazy workers went hungry, while stakhanovites were well-fed and clothed and received varied privileges. The family was re-established as the basic unit of society. Many nurseries and kindergartens were built, but most Soviet children were brought up in private homes and often cared for by domestic servants.

Those who opposed Stalin were dealt with as 'enemies of the people' — arrested, imprisoned, shot. Thousands of Red Army commanders were purged, along with tens of thousands of industrial administrators and party functionaries. Stalin became synonymous with the Communist Party, and the Party became the accredited and official guardian of the interests, rights, and desires of the Soviet people. In the course of the purge the old Bolsheviks — remnants of the nineteenth century, or, perhaps, heralds of the twenty-first — disappeared almost to a man. Professional politicians were replaced by engineers. The old Bolsheviks no longer ran the Soviet Union. Every major question of policy was settled by Stalin, and the country was administered by tough young patriots, many of whom were trained technicians.

Concessions were made to the Church in the interests of national unity. Sundays and Christmas were again celebrated as of old. State pharmacies sold oil for religious lamps. When Russia absorbed the Baltic States, no anti-religious measures were instituted. In 1941, both the Orthodox and Moslem churches officially supported the Soviet Government, and co-operated fully in the war effort.

History was rewritten. Ivan the Terrible and Peter the Great were revived as national heroes. Field Marshal Kutuzov and General Suvorov joined revolutionary Chapayev and Budenny as popular idols. Operas and plays about the Revolution were quietly pushed from screen and stage in favor of Pushkin, Chekhov, Shakespeare, Beaumarchais, Tolstoy. Soviet writers, cinema directors, and teachers adopted the new *mirovozrenia* (view of the world.) Marie Mishkova, Secretary of the Young Communists' League, stated it thus: 'Love of country is one of the basic things in life, and one of the most blessed. Without it a man has no place in society.'

The Stalinist Constitution of 1936 guaranteed many rights and freedoms to the Russian people. It held high the banner of a classless society. But the laws of the land provided for the strengthening of the state apparatus in order to compass its ultimate disappearance, and the solidification of Party leadership to bring about the extinction of all parties. These paradoxes were explained by the flexible Hegelian dialectic of the synthesis of opposites and the negation of negations. The *Communist Manifesto,* the Soviet gospel, continued to be read and quoted in Soviet Russia. *Das Kapital* and the works of Lenin were still taught in the schools. But to an increasing degree the credo was ossifying — was becoming a litany — believed, but not understood, much less applied literally. The functioning principles of Soviet life were: 'Work well and earn more,' 'Less talk, more work,' 'Love and defend the *Rodina* (Motherland) and the great genius, leader, and father — Joseph Stalin.'

Christianity began as a protest against the oppressive corruption of the Roman Empire and became stabilized as the Empire's official creed. It started as a revolution of slaves and poor men and developed as a great institution dominated by members of the Roman nobility. Originating in a total repudiation of the habits, customs, and beliefs of its contemporary world, Christianity reached power and equilibrium by a series of compromises with pagan rites, Greek philosophy, and Hebrew folklore. It became stabilized only after a series of bitter struggles between rivals for the monopoly of the *Word* — the credo which the Church could violate, but without which it could not live.

The French Revolution went through a similar development and the October Revolution in Russia followed the pattern. The leather-jacketed proletarian vanished as the legendary figure of the Soviet Union. Institutions, customs, and practices that the Revolution was pledged to destroy were allowed to survive and were even restored.

The material gains brought by the October Revolution to the people of Russia were enormous. The gap between Russian ideology and theories of capitalist enterprise narrowed as Russia and the capitalist nations borrowed from each other. To the world, Russia gave the first example of a planned economy which put all of its people to work. It stimulated the leaders of laggard nations to remember that a state's first obligation is to the welfare of all and not the prosperity of a few.

Some learned how to use Russian methods to promote their own selfish interests. From Russia, the first Fascist, former Socialist, Benito Mussolini, learned that a small group with a plan can take control of a disorganized country and remain in power — if it promises much, accomplishes a little, and is utterly ruthless. From the Soviet ideology which he denounced, Hitler derived a warped version. Upon the backs of a nation of believers he hoisted a Teutonic version of Russian regimentation. On a drum called fear of encirclement he beat into German minds the theory that the individual is negative — all that matters is the State.

Little by little, many of the ideas and techniques of the Russian Bolsheviks were accepted and adapted by other nations. During the nineteen-thirties five-year plans, seven-year plans, and ten-year plans appeared all over Europe. In Britain and America, Social Security Boards, Planning Commissions, and other agencies mushroomed, sometimes exact replicas of their Russian counterparts of a decade before. The idea of creating a society which would guarantee its citizens, not only freedom of speech, but freedom from want, was incorporated into the speeches of the leaders of the world's most powerful capitalist nations. The inviolable sanctity of private property was called into question throughout the world. Imperialism was subjected to attack by those who had formerly been its most ardent supporters.

In the early depression years of the thirties, when most of the world's leaders wandered aimlessly through an economic swampland, Russia sacrificed bread and lives to build factories. In the years after, when most of the world's leaders tootled a frightened prelude to the jangling, crashing symphony of World War II, Russia turned its steel into guns. Stalin pointed these guns at any nation which he believed threatened his country.

In world capital after world capital Maxim Litvinoff, properly garbed in white tie and tails, sounded a warning that fascism was preparing to strike in central Europe. Litvinoff was a stingingly witty, persuasive speaker, but his pleas for collective world security went unheeded. The world, shocked by Stalin's ruthlessness, had no reason to trust Russia, no historic perspective from which to understand her, and little trustworthy information on which to base empirical judgments.

The governments in European capitals neither believed Russian claims nor understood her position. To them, communism remained the great menace. Year after year they strove to provoke a Soviet-German war and to avoid recognizing the Soviet Union for what it was — a great, powerful country, interested, because of its geographic mass and its stabilized ideology, in maintaining peace. When the showdown came in 1938 and 1939, the gentlemen in London, spokesmen *par excellence* for the capitalistic world, refused to accept Soviet Russia and continued to hope that the October Revolution might be crushed. Said Lord Halifax to the House of Lords on December 5, 1939: 'Events have shown that the judgment of His Majesty's Government in refusing an agreement with the Soviet Government . . . was right.'

They were blind. Insurrections can be put down by force of arms, but great historic revolutions cannot be destroyed. The men of Munich could no more crush the October Revolution by defeating the Red Army than Nero could stamp out Christianity by crucifixion, than the Jesuits could destroy the Protestant Revolution by the Inquisition, or the monarchs of Europe wipe out the French Revolution by defeating Napoleon.

Reluctantly, Stalin was compelled to act to stave off a war brought on by 'capitalist encirclement' and give himself another year or two to build more tanks and planes. Lenin had made the same decision in 1918 at Brest-Litovsk. History had justified him. Germany had been defeated by other enemies. Soviet Russia survived and regained almost everything which had been sacrificed. Stalin had always thought of himself as Lenin's disciple.

By June, 1941, Stalin had prepared his country for total war. When the Germans attacked, the Russian resistance was courageous, effective, and superbly organized. To those who still contended that Stalin's Government would be overthrown at the first opportunity by those it tyrannized, the Russian people gave their own answer on the battlefields of the *Rodina.* Having had their land collectivized and their freedom limited, they fought with fanatic courage. Greater than Stalin, greater than the peasants' love for the soil, was the fury of a people defending the things they had built collectively, but in which each felt an individual pride.

Having become an ally of the democracies against Germany, Stalin made another bid for recognition. Litvinoff went to Washington and Molotov to London and Washington, to formulate a lasting agreement among the three great powers. A pact was signed providing for friendly co-operation during the war, and afterward in peace. There was a sound basis for this co-operation. Because of the extent of her territory, the richness of her resources, and the almost inexhaustible capacity of her own internal market, Soviet Russia could get along for generations without territorial expansion, without invading foreign markets. From any sane viewpoint, the Russian people merited recognition and acceptance.

Of all nations, the United States should have been the first to understand perhaps the only country in the world that equaled it in size and enterprise. Suspicion of Stalin, generated by his Asiatic impersonality, helped to prevent it. Other hindrances were old American prejudices and the antics of United States Communists dangling on the end of the Party line. As fighters against the common enemy, Russians proved to be magnificent. As post-war collaborators, they hold many of the keys to a successful peace. As people, their good points and their faults have shown through the barriers of Soviet secrecy and Western prejudice.

The two peoples in the world who indulge in the most grandiose talk and ambitious schemes are the Russian and the American. Both are capable of spells of maudlin sentimentality followed by outbursts of blazing anger. Both spend their money freely, drink hard, and argue interminably. Both are builders on a colossal scale. The United States erected mills and factories and tamed the land across a continent three thousand miles wide. Russia tried to catch up by performing the same task more quickly through a planned program that pioneer Americans would not have endured.

★ 2. RUSSIA TODAY ★

B Y 1945, SOVIET RUSSIA had changed greatly from its early days as the pioneer of the collective revolution. Many institutions outlawed in the twenties had reappeared, and many others, worshiped in the days of October, had been relegated to social museums. Its basic economic processes were similar to those in most other European countries. A State Bank issued money, backed by a reserve of gold. Together with the Industrial Bank, it furnished loans to trusts, co-operatives, and other organizations that wished to build or to expand operations. Savings banks received deposits from small holders and paid five per cent interest (the rate had to be high to induce old-fashioned Russians to keep their money in any place but their belts or their beds).

The State collected its funds from taxes, profits on state-owned industry, and customs duties. It spent money on the Army, the Navy, administrative machinery, and capital construction, operating through the commissariats of industry, transport, and agriculture according to a co-ordinated General Plan.

The ordinary worker went to a Soviet factory and was hired by a foreman who could fire him if his work was unsatisfactory. He was paid a weekly or monthly wage, according to the degree of his skill, or, more usually, according to the quantity of his production, as most Soviet workers were on piecework. The rate of pay was determined by the administration of the plant, together with the trade union, and fixed by a collective agreement.

The Soviet worker hired a flat from the city or town council, from the administration of his factory, or from a co-operative, or, in increasingly frequent cases, he built his own house. He paid a rental determined by law or by agreement. He paid a small income tax to the State and a very substantial turnover tax to the State every time he bought anything (except for a few basic articles sold at a state-compensated loss).

The Church, suppressed in the early twenties, heavily taxed, officially boycotted, and discredited by state propaganda, had come to life again and emerged into something approximating the State Church it had been before the Revolution. Even the Moslem Church came up with an unexpected speed reminiscent of Biblical miracles. One day in 1941, a gentleman named Abdul Rachman Razulev appeared in the city of Ufa, capital of the Tartar Soviet Republic, and declared himself to be the Grand Mufti, leader of all true believers of the Soviet Union. From the Soviet State he received a limousine with a chauffeur, technical facilities for the issuing of Moslem publications, and a fully equipped office. The new Grand Mufti went into business as the spiritual leader of some thirty million Soviet citizens who had been Moslems before the Revolution and many of whom were still, presumably, 'true believers.'

The motivation behind this official action was unquestionably to help the Soviet war effort, as the Grand Mufti devoted himself almost completely to exhorting the Eastern peoples of the Soviet Union to make greater sacrifices in the defense of the Motherland. However, its effect was to re-establish the Orthodox and Moslem churches under the wing of the Soviet State. The Government created a special 'Committee for Religious Affairs.' The newly reorganized Greek Orthodox Church, under its resurrected Holy Synod, together with the Moslem Church and some smaller denominations, became valuable instruments of the Soviet Government in carrying out internal policies within the Soviet Union. Furthermore, it was likely that the idea had not escaped the Soviet leaders that in dealing with Middle-Eastern countries like Iraq and Iran, as with Balkan countries like Greece, Bulgaria, and Yugoslavia, strong Moslem and Greek Orthodox churches in Russia could hardly fail to be useful.

In the early nineteen-twenties, at least among the more extreme Young Communists, the family had been declared an obsolete social institution, and great emphasis had been placed on state and cooperative nurseries and other educational institutions. By the late twenties, it was generally recognized in the Soviet Union that the family remained the basic social unit of the country. By the middle thirties, divorce and alimony laws had become as strict as they are in some parts of the United States. The divorce rate in Russia was greatly below that in most countries in western Europe. Newspapers, schools, and other educational propaganda institutions systematically urged young citizens of the Soviet Union to marry, build stable homes, and honor the 'Soviet family.'

In the Red Army, not only were pre-Revolution ranks re-established, but officers were given an authority which they had in few other armies. The Red Army officer was forbidden to carry a burden heavier than a briefcase. All packages were to be carried by orderlies or common soldiers. Iron discipline was the rule, particularly at the front, and uniforms of Soviet officers blossomed forth with epaulettes and other decorations, only less gaudy, perhaps, than the uniforms of Soviet diplomats.

In schools and from lecture platforms the population of the Soviet Union was still taught the principles of scientific socialism, but an even greater place in their education was taken by the national history of Russia. The pictures of Marx and Engels in Stalin's own conference rooms were in 1942 replaced by portraits of Suvorov and Kutuzov. The sixty-first anniversary of Karl Marx's death, which received considerable attention in leftist journals of Britain and the United States, passed without a word of mention in the Soviet press.

Patriotic devotion to Russia, to the Motherland, and loyalty to the great leader of the Motherland, Joseph Stalin, became the axioms of everyday Soviet life. Internationalism practically vanished from the everyday thoughts of the Soviet citizen. The Communist International, or Comintern, long senile, was formally dissolved on May 22, 1943, and its leader, Georg Dimitrov, of Reichstag fire fame, retired into obscurity, to turn up a year later in his native Bulgaria. Other remaining Comintern officials (many had disappeared during the purge years of 1936-37) were given various positions in the Soviet State apparatus.

In 1943, the first step was taken to make the Soviet Union eventually a commonwealth or federation of more or less sovereign states. A decree was issued in January, 1944, providing for the establishment of commissariats of foreign affairs and defense for the constituent republics of the Soviet Union. Among other things, this opened the way for a possible Soviet demand for sixteen seats instead of one at international conferences. This was foreshadowed in September, 1944, when the British in Moscow suggested that the Finnish-Soviet treaty be signed, not as an armistice, but as a peace. The Russians answered politely that in that case it would have to be ratified by all sixteen Soviet republics, which would involve considerable delay.

Overwhelming attention in the Soviet Union was devoted to the reconstruction of destroyed industries and the building of new factories from one end of the country to the other. Newspapers issued special bulletins on such accomplishments as the fulfillment of the manganese production plan by the newly liberated manganese mines in Nikopol, and the fact that by October 1, 1944, eight blast furnaces, thirty-seven open-hearth furnaces, twenty-three roller mills, and so on, had gone back into production in the liberated Ukraine.

In every way the Soviet Union had moved toward accepting the mode of life prevailing among the western European nations — in every way except one.

The one exception — and it was an extremely important one — was that in the Soviet Union the means of production and distribution remained in the hands of the State, and were operated, not for the profit of an individual or corporation, but for maximum production and maximum consumption. This one basic difference was probably more important than all the similarities put together. It made it possible for the Soviet Union to plan effectively the economy of the country and to subordinate, without difficulty, the interests of any one locality, one factory, or one mine to the fulfillment of a general economic plan. This one tremendously important difference was the legacy of the October Revolution, and there was no indication whatever in the Soviet Union of any intention or desire on the part of any group to go back again to individual or corporate ownership of the means of production.

Thus, the October Revolution, like its predecessors, had been extremist in its early stages. It had engaged in a variety of startling social, economic, and educational experiments. As the revolutionary tide receded, however, a series of compromises had been effected with the older institutions which were still generally accepted throughout the world. But it had stubbornly retained the primary idea of the collectivist revolution of the twentieth century, subordination of individual owners and productive units to the interests of the larger whole, and, as a corollary, detailed planning of the economy of the State.

Psychologically, the leaders of Russia had long since ceased to be revolutionaries. Their power was established and they were engaged in building up the country in terms of efficiency and prosperity.

Lecturing last year to the Rotary Club of a small town in Texas, I was asked what the Communist Party of a small town in Russia was like. The answer was easy. It was like the Rotary Club. The Soviet counterparts of the mayor of the American town, the director of the bank, the manager of the local grocery store, a teacher or two, four or five artisans, several farmers, were the members. Like their similars in the Rotary Club, they were chiefly occupied in building up the community and making it work, with seeing that the housewives got their groceries every day, that the currency circulation was maintained by the bank, that the schools were clean, and the streets sprinkled in dusty weather.

Russian Communists had become builders and, in a very real sense, proprietors of the society which they were building. Many of them felt exactly the same attachment and loyalty to their government-owned factory that an American or British manager feels to his firm. This was especially true because of the fact that, in many cases and with increasing frequency, the nominal owners of the British and American factories were no longer operators. The factories were run by high-salaried managers to whom the owners were stockholders, as misty and remote as any government, who often did not know the location of their own factories.

Many of these changes had taken place in the Soviet Union only after incredible internal difficulties. There was a purge in Russia in 1936-38. One result of that purge was the elimination from active leadership of hundreds of thousands of men and women who were inefficient or still adhered to the ideas of world revolution, absolute equality, and internationalism. In 1944, a prominent Soviet official said to me: 'We have had three revolutions in Russia — one in 1917, one in 1927 when we got rid of Trotsky, and one in the period between 1936 and 1938.' This was literally true. The revolution of 1936-38 was carried out against inefficiency and the failure to adjust to contemporary conditions. It was a fearful ordeal, but it left the Soviet Union stronger than it had ever been before.

In 1944, the Russians had a tremendous advantage over the other countries in Europe. They had gone through the violent stage of their collectivist revolution and then had discarded the extreme features which had proved unserviceable. With the aid of good engineers, they had put the entire State and its economy on a businesslike basis and made it produce results. The outcome was observed in the performance of the Red Army during nearly five years of war against Germany. Socialism in the Soviet Union worked.

II

The German Revolution

IN A NARROW SENSE, a revolution consists of (*a*) ousting one class from its control of wealth and power and (*b*) its replacement by another. In this narrow sense the changes in Germany during the last twelve years fulfil the conditions and satisfy the definition of the first phase of the German Revolution.

After the end of the first World War, the German people experienced economic suffering almost equal to that of the people of Russia immediately before the October Revolution. The conditions and causes of this suffering were, however, vastly different, and the reservoir of discontent broke through its banks in a very different fashion. One cause of the changes in both countries was the same — military defeat. But Germany was not a backward nation in comparison to its rivals, and its ruling clique, though short-sighted, was hardly inefficient. Fully industrialized Germany was defeated basically by Allied superiority of numbers, resources, and strategic position.

Although the German State emerged from the war in a weakened condition, it did not collapse. Several times, particularly in the early twenties, it seemed in a fair way to do so, but, bolstered by foreign loans, it managed to survive intact, and the groups that were powerful in pre-war Germany held on to their power for a while. Germany's advanced economic structure and the fact that the central administration was not ridden by the corruption and incompetence of Tsarist Russia prevented the complete disintegration of the social fabric that took place in the Russia of 1917, and saved the German ruling classes from a fate similar to that of the Tsarist nobility and bureaucracy.

All through the twenties, however, Germany remained a poverty-stricken, impotent, humiliated nation, racked by ceaseless civil and social conflict. When the crisis came in 1929, it suffered more than most European countries because the German nation was already burdened with debts and reparations which, although never paid, impeded its climb to prosperity and crippled its powers of recuperation. Inflation, chaos, and unemployment combined to weaken still further the diseased body of the German nation, and as it entered the critical thirties, it was obvious that some sort of drastic remedy would be required.

Around every large German city there had grown up Hooverville settlements known as *Laubenkolonie,* inhabited mainly by unemployed working men and office-holders who were unable to pay for the urban apartments they had formerly inhabited. Building after building in Berlin, Vienna, and other large Teutonic cities (many of them masterpieces of modern communally planned architecture) were emptied because no one could afford to pay the very modest rentals required to live in them. Construction workers could build no more houses because too many of those in existence were vacant. Unemployed and poverty-stricken, they, too, were turned out of the houses which they had helped to build and were forced to take up abode in the suburbs of the dispossessed. The inhabitants of these colonies lived in damp wooden shacks, raised a few vegetables, and went every week to the *Stampelstelle* to receive a miserably inadequate sum of unemployment insurance. These conditions prevailed for years. More clearly, perhaps, than in any other European country, it was evident in Germany that the economic machinery had broken down.

Under these circumstances it was only natural for the political parties of the extreme left to grow by leaps and bounds. Unemployed workers, students graduating from the universities into a world without prospects, storekeepers who had lost their shops, professional men without a paying clientèle — all were searching for a panacea for their distress. Many of them became convinced that communism was the solution. In the early thirties, the German Communist Party was, with the exception of the Russian, the strongest in the world. The German Communists had their own uniformed military units and a host of publications and subsidiary organizations. In 1932, they polled some six million votes.

Three groups in Germany were especially terrified by the rapid growth of communist influence. The Junkers saw themselves swept from their positions of power and influence, their vast landholdings divided, and themselves either jailed or killed. Industrialists — particularly the powerful magnates of the Rhineland districts where German heavy industry was concentrated — anticipated a similar fate. The Army officers, traditionally conservative, saw their rigid caste system and customs threatened by a revolution that would radically alter and perhaps destroy military institutions as they knew them.

With the example of Russia as a warning, they were willing to make some sacrifices to escape total destruction. In the twenties and thirties, these three groups bred and suckled the National Socialist movement in Germany. Despised and ridiculed until the late twenties, Adolf Hitler and his brown-shirted hooligans had much to offer to these hard-pressed but powerful sponsors. It was true that in many ways he, too, advocated ideas and used tactics that were not to their liking, but society as they wished it was doomed in Germany. If they were to cede any or all of their authority, it was better to yield it to a régime they had helped to create and believed they could control than to run the risk of complete annihilation.

Hitler opposed communism and was adept at lashing Germany's *kleiner Mensch* into an anti-Communist frenzy. Using lies, half-truths, invective, and hypnotic oratory, he showed himself able to persuade millions of little men in Germany to attribute the blame for their plight, not to the industrialists, *rentiers,* and profiteers whom the Communists said were responsible, but to the Jews, Bolshevik agitators, and the writers of the Treaty of Versailles. To each of his three sponsors he opened new vistas of profit and power. He promised the Army freedom from the restrictions of the Treaty of Versailles and money to rearm the country for world conquest. He offered the industrialists a foreign policy of expansion that would open up new markets and a gigantic program of rearmament which would mean good business and high profits. To the Junkers would go new jobs in an augmented Army and freedom from the fear of Communist expropriation. To all three, he promised a strong State which would smash the trade unions, destroy the radical parties, stop social strife and disorder, and put an end to strikes and agitation.

Hitler attracted growing numbers of the desperate German

people by promising full employment, national unity, and resurrection. For the pent-up violence generated by years of misery and frustration, he provided an outlet and a scapegoat. Conservative groups in France, England, and America, anxious to stem the growth of bolshevism in the second largest country on the Continent, gave him substantial aid. By 1932, the Nazis had become the second strongest party in the country, and were gaining hourly. For besides anti-Semitism and nationalism, Hitler had cleverly embodied in his program some of the concepts and aims that had proved so effective in attracting the desperate Russian masses. Parallel conditions called for Hitler to advocate some of the principles of the first collectivist revolution; in the program of 1929, for example, the Nazis proposed:

> Breaking the bonds of interest slavery.
> Abolition of all incomes unearned by work. In view of the enormous sacrifice of life and property demanded of a nation by every war, personal enrichment due to a war must be regarded as a crime against the nation. We demand, therefore, ruthless confiscation of all war gains.
> We demand nationalization of all businesses which have been up to the present formed into companies [trusts].
> We demand that all profits from wholesale trade shall be shared. With the aim of opening to every capable and industrious German the possibility of higher education and of thus obtaining advancement, the State must consider a thorough reconstruction of our national system of education.

By these demands he won the sympathetic co-operation of millions of left-thinking Germans and undermined the position of his left opponents.

In January, 1933, Hitler took power in Germany without resort to arms when the two major Marxist parties, the Social Democrats and the Communists, failed to unite effectively in fighting fascism. In power, Hitler destroyed both before they could rectify their mistake. He then went on to destroy the left wing of his own party. The blood-purge of June 30, 1934, freed him from a number of his associates who desired far-reaching social reform in Germany and who counted on the National Socialist Party to achieve it in the immediate future. At the same time the improvement of world economic conditions, plus rearmament in Germany, decreased unemployment drastically and improved the everyday life of millions of Germans. Had it not been for this fact, Hitler might have had serious trouble on his hands from disappointed Socialists in his own ranks, but he was able to point to rising employment, tranquillity in industry, and a whole program of social legislation, such as the *Kraft durch Freude* movement, which had a very wide appeal.

Having come to power largely on money from German industry, Hitler inaugurated almost immediately a series of measures which irritated industry to some degree. The first group which was displeased were those circles in German heavy industry who had gained a moderately safe position for their products in the world market, like the I. G. Farbenindustrie, and a number of wholesalers and bankers connected with them, whose exports were seriously endangered by Hitler's militarism.

On the whole, however, industry was satisfied during the early years of the Hitler régime. They took the minor inconveniences of National Socialism gracefully because class warfare in Germany had reached such a point that management felt it could maintain its position only with the aid of the Nazis. Among other things, Hitler had saved them from the full fury of revolution by introducing some Socialist elements into the German State. These elements expanded by their own inner dynamism, however, and as Germany found itself moving toward conflict with more powerful nations, as its economy became strained and creaked under the duress of heavy rearmament and later of war, they were extended and multiplied because of their superior efficiency in a tight situation. Ultimately, although in forms that were distorted by the Nazi State, the collectivist devices that were used to sustain the German war machine devoured, as fuel, much of the wealth and power of the very groups that had originally backed Hitler to forestall precisely this eventuality.

Orthodox German Communists hold that during the middle and late thirties the Nazis remained under the domination of monopoly capitalism. Certainly it is true that large concerns did expand under Naziism, particularly after the war began. It is also true that many big industrialists received administrative appointments in the state apparatus from the Nazis. On the other hand, a considerable group of German Nazis, like Hermann Göring, who previously had been lower middle-class or, in some cases simply hoboes, gained possession of large quantities of securities and became important capitalists.

Furthermore, in some cases the Nazis squeezed out monopoly capitalism, and as they grew stronger, the great private trusts became less and less free to run their businesses as they chose. Profits were limited. Exporters and importers sold to specific firms designated by the Nazis, who used the placing of orders to apply political pressure in foreign countries. Private enterprise and private competition were subordinated to the collective interests of the Nazi State as defined and interpreted by Hitler and his lieutenants. A number of new trusts sprang up, among them the huge Hermann Göring Works with about eighty per cent of its capital owned by the German State. The Hermann Göring Works became the largest single concern in Germany, and after 1939 stole and bought whole trusts and factories in Czechoslovakia, France, the Balkans, and the Lowlands. Later, it organized a special branch to operate heavy industry in the conquered lands of the East.

These new state trusts prospered and became powerful, under the protective aegis of the Nazi Party. It soon appeared that something in the nature of state capitalism was developing in Germany. The change was forcibly brought home to millions of small shopkeepers and small property-owners who found themselves forced to get jobs and become employees of state-owned and operated organizations.

These developments unquestionably increased the efficiency of Germany's economic machine, because it made it possible for the State to force all companies to give new inventions and processes even to their competitors; it enabled the Nazi leaders to plan the economy of their country and to enforce the realization of the plan upon individuals and privately owned companies that withheld consent or co-operation.

When the war started in 1939, the Nazis proceeded to force one country after another into economic serfdom to the Reich, or, as they euphemistically termed it, the New Order, or the New Europe. In this New Europe private German firms did very well, but the Hermann Göring Works and other state-owned firms did very much better. As each new country capitulated to German arms, or voluntarily crept under the wing of the German vulture, it was systematically robbed, and the Nazis and Nazi state-owned organizations received factories, fur coats, rare works of art, Riviera villas, patents and processes — in a word, whatever it pleased them to take.

But essentially the cream of the New Europe was skimmed off by the Nazi leaders. However, at the same time Hitler's New Order in Europe contained some progressive elements. Inefficient competition between companies and between countries was forbidden and economic activity planned. Frontier disputes were settled arbitrarily by the Germans, as, for example, the Transylvania dispute in August, 1940, in Vienna; and Europe's small states were permitted to fight each other only in those cases where it suited the German interests (Croats and Serbs).

A picture of eventual German economic plans for Europe was given by the President of the German Reichsbank, Doctor Walter Funk, in the German magazine *Signal* in the summer of 1944. Funk wrote as though the war were won, or at least as though the outcome were certain. In many of the statements the blurred outlines of sound economic principles were to be found:

> *Question:* What position will Germany have in the future European economic community?
>
> Within the European economic community, which will be based on absolute free will and which will work to the mutual advantage of all parties, without violating the sovereignty of the inner-European goods- and service-exchange, Germany will be the greatest buyer and seller.
>
> *Question:* You have particularly emphasized the social functions of money and mentioned the full employment of Europe as an aim. Are industrial agreements necessary in order to realize this European full employment? In this connection would Germany have to fear difficulty for its export industry?
>
> The social function of money has not been fully recognized hitherto. The aim is the economic expansion of the Continent into a real economic unity. The achievement of this aim should guarantee such advantages to its members that out of their own interest they would refrain from following short-sighted egoistic policies. In the development of industrial possibilities in Euro-

pean countries outside Germany, I do not see an obstacle to German export industry, but a desirable complement.

In the New Europe envisioned by Doctor Funk, natural resources would be exploited to the limit. Norwegian waterpower, for example, would be developed and harnessed to the non-ferrous metal industry. Primarily agricultural countries like Italy and Hungary would be virtually de-industrialized. All nations would be forbidden to engage in production of commodities which could be produced more economically elsewhere. Eventually such a Europe would have greatly increased its output. It would not have reached anywhere near the maximum of its capacity because the Germans would have wanted to make certain that the component parts of its domain could not become independent and that no combination of its subordinate states could become powerful enough to challenge it. Moreover, the lion's share of the output would go to the Germans. The lambs would get the remnants.

Thus, the architects of the New Order used basically advanced and progressive economic ideas as blocks in an edifice resting on a foundation of German national arrogance and planned from the imperial specifications of a band of degenerate megalomaniacs. Had the Germans been less conceited and more tolerant in their attitude toward the small nations of Europe; had the Nazis abstained from the vindictive cruelties they practiced in the countries they conquered; had Hitler accepted other peoples as equals and worked with them instead of over them; then a lasting European federation might have been built up around Germany. Millions of Europeans might have been willing to accept German leadership in organizing a planned Continental economy, if they had been allotted a reasonable share in its rewards and a reasonable participation in its government.

But Hitler never understood the difference between leadership and domination and never grasped the meaning of federation. He dreamed of a Europe united, not as a federation of free and sovereign states, but rather by a forced unification like that of Germany at the point of Prussian bayonets. Furthermore, his absurd racial theories antagonized every other people and made it impossible to maintain normal relations with Slavic or Latin countries. By his brutality, inhumanity, and worship of the mailed fist, Hitler alienated the sympathies which might have aided him to become the leader of a unified, organized Europe. Instead he became the tyrant. Tyrants, too, were the thousands of Nazi upstarts who had bcome the criminal but powerful leaders of German industry, transportation, and finance; and the Quislings through whom Hitler ruled the subjugated territories of his European fortress.

As a result of Hitler's abuse of what should have been the guiding principles of a federated Europe, a great proportion of the rulers of European states and the owners of European wealth were not only Nazi Party men, but frequently war criminals as well. They are being destroyed by the populations of the countries in which they tyrannized and enriched themselves or by Allied war criminal courts. Thus, to a great extent European economy has been automatically decapitated. Its owning and managing class have been eliminated without any revolutionary effort on the part of those classes which, according to Marx, should 'expropriate the expropriators.'

Not only did Hitler arouse the bitter hostility of other nations, but his policies begot strong opposition at home. Groups from the old workers' organizations maintained an unremitting if never very effective campaign against Nazi tyranny at home and abroad. Out of an illegal Rhineland Workers' Conference in 1942 came a manifesto which began:

> Gravely alarmed for the fate of our people, we Germans from the western regions of Germany, fully aware of our responsibility, have united, regardless of religious and political convictions. Overcoming many obstacles and defying all dangers, we arrived at the unanimous decision to issue the following statements to our people:
> The German people are being deliberately deceived.
> Germany approaches complete exhaustion.
> Hitler gambles with Germany's fate.

The manifesto continued with a 'program for liberation,' demanding immediate peace, the destruction of Hitler and the Nazis, arrest and punishment of German war criminals, and the return of Germany to complete democracy with improved social legislation. Illegal German newspapers, such as the *Freiheit* and the *Ruhr-Echo*

Essen, urged much the same thing, pointing out that the Allies had no designs on foreign territory and that millions all over the world would come to the aid of the Germans if they got rid of the Hitler régime before it was too late and established a free, democratic Germany.

Other elements joined the workers, particularly after it became obvious that Germany was doomed to defeat and that each battle and struggle was only plunging it deeper into the mire, condemning it to the status of a permanent outlaw among nations. From the Church, the officers' corps, and the industrialists, confirmed anti-Nazis or newly made recruits stepped forward to join the ranks of the opposition. The detailed account of this opposition and the fate it met is to be found in a later chapter.

One thing that should be stressed here is that among the innumerable difficulties that the opposition faced (difficulties so great that, at a stage of the war when most Germans were conscious that the Nazi régime was leading them to certain defeat, no serious revolt had yet developed) was the fact that, as the economic hardships the Germans had to endure increased, a great part of the distress was alleviated by the flexible institutions that grew up under the Nazis because of the collectivist seeds that were planted early in its history in response to the chaotic condition of German economy.

It is one of the theses of this book that all of Europe has been undergoing a revolution for some time now. Much as a democratic revolution began in the last half of the eighteenth century and continued to modify governments and institutions until well into the nineteenth, so the present century has been witnessing the gradual modification or drastic alteration of institutions and government along the lines of socialism or collectivism. In many ways World War I and World War II and the changes brought about by them are phases of that revolution. It is hardly a Communist revolution, although its first, most extreme expression was the October Revolution in Russia. It is a continuous process, and it is taking place in a vastly different manner from that anticipated by Karl Marx or that advocated by the earlier Communists. It is different because times have changed and conditions have changed along with them.

In Germany, this collectivist revolution was sidetracked and crisscrossed by various social and economic factors. It spiraled off into anti-Semitism and fanatic nationalism — both by-products of the attempt on the part of the great conservative elements in Germany to stop the leftward tide which by the early thirties had threatened to engulf them. It wound up in a warped, distorted state capitalism, dominated by a clique of half-demented Nazi functionaries.

But the collectivist revolution went on all the same. Even in the grotesque Nazi version, it still had enough power to help prevent German economy from cracking up quickly under the tremendous hammering of the Allies. In the long run it was probably accelerated by the Nazis. They destroyed and expropriated the old owning classes and large sections of the middle class. They pushed the working class, willy-nilly, toward the left. And, finally, with good German thoroughness, by fighting to the last ditch they set the stage in such a way that their own destruction left Germany without a ruling class, German business and industry without owners, and much of German property in the possession of an overthrown state.

III

Europe's Economic Revolution

★ I. MONEY ★

TWELVE YEARS OF NAZIISM, five of war, and two of systematic heavy bombing have caused a revolution in the economy of all Europe. Nearly every facet of the individual's relations to the means of production has been subjected to such changes that the very conception of these in the minds of men has been altered. Such fundamental axioms of the traditional European economy as the right of workers to dispose of their labor at their own free will, the use of money as a medium of exchange and the power to purchase as a function of money, the right to accumulate wealth and property and dispose of them according to law, have all been subject to extensive modification. In the last twelve years they have come close to being shattered, not only in fact, but even as guiding principles. A whole host of factors combined to bring this about in different ways in various parts of Europe.

In most of southeastern Europe, for example, by 1944 money had virtually disappeared as a medium of exchange. Slips of paper entitled farmers to exchange their agricultural products for iron, leather, textiles, tobacco, tea and coffee substitutes, and kitchen utensils. Money was sometimes used for purchasing these articles in shops, but with increasing frequency the routine transactions between groups producing different varieties of commodities were being carried on without money.

The situation was reported in detail by the Viennese economic and commercial weekly, *Sudöst Echo,* of April 14, 1944. According to its account, the situation was the result of a shortage of foodstuffs and commodities and an increasing quantity of paper money in circulation; in other words, scarcity and inflation. The ordinary machinery of distribution broke down as the peasant found that the sale of his produce did not ultimately yield the tangible goods in which he was accustomed to invest quickly whatever wealth he had. He then refused to part with his produce unless goods were offered in exchange. The situation was in many ways reminiscent of the so-called 'scissors' in the Soviet Union in the nineteen-twenties, when young Soviet industry could not supply the peasants with consumers' goods to buy with the money they received for their agricultural products.

In cities like Budapest and Bucharest, the surface appearance was unchanged. Business went on as usual. The shop windows were filled with astonishingly luxurious items of consumers' goods, but there were no customers. Prices for these articles had skyrocketed beyond the means of nearly everyone. Then, too, frequently the goods were really not for sale at all, or at any price, but simply on display. If the proprietor had sold them, his windows would have been as empty as his shelves.

To remedy the situation, Bela Jurcsek, Minister of Supplies for Hungary, proposed that compulsory delivery of goods by the peasants be combined with the right to definite allowances of industrial goods. The obligatory deliveries were to be divided into three groups and a corresponding classification of industrial goods would take place: in one class would come shoes and leather goods, in the second, textiles, and in the third, miscellaneous industrial products, fuel, and whatever else the peasant chose.

Doctor Szasz, Minister of Industry, went even further, and in a speech to Hungarian peasants about the shortage of textiles expressed his opinion that the peasants might supply their own needs. The situation was such that the Hungarian peasant was compelled to cultivate either three hundred square meters of hemp or one hundred and fifty square meters of flax. The old traditions of spinning and weaving were to be reviewed, which would mean that the peasants should be permitted to keep more wool for their personal needs. On the other hand, peasants who delivered more than fifty per cent of their shearing were to receive cloth in exchange. For delivery of twenty to fifty kilograms of wool, the peasant would receive three meters of cloth. This was especially intended to meet the demands of the small farmer. Under the shock of war and dislocation, European economy was reverting to its infantile stages. Domestic economy and barter were appearing everywhere.

In Croatia, where the circulation of paper money had soared to forty billion kuna, the direct exchange of goods had already begun to predominate. At the beginning of 1944, a complete systematization of this exchange had taken place in which state monopoly practices were combined with barter. According to the new rules, any peasant delivering more than his quota of pork, lard, cattle, milk, butter, cheese, eggs, or fowl would receive salt, tobacco, cigars, cigarettes, and matches from the State. Sugar, too, would be allotted to the peasants, usually in exchange for lard. For cattle totaling more than five hundred kilograms, the producer would receive leather soles for one pair of shoes. For cattle weighing more than five hundred kilograms, he would also receive an extra pair of soles. Again the arrangement was worked out chiefly to satisfy the peasant. Money economy was being overhauled as the result of the peasant's insistence on tangible commodities in preference to hard cash.

In Zagreb, the next logical step in the growth of barter took place. Factories were allowed by authorities to allocate portions of their output against foodstuffs. Since the peasants had previously acquired the right to exchange their produce for textiles and other goods, this supplementary provision allowed large-scale transactions to take place entirely without money. Townspeople continued to use money, but they were in a minority compared with the peasants. Moreover, the factory workers, who constituted a large percentage of the townspeople, were now trading through their factories and thus did not need much money. In fact, money remained a necessity only for civil servants and professional people. As a result, where money was being used, its abundance and worthlessness were all the more noticeable.

Barter first started on a large scale in Germany in 1942. After the fall of 1943, barter counters were common in the small shops and sometimes in the department stores of large towns and cities. Lengthy columns of personal advertisements offering household goods and clothing in exchange for similar articles appeared in the daily newspapers. The spectacle was not pleasing to the authorities. Doctor Funk, the Nazi economic chieftain, was against the practice and feared that it would upset the price structure of the country, which had been kept steady only with great difficulty. In his speeches he warned against the dangers of barter, but the practice was not formally forbidden. Instead, as gaping shortages and scarcities of every kind appeared in the Nazi economy, the practice of barter sprouted in the crevices. Increasingly, individual wealth came to mean personal possessions as money lost its utility.

After the first big raids on Berlin and other major cities, the Government was compelled to encourage barter officially because of the tremendous number of people in urgent need of goods of which the supply on hand for sale was utterly inadequate. Through the organs of the district governments (*Gauwirtschafts-kamwern*), public places were established for the exchange of goods at fixed prices. It was decreed that the prices of all articles exchanged must be determined by the official assessors or retailers who were empowered to do so.

In Berlin twenty-three shops were selected as sites for government-sanctioned barter to begin on January 23, 1944. The shops were conveniently located throughout the city — one in Colzstrasse, another in Berlin-Schönberg, still another in Charlottenburg. The retailers and functionaries who supervised the trading were forbidden to buy, sell, or barter for themselves. The shops engaging in this barter received fifteen per cent on every transaction. Nothing could be purchased for money, although an article could be obtained worth up to ten per cent more than the assessed value of the article received in exchange.

After the organization of these barter points, direct exchange of goods was not only tolerated by the authorities, but enthusiastically stimulated. In all probability, the Nazis had reached the stage where the alleviation of the hardships of vast numbers of people was more vital to their aims than safeguarding German money economy (an economy from which the authorities themselves derived considerable advantages). In any case the newspapers began to publish approving articles about these exchanges.

The *Deutsche Allgemeine Zeitung* of January 19, 1944, reported that the first woman to appear, at an early hour in the morning on the first day of official barter, had on one arm a complete set of coffee cups and on the other a suit belonging to her husband. She wanted a pair of boots for the coffee cups and a small radio set for the suit. Within a half-hour, she had made the exchanges to her satisfaction and returned to her home highly pleased.

Another anxious *hausfrau* arrived to inquire what she should bring in order to get bedclothes which she needed badly. The functionary hunted about and found a woman who was willing to exchange bedclothes for suits. The deal was consummated and both returned home. One by one others came of all ages, sizes, and sexes. They brought and took away express wagons, baby carriages, shotguns, boots, fur coats, cameras, cutlery, and plates.

In the Soviet Union during the difficult early nineteen-thirties, when consumer goods were scarce, barter was strictly forbidden, but other institutions existed which were officially sanctioned and performed very similar functions. These were the bazaars and the commission stores.

A bazaar was an Oriental market-place, usually situated just outside the center of a town. In some cities, such as Moscow, the bazaars had regular buildings like Les Halles in Paris. In new towns like Magnitogorsk, the bazaar was a bald hilltop with no buildings at all except a few kiosks. At these bazaars one could sell anything one had for as much as one could get for it. Collective farmers came to these bazaars and sold the agricultural products which were left over after their state quotas had been fulfilled. Sometimes the exchanges were made directly (that is, so many eggs for a pair of boots), but usually money was used as a medium of exchange. The militia kept a watchful eye for stolen goods and for new articles, which were not supposed to be bought and sold at the bazaars.

The commission stores were state-operated stores where one could take a new or used household appurtenance or article of clothing. The article was evaluated by an assessor. The seller then left the article at the store to be sold at the evaluated price. The store took ten per cent on a transaction for clothes, twenty-five per cent for jewelry, trinkets, works of art, and similar items.

In Russia these two institutions made it possible for goods to flow to those who needed them most at a time when there was not nearly enough new consumers' goods to supply the demand. In Germany and southeastern Europe the practice of barter developed under similar circumstances, but against a greater resistance. Its effects on people's economic habits were deep. Among other things, it forced large numbers of the bourgeoisie out of their class as shops became unprofitable and their function trivial.

★ 2. PROPERTY AND LABOR ★

EUROPE'S ECONOMIC REVOLUTION was not limited to monetary modifications. The status of private property was drastically altered as the Nazis subjected it to all sorts of decrees without precedent or legal basis. Individual ownership lost its stability as property was exposed to the arbitrary results of war and Nazi greed and oppression. The first serious weakening of the basis of private property occurred when the Nazis began their persecution of the Jews. For a whole decade, throughout Europe, with the sanction and participation of the State, the Jews were systematically robbed and despoiled. First their securities and business disappeared, then their houses and automobiles, and finally, their jewels, clothes, and personal possessions. Ultimately, this theft by the State and the Nazi Party reached a formidable total. By 1944, European Jews were fortunate if they could escape to some neutral country with their lives.

Then came bombings, which destroyed indiscriminately houses, household property of all kinds, automobiles — in short, everything. In some places, like Cologne and in some industrial suburbs like Siemenstadt in Berlin, everyone in the community lost nearly everything he had. These losses were less serious, of course, in the countryside, where farmers' houses were seldom destroyed by bombs, but among the urban and industrial population the losses were overwhelming and utterly irreplaceable. At the beginning of the bombings, the Nazi State made a pretense of compensating citizens who had lost their property. This virtually ceased by the beginning of 1944. By the end of 1944, it was no longer talked about. The only thing done was to provide those who had been completely bombed out with one knife, fork, spoon, cup, one pair of shoes and suit of clothes, if possible.

Since workers had to have some sort of shelter, they were often removed to other districts and supplied with crude prefabricated houses and wooden tents. Another measure made existence possible for those who had been bombed out, not at the expense of the

State, but of other citizens. The shelterless were provided with slips of paper classifying them as 'Hitler's guests.' These could then impose their presence on some one who was more fortunate than they and demand an equal share of whatever possessions had been left to their involuntary host. Hitler's guests would argue that, since they had lost their property through no fault of their own, but because of the communal disasters of war, they were entitled to equal shares of whatever remained.

Ultimately the chaos and ill-feeling that were created by these conditions made an even more drastic step necessary. In order to make sure that distribution of rooms in Germany would be carried out according to the best interests of Greater Germany, the distribution of all living space was given to the National Socialist Party. A decree to this effect was published in the *Dresdner Zeitung* for April 30, 1944. No one in Germany could now properly call his home or private apartment 'his own.'

Throughout the period of the war, in Germany factories and shops were frequently confiscated from private owners if it was considered that they were not being utilized to the best interests of the German war effort. Sometimes this confiscation was achieved by an act of law, sometimes it was done by the Nazi Party sending a representative authorized to dispose of industrial property and equipment in the best interests of the State. In Hamburg, after the great raids in July, 1943, high Nazi officials arrived from Berlin and arbitrarily denuded some damaged plants of all their equipment in order to restore production as soon as possible in other plants not so seriously damaged. Questions of property rights and reimbursements were waved aside to be taken up at some indefinite time in the future, perhaps after the war.

In the occupied countries, tremendous changes occurred in the structure of financial and economic institutions. Large German concerns such as I. G. Farbenindustrie, Krupp, the Hermann Göring Works, absorbed entire industries. This absorption was sometimes done by direct confiscation. For example, the Polish Steel Works, state forests, the port of Gdynia, were all simply confiscated and divided up among German firms, particularly the favored Hermann Göring Works. In similar ways millions of acres of Polish land, livestock, coal mines, were simply taken over, with all gold and foreign assets. This was done not only in Poland, but in many other countries as well.

Big German banks acquired other banks and financial holdings. Interlocked companies were created, partly financed by German capital and partly by capital from occupied territories, usually to the disadvantage of the non-German partner. Thus, I. G. Farbenindustrie and S. A. Francoleur (French Dyes Industry) became interlocked and numerous mixed German-Rumanian firms were created. In occupied and satellite countries, branches, agencies, and so-called 'daughter companies' of powerful German business concerns appeared to suck any profits back into the German vortex. Intense political pressure was applied to bring about the compulsory confiscation of foreign industry by German cartels so that the Nazis could regulate production and sales.

The aim of the Nazis throughout was to secure a maximum degree of control over all key industries, with a minimum expenditure of German capital. In general, the scheme was to draw into the network of Germany's powerful banking system and her great industrial combines all the major banking institutions and important industrial concerns of non-German countries. Outstanding examples were the Deutsche Bank and the Dresdner Bank, which by a widespread extension of control acquired powerful banking interests and holdings in all occupied countries and even in satellite countries. The most notable of the immense German concerns which expanded directly were the Hermann Göring Works, I. G. Farbenindustrie, Kontinentale Oel, AEG, Krupp, and Siemens, which to a large extent controlled heavy industry and the production of chemicals and mineral oil in Continental Europe, and within whose ring were to be found the great bulk of those metallurgical and chemical industries which formed the essential foundations of military power.

The Hermann Göring Works was founded in 1937, with a capital of only five million Reichsmarks, but in late 1944 had a capital of four billion Reichsmarks, and was the greatest and most powerful organization that Europe had ever known. It was originally started for the exploitation of low-grade iron ore in the Reich, but was soon extended to cover the production within the Reich of steel, machinery, and transport equipment. By 1938, its capital had increased to four hundred million Reichsmarks. During subsequent years its tentacles stretched not only far and wide within the confines of the German Reich itself, but into every country of the European Continent. In Austria nine big concerns were absorbed, and in Czechoslovakia the Skoda Works, the Brünner Arms Factory, and various iron and lignite interests were taken over. In Poland the concern acted as trustee for all Silesian heavy industries and took over various mining interests. In Rumania iron mines and steel works, accounting for four-fifths of Rumanian steel output, together with various important subsidiaries, were taken over by the Hermann Göring Works. Throughout Yugoslavia, Norway, France, and Belgium this vast organization spread like some parasitic monster, ingesting iron mines and smelting works, and absorbing whole industries. The concern also spread eastward, for it was arranged that the Göring *Werke im Osten* should take over certain industries in occupied Russian territory. As a first step, the iron workings of Krivoi Rog and the manganese deposits near Nikopol were incorporated.

I. G. Farbenindustrie, like the Hermann Göring Works, was a giant trust operated for the purpose of securing Germany's economic control of Europe. Ever since 1933, it had done noteworthy service in the furtherance of Nazi policies. It was originally founded in 1925, with a capital of 646,000,000 Reichsmarks, as a loosely knit association of six German chemical firms, mainly interested in drugs and dyestuffs. By July, 1942, its share capital had been expanded to 1,400,000,000 Reichsmarks and by 1944 its network was spread all over Europe.

One great aim of this all-inclusive German penetration of the Continent was stated by Göring in 1942: 'As regards the satisfaction of hunger and nutrition in general, the German people come first and foremost. I am in favor of the territories we have taken under our protection and those we have conquered not suffering hunger. But if, as a result of enemy action, difficulties of nutrition arise, then I want everyone to know this — if there must be hunger, it must under no circumstances be in Germany. Henceforth, one thing must be adhered to in all circumstances, namely, that the German workers and foreign workers laboring in Germany are to be given priority and precedence.'

As a result of this German incorporation of European wealth into its own body, the efficiency of the Nazi war economy was increased and its staying power enormously augmented. Tremendous clearing debts were established in Germany's favor which will remain as a vexing hangover after the war. Most important of all, perhaps, it resulted in a complete change in the structure and ownership of industrial property throughout Europe. Former owners of productive assets — money, real estate, businesses, agencies, securities — found themselves in much the same plight as those who had never had anything. Their property either had been completely destroyed by bombs and shells, fire and pillage, or else had been confiscated and become the property of the Nazi State or one of its subsidiaries. In either case there was little chance of ever getting it back.

As the Nazi tide ebbed, the governments of liberated countries discovered their economy to be saturated with Nazi ownership. Measures similar to those taken by the Nazis but opposite in effect had to be decreed, and as the property dried, it was discovered to be virtually ownerless. In Yugoslavia, for example, on November 24, 1944, the Vetchi, or parliament, decided on 'the turning over to the State of all property of the enemies of the people.' This decision provided for the confiscation of all property of the German State or of German citizens presently on Yugoslavian territory, and also all personal property of all Germans with the exception of those who had fought in the ranks of the people's liberation army and its auxiliary units. Exception was also made apparently for property of Germans who were citizens of neutral countries. The decision further stated that the property of people who during the occupation were forcibly deported by the enemy, or who departed of their own volition, goes into the custody of the State. The State treats this property simply as a custodian until the ultimate invesigations as to its proper ownership can be carried out.

According to this law, the State in Yugoslavia is to inherit a very considerable portion of the property in the country, because most valuable industrial properties were taken over by the German State or German firms, a large part of the rest remained in the hands of local citizens who did business with the Germans, were branded as Quislings, and were liquidated by their liberated fellow countrymen if they had not hastened to join the retreating German armies. Personal property will be affected to a lesser degree, but certainly many small businesses will become the property of the State as a result of this law. Similar laws are being enforced in Greece, Poland, and many of the western European liberated countries.

All over Europe, too, measures adopted by the Nazis remained, simply out of inertia and because their repeal would create additional confusion or dislocation. Often similar measures were passed as the only conceivable ones to ameliorate hardships or solve parallel wartime urgencies. Thus, nearly everywhere in Europe, housing has become subject to requisitions that spare neither the highest nor the lowest.

When I was last in Finland, in October, 1944, I visited the home of General Kekoni, chief of Finland's state tobacco monopoly, major general of the Army, and chief of the State Information Bureau. He had a largish apartment well-furnished and partly empty, because one son had fallen in the Winter War and his daughter was busy in the Lottas, or Finnish WACS. One fine day the Helsinki city housing commission sent several people with an order entitling them to live in some of Kekoni's rooms. Kekoni telephoned the Minister of Internal Affairs, Hillilae, a good friend of his, who told him regretfully that he could do absolutely nothing. No exceptions could be made. The demobilized Finnish Army was coming home and had to have rooms to live in. There was no redress. Others, more provident, moved distant cousins, aunts, and friends into their apartments before the State got around to allotting them to complete strangers, but the effect was virtually the same. With very few exceptions in Finland, no one can have more than one room per member of his family.

Perhaps the greatest disruption in the relations of the individual to his community and the means of production was caused by the ruthless Nazi conscription of labor power. In Germany itself a major transformation took place as the result of the attempted integration of a tremendous number of foreign workers into the economy. At the end of January, 1945, it is probable that there were some eight million foreign workers in the Germany of 1937 frontiers, some twelve million in 'Greater Germany.'

As early as the spring of 1942, Sauckel, the newly appointed

German Controller of Labor, stated that Germany was faced with the greatest labor problem of all time. Subsequently, many catastrophes occurred to intensify difficulties. The Wehrmacht suffered crippling losses in men and matériel in Russia and also in the Mediterranean and in the West. The need for replacements became urgent at a time when, owing to the growing strength of the United Nations, the general commitments of the Reich were increased. On January 27, 1943, total mobilization within the Reich of all men between the ages of sixteen and sixty-five and women between seventeen and forty-five for compulsory labor was decreed, in order to release 'essential' workers for the fighting services. This compulsory mobilization of women was the first large-scale official departure from the Nazi ideological tenet that women should be kept in the home. German women, however, apparently found numerous means of obeying the tenet and avoiding the decree, since the first six months of its application yielded only some three hundred thousand, a figure far below the potential. It was generally admitted that inducting 'essential' workers was bound to lead to a considerable lowering of productive efficiency. In the autumn of 1943, Speer, the Minister for Armaments and War Production, demanded still more ruthless mobilization of labor in order to provide at least another one hundred thousand workers. In the circumstances, it was obvious that desperate drives would be made to harness foreign labor to the Nazi chariot.

Up to the middle of 1942, open compulsion and mass deportation had been used to recruit foreign labor, chiefly in eastern Europe among the so-called 'inferior races.' In the western occupied countries the Germans had magnanimously restricted themselves to propaganda and various forms of indirect pressure, except for Norway and the Netherlands, which, like Poland, had been subjected to labor conscription. This policy was abruptly terminated by Sauckel's decree of August 22, 1942, when all pretense of 'voluntary' recruitment was abandoned and the German labor authorities were given wide powers of compulsion. Henceforth, according to the decree, all available labor in territories occupied by the German armed forces, in so far as they were under German administration, must be used primarily to satisfy the requirements of the war machine within the Reich. The application of this principle varied from the brutal compulsions adopted in eastern Europe to near laxity in Denmark where some unemployment actually existed. On the whole, however, enforcement was complete and merciless.

In Belgium, for example, by an order of the German military commander of Belgium and northern France, dated July 10, 1942, all men between the ages of twenty-one and thirty-five became subject to conscription for work in Germany. Workers unable to prove their employment to be of importance to the Reich could, at any time, find themselves transferred to such work in their own country or deported to work in other occupied territory or in Germany. All unemployed workers — and as a result of Nazi economic policy in Belgium there was an increase in unemployment — were forced to accept work in Germany or risk having their relief cards withdrawn and facing, in consequence, destitution and starvation. A similar alternative confronted those who failed to comply with the orders of the Nazi manpower chiefs. Transportations and deportations were carried out on a large scale and some four hundred thousand Belgian workers were requisitioned and sent to Germany and elsewhere.

In France, the Germans were aided by the Vichy Government in their exactions of forced labor. Until shortly before the extended occupation in November, 1942, there was still a volunteer element in the recruitment from France. On September 4, 1942, however, a French law was passed governing conscription. By November the voluntary element had disappeared. By March, 1943, a series of decrees issued by Vichy indicated that the collaborationist Government had thrown off all restraints in its attempt to force all French workers to meet German demand. Increasing resistance was met by the most violent methods. No exact figures for the number of French workers in the Reich are available, but it seems probable that the total of skilled and unskilled men and women amounted to roughly 500,000, in addition to over 750,000 prisoners of war.

Laval openly collaborated with the Germans and gave every encouragement to the drafting to Germany of complete teams of workers and technicians from French factories, while the Germans themselves resorted to various drastic measures for rounding up all available labor. In France, as in Belgium, no able-bodied individual was safe from this form of persecution and there was no legal redress. European civilians trembled in fear of 'roundups,' much as Africans must have dreaded, at one time, the appearance of the slave ship.

The situation in Holland was described by a pastoral letter of the Dutch Roman Catholic bishops, read in all Catholic churches in the Netherlands on May 16, 1943: 'Greater than the privations, which assume in many cases the character of dire want, is the suffering caused by deportation and enforced employment abroad. Now the limit has been reached. All able-bodied men who can be spared are deported. This is deportation on a larger scale than the Christian world has ever known.' The reading of this letter followed the general strike declared throughout Holland in resistance to new German measures of internment and deportation and the imposition of martial law as a counter-measure.

Lest such measures be thought wanton and unregulated, the guiding principle of Germany's foreign labor policy was explained by Sauckel when he visited Brussels on January 14, 1943. He claimed that Germany had the absolute right and even the duty to mobilize Europe in the same measure that she was sacrificing her own blood.

The total number of foreign workers within the 1939 boundaries of Germany, including both civilians and employed prisoners of war, had climbed by the autumn of 1943 to near seven million. They formed about one-fifth of the total number of gainfully employed persons, and in certain sections of the armament industry accounted for two-thirds or more of the workers employed. Poles and Russians, deported wholesale from their own countries, were the biggest groups numerically, but a large proportion of the skilled workers came from France, Belgium, and the Netherlands. The satellite countries also were called upon to supply their quota of skilled workers to keep the wheels of German industry turning.

In addition to deporting labor to Germany, the Nazis made great use of forced labor in the occupied countries for local essential industry, agriculture, and the building of fortifications. In Norway, for example, it suited the Nazis best to keep conscripted Norwegian workers in their own country and there was no large-scale deportation to the Reich. Forced labor from any country was liable to be employed in any of the occupied countries. Thus, men in the Netherlands could be put to work on fortifications, either in their own country or in another conquered territory. Russians and Danes were employed in Norway. France had Belgian factory workers and several thousand Russian miners.

While the Germans were forced by acute shortage of manpower to employ foreign labor on an extensive scale, this could not be done without risk and without expense. It opened the way to sabotage and revolt. The employment in the Reich of forced labor, not in thousands but in millions, created a grave potential danger for the Nazis. Extensive precautions had to be taken against this menace.

An interesting sidelight on Nazi methods is provided by the fact that remittances sent home by foreign workers in Germany were credited in Reichsmarks to the clearing account of the country from which they came. If the recipient at home wanted to buy anything, he or she had it debited by the local bank in local currency which was spent on local goods. Thus, the occupied countries provided, not only the worker who was sent to Germany, but actually had to pay part of his wages.

Thus, in the period of reconstruction, when Europe will be faced with economic hardships of every kind, it will find ready to hand, so to speak, methods which have taken root in the soil of war and chaos. It seems highly unlikely that short cuts around money will not be devised when the destitute and impoverished people of Europe have to be fed and clothed. New and different labor relations will probably have to function in the difficult task of reconstructing the devastated areas of the Continent. Control of housing will doubtless continue into the indefinite period of shortage that confronts all of Europe.

Particularly, the end of the war found the ownership of business and industry in a condition of irremediable confusion. Former owners who had become involved with the Nazis have been eliminated by their own population. Former owners who have been driven out by the Nazis and have fled to America, where they sat out the war, will stand little chance of coming home and reclaiming property. The Nazi owners, indeed the entire Nazi clique, which stood at the head of Europe's industrial and economic machine, has been swept away and destroyed by victorious Allied armies and by the populations of their own countries.

In this way there is really today no legitimate claimant to much of Europe's economic wealth. Millions of Europeans consider its nationalization or socialization a most natural and obvious measure. This is what is being done, as I am writing, with mines, factories, banks, and insurance companies in France. It is a step in the direction of socialism. It is a part of the European revolution of the twentieth century, and it has been brought about directly by the war.

IV

The Communist Parties of Europe

A GREAT NUMBER OF PEOPLE who formerly had a fanatic fear of Bolshevik Russia have had their trepidation allayed by the events of the last few years. They have discovered that the Russia of today is vastly different from the country that emerged from the last war and the October Revolution. If a historical change occurs over a period of twenty years, it often takes people another twenty to realize that it has happened. Some who have lost their anxiety about Russia, however, have transferred it to the Communists of the other countries, without realizing that a parallel change has taken place in the orientation and status of communism the world over.

Communists today sit in the governments of most liberated European countries. In France, Belgium, Finland, Greece, and Italy, Communists hold positions of responsible leadership. In most countries, perhaps by pure accident, the Ministers of Public Health are Communists. As a writer in the English periodical, *The Economist,* expressed it: 'One might almost say that Public Health has become the classic ministry of Continental communism.' The policies and attitudes of these Communists vary from country to country. In most cases there is no official, detailed Communist Party program published, but nevertheless the direction of Communist activity is usually sharply defined.

By its own account, the Communist Party of any country is supposed to be the vanguard of the working class of that country, its most active, conscious, and effective element. Orthodox Communists of the old school are dedicated to the intensification of bitter class warfare and to the struggle for the dictatorship of the proletariat as a necessary stage on the road to socialism.

Until recent years European Communists tended to be sectarian, doctrinaire, and highly disciplined. They were completely subservient to their leadership in Moscow, which passed orders down from the Communist International or Comintern, to its fifty-odd member Communist Parties. Theoretically the Communist Party of the Soviet Union was also a member of the Comintern, and should have received orders from Manuilski, Dimitroff, and other Comintern leaders. Actually, of course, it worked the other way around.

This blind obedience, this iron discipline, made the Communist Parties extremely effective. It made it possible for them to use faction politics and, by voting in a bloc, to exercise an influence out of all proportion to their numerical strength. It also resulted in disastrous stupidities, because the leadership in Moscow was often not familiar with, nor equipped to handle, local problems in foreign countries.

A glaring example which Communists dislike discussing now was the Communist Party collaboration, in some instances, with the Nazis in 1932, when Moscow believed that Naziism would break the resistance of the big bourgeoisie and then, because of its inability to stay in power, that it would open the road to revolution in Germany. As a matter of fact, this is, more or less, what happened; but it took thirteen years instead of the few weeks that the Comintern leaders in Moscow had anticipated, and involved the complete destruction of the German Communists and indescribable suffering to the German working class during these years.

Again, immediately after the signing of the Soviet-German nonaggression and friendship pacts, the war was branded by most European Communist Parties as an imperialist war. After the Polish campaign, Communist Parties in many parts of Europe supported Hitler's peace offensive and accused Britain and France of fomenting an aggressive and criminal war in the interests of imperialism. I do not believe that these Communist Parties had any concrete instructions from Moscow. War had shattered communications to a considerable degree. Over a long period, moreover, the Comintern had been gradually lessening its activity for the simple reason that Stalin had increasingly found it an embarrassment rather than an advantage to him. The foreign Communists reacted as they did because they had been schooled.

Catholic leaders have stated that if the Catholic Church has a child until he is seven, he will always be a Catholic. I have noticed that Englishmen who have gone through any one of half a dozen schools, then through Oxford or Cambridge, rarely have to be told after that what to do. They sometimes err, of course, but even when working for years in completely foreign countries out of all contact with home, they remain English and they think in terms of His Britannic Majesty.

The same thing is true of the Communists. When a young worker in a mill or mine in the Rhineland, France, or Austria joins the Communist Party, attends study classes for several years, works in committees, conferences, factions, and finally, perhaps, attends the Lenin School or University of the Workers in the West or the East in Moscow or Leningrad for a year or two, he no longer needs to be told that his chief task is to promote the survival and development of the Soviet Union, the Fatherland of the working classes of the whole world. He can get his basic information from the *Daily Mail* or the *Chicago Tribune* if necessary, but his intellectual and emotional reactions are fairly well predetermined.

This was the case in 1939. There were some exceptions, of course. Harry Pollitt, the leading Communist in England, refused point-blank to go along with his Central Committee and tell the working classes of Britain that fascism was a matter of choice, that this was an imperialist war and the working class had no part in it. As a result, Pollitt was removed from leadership and only returned to a position of responsibility after 1941.

In April, 1940, when the Germans invaded Norway, the Communist newspaper in Oslo told Norwegians to collaborate with the Germans and to avoid contact with Anglo-French militarism which was plotting in northern Europe. In northern Norway, however, two small Communist newspapers took a completely opposite line. In Denmark, Communist newspapers attacked Pollitt as a lackey of British imperialism. In France, the Communist Party urged its members to desert and not to support the war against Germany.

But in 1941, everything changed. Germany attacked the Soviet Union. The Communists the world over reacted overnight. In a great orgy of patriotic unity they threw their entire weight on the side of the governments of their countries, conservative, center, or radical, to further the effective prosecution of the war against the Nazis.

Europe's Communist Parties have become increasingly respected, more united, and considerably stronger than they were previously. During the past few years, their program, viewpoint, and strategy, have been profoundly modified as well. An interesting example is the Finnish Communist Party, which was founded in August, 1918, in the Soviet Union. At that time a White Terror ruled Finland, and, consequently, the party could not be formed on Finnish soil. During the next twenty-six years, the Finnish Communist Party was compelled to operate more or less underground and against the implacable enmity of the Finnish bourgeoisie. Its members were punished and imprisoned, but the activity of the party continued. The Finnish Communists always believed that the differences between workers and capitalists were irreconcilable. The Fascist bourgeoisie and the Fascist-oriented Social Democratic right wing always regarded the Communist Party as their most dangerous and permanent enemy.

In November, 1944, however, after the Finnish Communist Party had emerged and become legal, it issued a program calling for 'the immediate establishment of complete democracy in the country.' It demanded the elimination of the Fascists from all important national institutions and the amnesty of all Finnish anti-Fascists. In its statement on foreign policy, it advocated 'close and friendly relations, particularly with the Soviet Union, but also with other democratic countries.' Economically, it wanted 'work for everybody,' increased aid to the unemployed, higher real wages, and demanded that the cost of the war be borne by the upper and middle classes.

Thus, Finnish Communist leaders, having been in jail for nearly two decades for their convictions, had, at least temporarily, abandoned many of them. Not a word was to be found in the entire program about the 'class struggle' or the 'dictatorship of the proletariat' or the seizure of power by soviets. The demands were of a democratic, left-wing reformist nature and its whole program had undergone a startling transformation since the early twenties and even since as late as 1940.

The British Communist Party had changed to a similar degree. In 1943, in London, I sat down at a table in a fashionable restaurant with a well-dressed, dapper young man, who was a Communist Party organizer for an industrialized north country district. His wages were paid by the factory where he formerly worked as a draughtsman. His activities were not interfered with by the civil authorities. On the contrary, he was given many facilities because he devoted all of his considerable energies and most of his time to persuading the British working class to work overtime, accept economic and physical hardships, forget the awkward labor issues which tended to destroy unity, and concentrate on winning the war. By the nature of his work and by all appearances, this particular 'comrade' might have been a well-paid functionary of the Federation of British Industries.

A more general picture could be seen at a recent conference of the British Communist Party. Mr. Harry Pollitt made an opening speech expressing the well-disciplined and crusading spirit of the 'win-the-war-and-the-peace' policy of the British Communists. The emphasis was 'British' rather than 'Communist.' Propaganda was patriotic, straightforward (the use of party jargon was frowned upon), and attractively presented. The traditional picture of the long-haired Bloomsbury parlor Bolshevik had been replaced by that of the trade-union-conscious shop steward. One-third of the delegates at the conference were engineers, and miners and office workers were well represented. The Communist Party proposed to put forward thirty-two candidates at the next general election, but it was still hoping for affiliation with the Labor Party. Labor was still suspicious of 'dictation from Moscow,' but to the outsider it seemed that the advantages to labor of having the off-white sheep within the fold were more important than the disadvantages.

On November 24, 1940, Axel Larsson, leader of the Danish Communist Party, wrote: 'Germany does not think of giving up its declaration of April 9, in which it is stated among other things that the freedom of the Danish people would be respected and the independence of the country guaranteed.' After June 22, 1941, however, the Danish Communist Party became an extremely active and effective underground organization. The same Axel Larsson became one of the chief leaders of the Danish underground, and worked in harmony with conservatives and moderates. Both in Denmark and Norway, after June 22, 1941, the old Communists were invaluable to the resistance movements, because they had long experience in illegal activity. They knew how to go about organizing the publication of secret newspapers and arranging illegal meetings. The result was that while well-meaning, inexperienced Social Democrats and conservatives were frequently caught, imprisoned, and tortured, the Communists usually did their work and remained at liberty.

In Norway there was a certain amount of suspicion of the Communists, who were still not admitted to membership in the Hjemfrontledelse — the Home Front Council. This was due to the fact that the old-line Labor Party functionaries who ran the organization admitted only those who had fought the Germans from the beginning. This was necessary, they said, in order to keep spies and Nazis informers out of the organization. The Communists began fighting the Germans only after June, 1941. When these issues were discussed, the Communists pointed out that almost all the leaders of the Communist Party of Norway of the period of 1940-41 had died in the struggle since, and that it was simply bad taste to bring the matter up now. Nevertheless, some suspicion continued to exist and the Communists were not admitted into positions of leadership in the underground.

In Norway and in England, the Communist Parties are making every attempt to join the Labor Party. This is being resisted by the Labor Party leaders, because they fear the impact of a strong, highly disciplined group, skilled in factional politics, and vested with great authority because of the performance of the Red Army and of the Communist Parties themselves during the last three years. In my opinion they would do well to admit the Communists and probably will do so.

The program of the Norwegian Communist Party, or the nearest approach to it which I have been able to find, was published in a book entitled *Norges Vag till Frihet*. Its chief thesis was that 'Norway's way to freedom lies in united struggle with the patriotic active forces of the home front and the Norwegian invasion army, supported by the military force of the Allied nations.' In the period immediately after the war, the Norwegian Communists wanted the Quislings punished and their property confiscated, annihilation of all Fascist organizations, and an increase in the influence of the working class in the political and economic life of the country. Its more long-range demands included the building-up of a collective system of safety, freedom from want through increased production of consumers' goods under public control, state control of banks, and the prohibition of private profits from the manufacture of armaments. More or less the same program was being advocated by Communists in all the other occupied or liberated countries of Europe.

The Swedish Communist Party crashed through with twelve new seats in the Swedish Riksdag in the last election, thus bringing their representation up to fifteen. This increase was the result, in my opinion, in great measure, of the stupidity of the Social Democratic leadership in not permitting the Communists to have positions of responsibility. It was also unquestionably the result of the general feeling of many people in Sweden that Europe is swinging left and that further socialism is necessary and desirable in Sweden.

The German Communist Party is obviously the most difficult of the Continental Communist Parties to examine. Almost all German anti-Nazis agreed that the Communists were virtually the only ones in Germany after July, 1944, who still had some sort of illegal organization in operation. It was small, it was badly crippled, but it was still there. I talked to German Communists in Sweden, who had been back and forth many times on illegal missions to Germany. They were courageous beyond measure and they had learned a great deal in the course of the war.

In Stockholm, in the summer of 1944, the German Kulturbund was organized. In it almost all anti-Nazi groups except the monarchist were represented. The Communists made the suggestion that their eight-page magazine, *Die Politische Information,* should become the organ of the Kulturbund. They offered to place this German-language weekly at the disposal of a group in which they were far from having a majority. The more numerous Social Democrats refused. They stated that they did not wish to become associated with a magazine which was already regarded in the minds of the public as Communist. In discussing this matter with a leader of the Social Democratic Party, I pointed out that there were several hundred Social Democratic publications in Sweden, that the Swedish Social Democratic Party was the largest party in the country, had plenty of money, and that there were more Social Democratic German refugees in Sweden than Communists. Why was it, then, that the Communists had a German-language publication and the Social Democrats did not? If the Communists were going to display more initiative and work harder, of course they would seize the leadership of the German revolutionary movement, and there was nothing the Social Democrats could do except to take the initiative and work hard themselves instead of complaining about unscrupulous Communist methods.

The Social Democratic leader shrugged his shoulders helplessly: 'I know. It is quite true, but the point is this: There are fifty Communists here. They decide to start a publication. The leadership decides that every member shall give ten crowns a month for this purpose. The Communists are disciplined and obey, and they have five hundred crowns a month, which is a good beginning to cover the expenses of a small weekly publication in Sweden. We tried to do the same thing. What happened? The group unanimously voted that any arbitrarily fixed sum would be dictatorial, undemocratic, and generally intolerable. Contributions must be voluntary. The result was that we got some 115 crowns the first time, and since then nothing.'

In trying to make an opposition political movement function, discipline is an important thing, and the Communists in this respect were far ahead of most of their colleagues and competitors. In their current work in Sweden, the German Communists were well to the right of some groups of Social Democrats, but they were much better organized. Some accused the German Communists in Stockholm and elsewhere of being in constant contact with the local Soviet Legation. I doubt this very much. As I stated above, the Communists are supposed to figure out things for themselves. The way they have done it in Stockholm is largely along the following lines: The future of Germany lies in the people's movement, perhaps led by and certainly participated in by the Free German Committee now organized in Moscow. This should be taken from all layers of the population. The work of this people's movement will be to liquidate the organizations of the Nazis in Germany and get the country back again to a situation where the people will have enough to eat and somewhere to sleep. 'No talk of socialism can be tolerated until these jobs are done. It will be much easier to get the country working again on a basis of controlled *Freie*

Wirtschaft — free economy — than the dictatorship of the proletariat. Anyhow, the German people have had enough of dictatorship for a while.'

German Communists were interested in collaborating with Social Democrats to fulfill the basic aim of peace and order for Germany and to destroy the remains of National Socialism. The Communists realize that they will be far from a majority in post-war Germany and therefore seek to collaborate with the S.A.P. — a halfway party between the Social Democrats and the Communists — and also the Social Democrats themselves, on an extremely democratic basis. It is probable that this general aim of the Communists is based on concrete information from Germany to the effect that German workers today aim to try and avoid Weimar sectarianism in the labor movement, which everybody now realizes made Hitler's *Machtangriff* possible. I talked to many German Communists, but not one of them wanted to raise the slogan of the dictatorship of the proletariat in Germany. They advocated class collaboration. As their political line has changed, so their political organizational forms have also changed, and Communists have even modified their fraction discipline when working in other organizations like the Kulturbund, in order to avoid antagonism from less well-organized Social Democratic colleagues.

The basic aim of German Communists seems to be to avoid social strife in order that Germany shall be able to get back on her feet and be in a position to send the machinery and other manufactured goods necessary to the Soviet Union for the rebuilding of damage done by the Germans. Communists with whom I talked realized that this policy, if strictly enforced, might well mean dragging the German workers' standard of living down to or below that of the Russians. The Communists realize, better perhaps than others, however, that the war and bombings have brought such suffering to the German working class that the day after the armistice, peace and security will mean infinitely more than the previous high standard of living which is already forgotten now, and which they know will not return for many years, under any circumstances.

One idea which I consider of great interest, was expressed to me by one very able German Communist leader:

'Communists aim at socialism and later at communism, not because we like the sound of the words. Both communism and socialism are means to an end — the greatest good of the greatest number of people. We Communists have always believed that socialism and communism would ensure, in the best possible manner, the greatest good of the greatest number. We also believed that socialism could be achieved only by means of revolution and the dictatorship of the proletariat. These concepts were based on Marxist Leninism and Stalinism as they developed until the beginning of the present war. These ideas were correct for that time. Now, however, the situation may well have changed. Great sections of the bourgeoisie have been destroyed by Naziism, by war and by bombings. Other sections of the bourgeoisie have learned a great deal. Some sections of the bourgeoisie in Germany, for example, would be delighted today to accept socialism without any resistance. They would be only too pleased to adapt themselves to the nationalization of wealth and socialization in their own country because the example of the Soviet Union's economic and military might have persuaded these individuals that socialism works better than capitalism.

'Just as the British aristocracy accepted over a period of a couple of generations the ideas of the French Revolution and incorporated them into English life without a revolution in England, so today the bourgeoisie in many European nations may accept, even lead, socialization movements on the Continent of Europe. This is all the more probable because the bourgeoisie has lost its property in the war and bombings. It is always easier for a man to give away without regrets something he has already lost.'

These basic ideas, I believe, embody the germs of the synthesis of the collectivist revolution in Europe. Similar notions, in various degrees of articulation, are present in the minds of many progressive European political leaders today.

Communists throughout Europe aim at participation in progressive democratic governments, although unquestionably, if the interests of the Soviet Union become involved, the Communists will adapt their own policies to the defense of the Soviet Union. Although the Government of the Soviet Union does not tolerate opposition groups at all, Communists will not hesitate to oppose their own governments if they threaten the Soviet Union. The policies of the Communist Parties resemble to a certain degree the policies of the Catholic Church. In parts of the world where they are not in control, they stand up for the rights of minorities, the freedom of expression of minority opinions, collaboration, liberty, friendship. Where they have gained control, they tend to neglect the defense of the rights of minority opinions and of freedom of opposition in general.

The best-known expression of the new 'dialectic' Communist line was made by Earl Browder in a speech in New York on January 10, 1944. Browder spent a great deal of time discussing the decisions of Teheran. Said he:

'Churchill, Stalin, and Roosevelt in Teheran expressed the determination to "work together in the war and in the peace that follows." . . . The difficulties which stand in the way of such an agreement are known.

'Not so widely understood is the fact that the motive for agreement for the post-war period is equally as forceful as the motive for agreement on joint war. There is an equally strong motive that, without coalition peace, the alternative is the spread of civil wars over vast areas, culminating finally and inevitably in a new world war between nations.

'Those who have said light-heartedly that it was the pressure of Hitler that forged the Anglo-Soviet-American coalition, and that as soon as Hitler is gone, the coalition will fly apart overnight, were but shallow thinkers who underestimated the depth of the world crisis through which we have lived. Likewise they underestimated the amount of effective intelligence that has been achieved by mankind. Roosevelt, Stalin, and Churchill at Teheran were representatives of the collective intelligence of mankind facing the threatening supreme catastrophe of history and determined to avert it. . . . *Capitalism and socialism have begun to find the way to peaceful coexistence and collaboration in the same world* [my italics]. The broad over-all joint policy now agreed upon carried with it the duty jointly to work for the settlement of inner problems affecting the defeat of the Axis forces and their Quislings. A broad all-inclusive anti-Fascist democratic camp must be established in each country within which all relations are determined and problems settled by free discussion, free political association, and universal suffrage. Such a democratic camp of necessity must include Communists.'

Browder then went on to pledge that Socialist issues would not be raised either during the war or the post-war period, because they would tend to divide and weaken the democratic and progressive forces. 'Even such elementary measures as the nationalization of the banks, railroads, coal, and steel' would not be advocated because they 'would be resisted desperately by certain circles' and would not even have the 'united support of the labor movement.' Economic unity in America, he stated, would require huge foreign markets and such markets were 'unthinkable except under stable conditions, free from international or civil wars of major proportions.'

Browder then advocated the liquidation of the Communist Party as such, indicated that he had no objections to the Communists joining other parties, and renounced any desire to proceed any further toward socialism than the New Deal had already taken the United States. He was willing to work with practically anybody toward the object of winning the war and fulfilling the aims of the Teheran Conference. In many respects his program was far to the right of other non-Communist, moderate, and Socialist labor groups throughout the world, which were at the same time advocating such steps as the 'nationalization of mines, railroads, and banks.'

Communist Parties in other countries were apparently following a line similar to Browder's. The new program produced some unusual phenomena. Within the Communist Party of Italy, for example, a Catholic section was established, headed by Miggioli, the former representative of the Catholic Center in Parliament. This Catholic movement began with the slogan that Christ was the first Communist. On the anniversary of the outbreak of the first Soviet Revolution, Miggioli arranged for services in one of the churches of Naples and had an altar draped with the Red Banner bearing the hammer and sickle emblem of the Bolsheviks.

Thus, although the Communist Parties throughout the world are becoming stronger, the influence is not at all the influence that it would have been years ago when Georgi Zinoviev, collaborator of Lenin and head of the Comintern, wrote: 'Now, as we write these lines, the Third International already has as its foundation-stone three Soviet republics — Russia, Hungary, and Bavaria. But no one would be surprised if, when these lines appear in print, we had, not three, but six or more Soviet republics. In a year's time we shall already be starting to forget that a struggle for Communism was raging in Europe: for within a year the whole of Europe will be Communist.'

Within less than seventeen years after writing these lines, Zinoviev was shot by a Soviet executioner for treason against the Soviet Union. The Communist of today is a far different man. The Communist Parties of Europe have become reformist, collaborationist organizations after the pattern of the Social Democratic Parties of World War I. They speak of peaceful collaboration, of capitalism, and of maintaining stability, law, and order in Europe under a system of democratically controlled private enterprise.

But whatever the Communist Parties may do or not do in Europe, the leftward trend goes on. Infringements on individual enterprise, nationalization and socialization of industries and businesses, have been legislated in many countries by governments virtually free of Communist influence. The Communists go along with this leftward swing. They cannot allow themselves to fall too far behind the left wing of the labor movement of their countries. If they did, extreme Marxists — so-called Trotskyists — would threaten to seize the leadership of the labor movement from them, just as they threatened, some years ago in some countries, to seize it from the Social Democrats.

This the Communists realize only too well. Browder's speech caused some Swedish Communists of my acquaintance considerable anxiety. They were working along the orthodox class-struggle line trying to lay the foundation for socialism in Europe. In doing so, they were fighting in a democratic, characteristically Scandinavian style, against the right wing of the Social Democratic Party and against the big industrial and financial interests in Sweden. Then suddenly Browder made a speech about liquidating his own Communist Party. The Swedish Communists with whom I talked were not sure whether this was to be taken as a hint that they were to liquidate themselves or not.

Of course, Sweden was a neutral country and therefore the need for national solidarity to help defeat Hitler did not affect them. Most European Communists were living and working in belligerent countries, countries where the class structure had been shattered. The policies of these Communists tended increasingly toward collaboration with other groups on a broad, democratic, reformist program of national unity. Of course, all this does not preclude the ever-present possibility that the political line of European Communists may undergo a sharp, sudden alteration in the interests of Soviet foreign policy should the necessity present itself.

To estimate this possibility properly a detailed study of Soviet foreign policy is essential.

V

Russia's Three-Dimensional Foreign Policy

★ I. HISTORIC FOUNDATION
AND DEVELOPMENT ★

SOVIET FOREIGN POLICY was described by Winston Churchill as a riddle wrapped up in a mystery, inside an enigma. Stalin has repeatedly insisted that Russian foreign policy is 'clear and simple.' To most Americans, Churchill's characterization seems the more accurate of the two. Enigmatic or not, Soviet foreign policy was part of, and a major influence on, the development of the European Revolution, and will continue to be for many years.

A frequently neglected truism about Soviet foreign policy is that it is basically Russian. For several hundred years, Russia has been a large country with a high birth rate. After throwing off the 'Tartar yoke,' Russia began to expand. After Peter the Great brought Russia to the shores of the Baltic and Alexander incorporated Finland, Russian expansion proceeded largely eastward. It was a rapid expansion. Historians have calculated that Tsarist Russia increased territorially by about thirty square miles a day during the reign of Catherine the Great and by about forty-eight square miles a day during the eighteenth century. Its speed is best compared with that of the United States in its westward expansion.

By 1815, Russia had acquired Siberia, the Caucasus, the Baltic coast, Poland, most of Rumania, Bulgaria, Finland, Alaska, Sakhalin, and part of Manchuria. In addition to this, Russian spheres of influence were established in northern Iran and parts of Mongolia. So powerful had Russia become that Britain expended a great deal of energy in arranging to counterbalance Russia (Austria, Turkey) and fighting (the Crimean War) to prevent it from dominating the Middle East and the Balkans.

During the late nineteenth century, Russia lost considerable ground as a great power. British effort was partly responsible. More importantly, Russia continued to suffer from ailments that the democratic revolution had cured in most of the other great powers. A stubborn, corrupt, and inept small band of aristocrats held most of the country's wealth in its hands, and dominated, not only its administration, but the educational system and national culture as well. As a consequence, while the other great powers became rapidly industrialized, Russia remained a technologically backward, largely agricultural nation. In the early eighteenth century, the Urals produced more pig iron than England. At the end of the nineteenth century, while the Ural iron industries had remained static, Britain, Germany, and the United States had increased their output many times over.

Russian territory began to contract. Alaska was sold, Wallachia and Moldavia lost. Russian weakness was evident in the Crimean War. Some efforts were made to remedy its technological and cultural backwardness, but they were not very successful. In 1905, Japan inflicted a serious defeat on Russia and took away southern Sakhalin, Port Arthur, and other Manchurian areas, as well as a number of islands. Defeat in 1917 was even more costly. In the words of Shcherbakov, Moscow Party Secretary, in 1944, 'Tsarist Russia was traveling along a road which would inevitably have brought it to the loss of its independence.' Today most Russians believe that the overthrow of the Tsarist régime not only changed the economy of their country, but preserved its identity.

In 1917, forces of change that had been accumulating for more than a century exploded in defeated, chaotic Russia. During the next three years, the land was devastated and more than fifteen million Russians killed by civil war, terror, invasion, and famine. Industry, agriculture, and communications were all but destroyed.

During these years of weakness, Finland and the Baltic countries, previously part of the Russian Empire, became independent. So did Poland, taking with it large areas of the western Ukraine and western White Russia. Bessarabia was incorporated into Rumania. Russia lost Turkish Armenia and its treaty rights in Persia.

In all, it was not quite so bad as it might have been. At various times during the Civil War, Russia had lost the Caucasus, the Ukraine, most of Siberia, and the Murmansk and Archangel districts as well. Chance, rivalry among the great powers, war-weariness everywhere, and hard fighting pulled Russia through, weakened, despoiled, but still a major power in territory and population. Its new, inexperienced Soviet Government set about trying to regularize its relations with foreign nations in preparation for regaining its place as a great power.

For most Russians the Revolution of 1917 meant 'peace, land, and bread.' It was not an ideological revolution, but an upheaval against a tyrannical régime that had brought the country to disaster, a desperate attempt to put a group in power that would make things work. To the leaders, however, it was very much an ideological revolution. The country's leaders (Lenin, Stalin, Trotsky, Zinoviev, Bukharin, Radek, Rykov, Dzherzinsky) believed in a world revolution, the establishment of dictatorships of the proletariat as a transition to world-wide socialism. Fearful of the capitalist governments by whom they were spurned and menaced, confident that these governments could and would soon be ousted by revolutions in their own countries, they tied Russian foreign policy to the revolutionary parties abroad. For some ten years Moscow's formal diplomatic relations with foreign governments were incidental to direct appeals to the masses of foreign countries.

The Comintern or Third International, linking together all the Communist Parties of the world, was organized in Moscow. Many of Russia's best organizing brains were sent to foreign countries to aid in bringing about proletarian revolutions. Radek went to Germany, Borodin to China. Under the leadership of such men as Zinoviev and Trotsky, who believed that socialism could not survive in a single country, the Comintern was feverishly active all during the nineteen-twenties. Results were not encouraging. Two insurrections in Germany were crushed. The Red Hungarian Government of Bela Kun collapsed after a few weeks in power. In 1927, the Canton Commune in China went down to defeat; to defeat likewise fell Leon Trotsky's theory of permanent revolution and the policy of devoting Russian effort to fomenting revolutions abroad.

Stalin's policy, clarified all during the twenties and finally formulated in 1927, was based on the attempt to construct and maintain socialism in one country. If Communist revolutions took place in other countries, well and good, but Russia was to depend for survival on its own internal strength, on the development of which all energy was to be concentrated. In power, Stalin proceeded to launch a non-ideological policy based on Russia's national interests, and attempting to promote them by establishing good relations with every country disposed to accept them. With Fascist Italy, for example, the Russians maintained cordial diplomatic relations and mutually beneficial commercial intercourse from the late twenties right up to the outbreak of World War II, despite such occurrences as the Spanish Civil War. Soviet-German friendship dated back to the Treaty of Rapallo in 1922, when both Germany and Russia were weak, unpopular countries, territorially denuded, and still suffering from the results of an economic blockade by the Western Powers.

During this period, the importance of foreign Communist Parties in Soviet foreign policy decreased rapidly. Whereas in the early twenties the development of Communist activity in other countries was a primary consideration of the Kremlin, by the early thirties it was secondary or tertiary. Stalin was banking on the military and economic strength of the Soviet Union, rather than on Union Square and Hyde Park demonstrations, to save the Soviet Union in case of war. He was beginning, too, to believe that the good-will of the governments of the other great powers was worth more to Russia than the small revolutionary groups inside them. The activity of the Communist Parties was often a hindrance to obtaining that good-will.

When Hitler came to power, a much greater effort was made to develop favorable relationships with the democracies. Maxim Litvinoff made desperate attempts to get the other governments to join that of Russia in a collective security arrangement against Fascist aggression. Alliances were made with Czechoslovakia and France (curiously enough, the Franco-Soviet Pact of 1935 was signed by Pierre Laval). At the same time, Litvinoff repeatedly called for progressive proportional disarmament of all European countries, and several times caused a sensation by proposing disarmament at Geneva conferences. He met with suspicion, hostility, and failure.

At the very same time, the Communist Parties the world over began to follow a 'popular front' line, working with bourgeois liberal parties and Socialist Parties (once regarded as their greatest enemies) to bring governments into power that would be anti-Fascist, no matter what else their character.

With the outbreak of the Spanish Civil War, Moscow made a valiant gesture toward supporting the far-off republic. Despite geographical difficulties and the virtual blockade of Spain resulting from the British policy of non-intervention, Russia sent military supplies, anti-aircraft equipment, and some officers to Spain. After three years of bitter warfare, Franco, with the help of sizable military forces from Italy and Germany, emerged victorious. Neither Britain nor France realized that the first battle of World War II had been lost.

Appeased at Munich by London and Paris, Hitler began a campaign of active aggression in Europe. The annexation of Austria was almost immediately followed by the fall of Czechoslovakia, which was a major calamity for the Soviet Union, since Czechoslovakia was regarded by Russians as an outpost of Soviet defense, much as the Philippines are for the United States. After these smashing defeats to the policy of collective security, Stalin began to develop the alternative one of reaching an agreement of expediency with the aggressor. After Munich, it became obvious to Stalin that the Governments of Chamberlain and Daladier were bent on avoiding war with Germany by attempting to persuade Hitler to attack the Soviet Union. Stalin pushed his new alternative policy all the more industriously.

★   2. THE MASTER PLAN IN
WAR AND PEACE   ★

AFTER 1937, when internal problems of collectivization and industrialization were on the way to being solved, Stalin was able to turn more attention to foreign affairs than he had hitherto. Until then, his words on foreign policy had been few. Early in

1939, in his report to the Eighteenth Party Congress, for the first time Stalin outlined what amounted to the master plan of Soviet foreign policy. Among other things, he said:

> The majority of the non-aggressive countries, particularly England and France, have rejected the policy of collective security . . . and have taken up a policy of non-intervention, of 'neutrality.'
>
> Formally speaking, the policy of non-aggression might be defined as follows: 'Let each country defend itself against the aggressor as it likes and as best it can. That is not our affair. We shall trade with both the aggressors and with their victims.'
>
> But actually speaking the policy of non-intervention means conniving at aggression. They [England and France] have begun egging the Germans on to march farther east, promising them easy pickings and prompting them, 'Just start a war on Bolshevism and everything will be all right. . . .' They are saying quite openly, however, that the Germans have cruelly 'disappointed them,' for, instead of marching farther east, against the Soviet Union, they have turned to the west and are demanding colonies. . . .
>
> Far be it from me to moralize on the policy of non-intervention, to talk of freedom, treachery, and so on. . . . Politics is politics, as the old case-hardened bourgeois diplomats say. It must be remarked, however, that the big and dangerous political game started by the policy of non-intervention may end in a serious fiasco for them. . . .
>
> The foreign policy of the Soviet Union is clear and explicit:
>
> 1. We stand for peace and the strengthening of business relations with all countries. . . .
>
> 2. We stand for peaceful, close, and friendly relations with all neighboring countries. . . .
>
> Our tasks in the sphere of foreign policy are:
>
> 1. To continue the policy of peace and of strengthening business relations with all countries. . . .
>
> 2. To be cautious and not allow our country to be drawn into conflicts by warmongers who are accustomed to have others pull their chestnuts out of the fire for them. . . .
>
> 3. To strengthen the might of our Red Army and Navy to the utmost.
>
> 4. To strengthen the bonds of international friendship with the working peoples of all countries, who are interested in peace and friendship among nations.

This was a clear, explicit statement of a completely realistic foreign policy. It was a warning that Stalin was through accepting the vague promises of London and Paris because they were supposed to be or might become anti-Fascist. It meant that Stalin, if he could get more favorable terms from Berlin, would accept them. Few heeded this warning. Later, some scholars and journalists re-reading the speech found in it the answers to at least a few of the riddles and mysteries to which Churchill referred. Quite simply, Stalin had enunciated the tenets of a three-dimensional, master foreign policy. In it the foundation was laid for two alternative courses of action to be pursued as need and circumstances dictated. The use of Communist Parties and Communist influence on the working classes of the world was relegated to a subordinate level, depending on which policy was adopted. Internally, Stalin had long since developed the technique of dual policy to a high point. If any road became blocked, he had always managed to leave himself free to take another. Exactly the same principle was now applied to his foreign policy. Stalin carried on simultaneous negotiations with Germany and with the democracies. He kept himself free to maneuver and temporize, and finally chose the road that seemed most suitable for the safety and prosperity of Russia.

It seems obvious that Stalin would have preferred co-operation with Britain and France, if only for the reason that neither was a direct military threat to the Soviet Union, while Germany was a constant and major one, with specific commitments against Russia. But, beginning with Munich, the Daladier and Chamberlain Governments made a series of moves which resulted in Stalin's complete alienation. In August, 1939, for example, an Anglo-French Commission arrived in Moscow to negotiate the terms of a three-power alliance against Nazi aggression.

The commission came without plenipotentiary powers to sign anything and with instructions to mark time as long as they could, if possible until the German campaign season was past. At the very first meeting, the Russians said: 'If we are to oppose German aggression, we must be prepared to fight Germany. Having no common frontier with Germany, we must go through intervening countries, notably Poland. We consider it absolutely necessary that, immediately upon the outbreak of war, the Red Army should enter Poland to operate against Germany.'

The Russian generals then designated the specific areas in Poland in which they wanted Red Army troops to operate. The British and French informed them that they were unable to comply with these Soviet requests because the Polish Government was unwilling to allow Soviet troops on Polish territory and was convinced that it could deal with any German aggression alone. All the Poles wanted from Russia was military matériel. To the Russians this was utterly unsatisfactory. It meant that Russia could not begin fighting until the Germans had reached the Polish-Soviet frontier, a very poor line of defense, only a few miles from Minsk and not far from the important industrial areas of the Ukraine.

When Stalin became convinced that neither London nor Paris desired or intended to co-operate effectively with Russia in a war against Germany, his alternative had been long prepared. On August 23, with only a few hours' warning, German Foreign Minister von Ribbentrop flew to Moscow to sign a non-aggression pact. The German rear was secure and World War II began on September 1 without the Russians being involved in it. In essence, the choice was simple and dictated by self-preservation. Had the Russians signed the alliance with Britain and France, they might well have had to fight Germany immediately and perhaps alone. Signing with Germany, Russia had only to maintain a neutrality, every month of which was so much time gained in which to prepare and strengthen her defenses.

During the twenty-month period of Soviet-German friendship, Stalin again pursued a dual policy. Diplomatic relations with Germany were cordial and the commercial turnover was heavy. Comintern propaganda was adjusted to the new situation. On the other hand, a resolute campaign went on to strengthen Russian defenses against Germany. Dead wood was cut out of the Russian High Command. Equipment was brought up to date and the military budget was more than doubled. Soviet leaders made speeches to the effect that Soviet-German friendship was based on the real interests of the peoples of both countries and was not a transient affair. But the locks on the Dnieper-Bug Canal on the new Soviet-German frontier were made out of wood instead of concrete, while the fortifications on the same frontier were built solidly. Russia cultivated and profited from German friendship and engaged, at the very same time, in extensive, systematic preparations for hostilities with Germany. During the same period, Russia was extremely careful in her relations with Japan and resisted, on several occasions, German attempts to bring the two countries closer together.

Until 1939, Moscow had been constantly on the defensive in its foreign relations. Never once was Stalin in a position to step across the frontiers imposed on the weak Soviet Union in the early nineteen-twenties and re-establish Russian pre-war frontiers. But the desire to do this was a basic national undercurrent which became more powerful during the nineteen-thirties as Soviet internationalism was modified into active nationalism. Only after the outbreak of World War II was Stalin able to do anything about satisfying this national desire.

In the confusion concurrent with the fall of Poland in September, 1939, the Russians marched approximately to the Curzon Line — an ethnological watershed separating roughly the Polish from the Ukraine and White Russian districts in Poland. Shortly afterward, the three Baltic States were incorporated into the Soviet Union, almost without a shot being fired. In Finland, the Russians blundered badly, and after a colossally stupid war, got slightly improved frontiers on the other side of which lay an almost irrevocably hostile Finland. From Rumania the Soviet Union took back Bessarabia and, for good measure, annexed northern Bukovina. It was noticeable that the new Soviet boundary included northern Bukovina, which had never been part of Russia, but was predominantly Ukrainian in population, and did not include central Polish districts which had been Russian before 1914, but were inhabited by Poles.

On June 22, 1941, having failed to subdue England, Hitler invaded the Soviet Union. Well-informed members of the German Embassy in Moscow were opposed to the move. They were convinced that the Russians would fight hard and effectively and that the Soviet régime would not collapse in a few weeks as its more severe critics believed. Nevertheless, during the first few months Germany achieved a series of spectacular victories.

Instead of the hostile glee which some Soviet cynics in Moscow expected to hear from Britain and the United States, Churchill extended a friendly hand across Europe, declared Russia an ally, and promised as much aid as possible as soon as it could be delivered. The United States offered credits, and within a few months the Soviet Union was receiving a stream of military materials which rapidly broadened into a torrent — one of the major factors in Russia's successful defense against the Nazi invasion. The surprised and delighted Russians signed a twenty-years' alliance with Britain, pledging full co-operation both during the war and after it.

During the early critical years from 1941 to 1943, Soviet foreign policy was wholly devoted to winning the war. Until June, 1944, the second front was the touchstone of Russian relations with her allies. Many Russian pin-pricks, interpreted as Machiavellian, were merely attempts to goad the Anglo-Saxons into the more active military co-operation desired by the Russians. Stalin emphasized the importance of the second front repeatedly, stating that 'We know from history that Germans have always won wars fought on one front and lost them when forced to fight on two fronts.'

During this period, Stalin made several reasonably acceptable statements of Russian war aims. In 1941, he declared that the first task of Russia was the liberation of its own people and territory from the Nazi invaders. Disclaiming any intention of conquest or the imposition of the Russian régime on any European or Asiatic nation, Stalin offered to help the other people of Europe in the fight against Hitler and to assist them in restoring their own sovereignty on their own territory. In November, 1943, Stalin defined the tactical aims of Soviet foreign policy during the war as:

1. To liberate European peoples from Fascist robbers and to help them re-establish their national states. France, Belgium, Czechoslovakia, and other countries under the German yoke, must be free and independent.

2. To give European peoples full liberty to settle their own form of government.

3. To take the necessary measures to punish Fascist criminals responsible for the present war and its attendant suffering.

4. To establish a European order which will make it impossible for Germany to undertake new aggression.

5. To establish lasting political and economic collaboration between the peoples, based on mutual confidence and aid,

and re-establish economy and culture destroyed by the Germans.

Nevertheless, all through World War II, Soviet foreign policy remained three-dimensional. The desired policy was pursued zealously, but never to the complete exclusion of an alternative policy to be followed if Russia was forced to give up its preference. Thus, Russia maintained a precarious neutrality with Japan. Of course, no one but a few extremists expected or desired Russia to attack Japan at a time when the Red Army was bearing the brunt of the war against Germany. It might have been suicidal for Russia and catastrophic for the Allies. But apart from strategic considerations, continued neutrality toward Japan left a chance for a new orientation in the unlikely event of the present arrangements breaking down.

To China, too, Moscow's approach was dual. In North China, large Communist forces were operating virtually independently of Chiang Kai-shek's Government in Chungking. Russia said nothing until 1944, and then very little. It refrained from doing anything to bring the situation to a head. But Russian prestige was maintained in China because of the previous considerable aid rendered during a period when Britain, for example, had closed the Burma Road. This had not brought Russia into open conflict with Japan. Stalin was free to throw full support to Chiang Kai-shek and also to pursue the opposite policy of intervention in a Chinese civil war; an intervention which many thought could be decisive, if Moscow so desired.

In Europe and in the Western Hemisphere, Communist Parties supported the Allied cause against the Germans. They invoked support for all the Allied governments, and remained utterly silent about socialism, the class struggle, and all other disputes which might provoke dissension in whatever country they were, or between Russia and the Anglo-Saxon powers. It did not seem likely that they would change unless Russia were suddenly menaced by the countries with which she was friendly.

In his dealings with America and Britain, Stalin was, I believe, unfeignedly cordial. Probably outweighing every other consideration is Stalin's desire for a period of prolonged peace and friendship with Britain and the United States. As the Russians went about trying to dispel ideas about their indifference or essential antipathy to the democracies, some situations gave them considerable difficulty. To millions the world over, a great question mark hovered over the Red Army, when, in the summer of 1944, it reached the frontiers of the Soviet Union.

Would the Red Army stop or go ahead? In Sweden, where I was at the time, Right extremists had, as they did elsewhere, answers ready for both contingencies. If the Red Army stopped, then Stalin had betrayed his allies and gone back into his bear's lair of isolation and self-interest. If the Red Army advanced, then the Bolshevik Bear was out to gobble up Europe and had already begun. As the Red Army advanced, liberating occupied nations and invading enemy territory, Stalin was confronted by a number of delicate problems. In general, they were solved in a manner calculated not to cause a breach in the Anglo-Soviet-American coalition, but with an eye on Russian post-war security.

In the background, prepared for as far back as the report to the eighteenth Party Congress mentioned previously ('To strengthen the bonds of international friendship with the working peoples of all countries'), Stalin always had an alternative based on the popularity and prestige of the Red Army among the poor suffering people of Europe, particularly those in the eastern and southern backward, agrarian areas. If he wished, at the turn of a hand Russia could have millions of supporters throughout Europe who would place the interests of the Soviet Union above their own national or regional interests. Stalin, I believe, never forgot that he could, if necessary, give this signal, although he hoped that it would not become necessary.

As the war drew to a close, Soviet foreign policy broadened out to include other desires and aims than winning the war. Among them, Russian post-war security; the economic reconstruction of Russia and Europe; and the promotion of peace and stability in Europe, and, if possible, throughout the world. Russia shaped her relations with her allies and with their defeated and invaded neighbors with the object of fulfilling these basic aims. At Teheran and other conferences, Russia held out for decisions that would implement them. At Teheran, Russia made commitments for future activity against Japan. It is also likely that Churchill and Stalin agreed that Yugoslavia and Greece were to be included in the Russian and British spheres of influence respectively. We know little enough of the specific arrangements made at the international conferences, but the Russians have said and done enough to give a fairly concrete picture of the way Stalin proposes to achieve the security, reconstruction, and stability which Russia so desperately needs.

The official version of the measures taken by Russia and Britain to ensure security may be found in Articles 5 and 6 of the Anglo-Soviet Treaty of May 26, 1944. Behind the rather vague and un-illuminating official language of these articles is a very concrete Soviet plan to create in eastern Europe a security belt, a *cordon sanitaire* in reverse, including Finland, Poland, Rumania, Bulgaria, Czechoslovakia, and Yugoslavia. These nations were envisaged as independent sovereign states, free to organize their internal lives as they chose. But their governments were not to be hostile to the Soviet Union and their foreign policies and military plans were to be cleared through Moscow, much as those of small European states were cleared through London and Paris at the end of the first World War. Russia's security belt might equally well be called her 'good neighbor sphere,' for the component nations, though designedly friendly to Russia, were not necessarily anti-British, anti-American, or anti-Western.

In this way Stalin hoped to get what both the United States and Britain had long ago secured for themselves in one way or another: a group of friendly small nations situated in strategically vital areas, ready to help out with votes at international conferences in peacetime, and with armies and bases in case of war. These Russian desires were expressed in the Soviet-Czech Pact.

Just as Britain had its trouble keeping Ireland friendly, just as the United States had problems in the Argentine, the Russians ran into trouble in Poland and Finland. The London Poles did not come up to the Russian specifications for a 'friendly' government. The Russians made every effort to have it changed, then gave up, and installed another government friendly to Russia. In Finland they were more successful. In following the changes in the Russian attitude toward Finland, it is possible to get a picture in miniature of Russian policy toward eastern Europe.

Like most countries, Soviet Russia wants friendly neighbors. Finland was dominated by a government obviously irrevocably hostile to Russia and friendly relations between the two countries seemed impossible. What could Moscow do about it? It must be remembered that Russian actions in Finland were the result of a situation very much like that in which the United States would be placed if Mexico or Canada should enter into a conspiracy against it with a powerful third party. One way of getting around the difficulty was to let Finland have whatever government she wanted, but to weaken the country strategically and economically, to a point where it was harmless and could not serve as a springboard for a third power to use against Russia. The British have used this method in Ireland. The United States has tried it in its dealings with Argentina. It was the one the Russians used in Finland in 1940, when, by taking Viipuri, Hangoe, and the Saima Canal, they thought to place Finland in a position of dependency. They found they had erred. In 1941, Finland became just that *place d'armes* which Russia had sought to prevent. Leningrad was shelled by Finnish batteries; the Murmansk railroad was cut by Finnish and German troops operating from well-prepared positions in Finland.

On the other hand, Finland could have been made friendly by the setting-up of a Soviet régime inside it or at least a Soviet-friendly government. The United States tried something similar in Nicaragua; the British in Iran in 1941. In 1940, Russia tried it in Finland with the Kuusinen Government, but was prevented by the world situation and the tough, stubborn hostility of the Finns. In 1944, Moscow was again free to choose between a friendly Finland and a weak but hostile Finland. A compromise was finally worked out in the armistice terms of September 13, 1944.

In pursuing their security-belt policy, it became obvious that the Russians would not tolerate any Eastern, Balkan, or Scandinavian federation in Europe. The reason is quite plain. Russia does not want any large units in Europe. She wishes to be able to maintain an army of only a million or so and still have far and away the largest in eastern Europe. Federations would mean an increase in the Russian armament budget and add to the number of uncertainties inherent in the post-war situation.

Nor did Russia desire to annex large parts of eastern and central Europe as an alternative to the complex task of forming the security belt. The annexation of a country like Poland, for example, would mean incurring the permanent hatred of the Poles as well as additional administrative and economic burdens. Whoever annexed Poland or any similar nation would have to put money into the country for reconstruction and relief. Russia has more than enough of both to do at home. Moreover, any such annexations might lead to a serious breach with the Anglo-American powers, something which the Russians want, above all, to avoid.

To rivet its good-neighbor belt securely into place, Moscow planned to help each country in it to take some territory from its western neighbor, thus making it forever dependent on Russia for protection. By this method, Poland would get part of eastern Germany, Rumania would get Transylvania, Hungary might get part of Austria or Germany, Bulgaria part of Yugoslavia, and Yugoslavia part of Italy and Greece. It would not be at all surprising if Finland asked for some transit or port rights in Norway and received the backing of Russia.

As the war drew to a close, it became obvious that no world organization effective enough to guarantee security and peace to Europe was likely to be formed. To be effective, the central organization would have to be stronger than any of its component parts. Neither Russia nor America nor Britain was likely to consent to submerge its power in such an organization. As a consequence, Russia felt compelled to take steps to guarantee her own security. The security belt of small nations was the answer. By it Russia would get the equivalent of what Britain had in the Empire and the United States in South America — strategic positions and a sphere of influence. Moreover, the economies of these nations could be geared into future Soviet five-year plans, thus contributing toward the reconstruction of Russia, which was now a major consideration of Russian foreign policy.

Defeated countries — Finland, Germany, Rumania, Hungary, Bulgaria, are to pay substantial reparations to the Soviet Union for damage by their troops in Russia. These reparations will be demanded in kind — that is, in machinery, semi-manufactured products, ships, rolling stock, and labor. In this respect the Soviet Union has an enormous advantage over the United States and Great Britain. For Britain and America reparations in kind would in most cases undermine British or American business, create unemployment and instability at home. The Soviet Union can consume any conceivable quantity of practically any kind of goods from Europe for perhaps a generation without satisfying its own gigantic demand.

But countries like Finland, Bulgaria, and Rumania are not in a position to produce the things which Russia most wants — ships, lathes, diesel motors, and machinery. Therefore, say the Russians, Finland and Rumania must industrialize their countries in order to produce these goods. Where will the Finns and Rumanians get the capital and machinery to build these factories? At conferences in Helsinki, Bucharest, Sofia, Budapest, Russia let it be known that she wanted these countries to get the necessary credits and machinery from Britain and America. By this plan these small countries would become industrialized, Russia would get the products of the industries for several years, and the American machine-building industry would be saved from post-war depression. It would be a form of indirect aid to Russian reconstruction by America and England.

A serious limiting factor in the economic relations of Russia with the rest of Europe is the fact that the Russian standard of living, never too high in relation to her Western neighbors, had by the war's end fallen very low. To have neighbors, many of them defeated countries, living at a higher standard than victorious Russia will be awkward and embarrassing. The Russians do not mention it, but their basic criteria for the amount of reparations demanded from defeated enemies is based on the consideration that the amount be great enough to prevent the standard of living in the countries surrounding Russia from rising inconveniently higher than that of Russia herself.

One instrument by which the Russians can govern the standard of living in defeated countries is currency manipulation. In Rumania, the Russian policy has been significant. In November, the Bucharest radio stated that all holders of rubles and Soviet occupation lei were to present these for exchange into ordinary Rumanian lei. The rate was one hundred Rumanian lei for one ruble and five Rumanian lei for one Soviet lei. Overvaluation of one's own currency when entering into a defeated country has been the general rule throughout Europe in most wars and the Russians have made no exception in Rumania. Before the war the Russian ruble was equal to about twenty-six Rumanian lei. Since the beginning of the war, Rumanian prices have been increased by several times, but so have Russian prices. In 1940, a liter of fresh milk in Russia cost two rubles and ten kopeks. At the same time a liter of milk in Bucharest cost ten lei. Thus, the Russian soldier purchasing milk in Bucharest today with rubles receives two and a half times as much milk as he could purchase at home for the same amount of money. It is probable that the same thing is true of other commodities. In Helsinki at the end of 1944, Red Army soldiers were coming to town on leave from the garrison of Porkkala with Finnish marks to spend. I was unable to ascertain what they paid for their marks, but I do know that they were spending money in restaurants and buying furs to send home to their wives in a way which few could permit themselves in the Soviet Union.

Russia desires stability in Europe. Stability means no revolutions, no civil wars. In Rumania, Bulgaria, and Finland the Red Army has partly or wholly occupied countries which have proceeded with the fulfillment of the armistice conditions without revolutions or civil wars. I think the Russians will do likewise elsewhere. They are anxious to avoid the trouble which usually follows in the wake of civil disorder. It seems likely, then, that the Russians will oppose extreme revolutionary tendencies anywhere in Europe and will support moderate agrarian reforms and reasonable democratic governments. They will support and encourage only those Socialist measures which can be legislated democratically, and the realization of which will not arouse critical controversies with the Anglo-Americans. In some cases this policy may even involve the suppression of left extremists. The Russians did not hesitate to suppress the extremist POUM in Spain during the Civil War, and it is hardly likely that they will hesitate with other left extremists now. Following this Soviet desire, European Communist Parties are pursuing policies of social reconciliation and class collaboration and will continue to do so unless Soviet foreign policy changes.

For Russia, as for other countries, Germany presents a special case. Russia's policy toward Germany has zigzagged through World War I, Rapallo collaboration, hostility from 1933 to 1939, collaboration, and then hostility again. Economically, Germany and Russia complement each other, and, all other things being equal, might be very friendly on the basis of common interests.

But all other things are not equal. For one thing, the average Russian today hates the Germans; not just the Fascists or the Nazis, but the *Germans*. This has resulted from the activities of the German invasion forces in Russia, and far from trying to prevent this hatred or softening it, the Soviet Government has stimulated it by every kind of propaganda. In sharp contrast to the inculcation of this attitude and despite Russian acceptance of the Casablanca unconditional surrender formula, the Soviet Government has pursued a careful, energetic, and probably effective policy of political warfare aimed at splitting the German people and creating an opposition to Hitler. The main instruments of this warfare were the Seydlitz Committee and the 'Freies Deutschland' National Committee.

The 'Freies Deutschland' National Committee was formed in the middle of July, 1943, in Moscow, when German war prisoners, soldiers and officers, met with the German Communists who lived in the Soviet Union. 'After a lively discussion they unanimously decided to organize a national committee of free Germany,' the official report stated. Erich Wiener, a Communist writer, was elected president. Major Karl Hetz from Königsberg was elected vice-president and Lieutenant Count Heinrich von Hinsiedel, a great-grandson of Bismarck, was elected second vice president. In the summer of 1943, it was decided to publish a manifesto to the German people. This manifesto gave a picture of the war situation at that time, and exhorted all Germans to work for an immediate end of the war. If Hitler should be overthrown only by Allied arms, this would mean the end of national freedom and the splitting-up of Germany. The manifesto urged the formation in Germany of a new, strong, anti-Nazi government in order to overthrow Hitler. This government should immediately make peace. The manifesto concluded with the words: 'For people and country. Against Hitler and his war. For immediate peace. For the saving of the German people. For a free and independent Germany.'

The manifesto also contained an internal program for Germany with demands for freedom of speech, press, organization, conscience, and religion, and the confiscation of the property of war criminals. It also promised 'amnesty for all Hitler supporters who at the right time, by their deeds, renounced Hitler and joined the movement for a free Germany.'

As a bait to the middle classes, the manifesto urged 'economic, industrial, and commercial freedom, guarantees of the right to work, and to own lawfully earned property.' It is quite obvious that the National Committee and this manifesto were designed to unite all anti-Nazis in a common fight to overthrow Hitler and to accelerate German demoralization on the fighting fronts. The statements in the manifesto did not bind the Soviet Government, but they did serve to undermine Hitler and weaken the German war effort.

The 'League of German Officers' was formed in September, 1943, in Moscow, chiefly with the purpose of contributing to the demoralization of the German Army. General Walter von Seydlitz was appointed chairman. The league joined the organization of the 'Freies Deutschland' National Committee. The chairman of the National Committee, Weinert, also made a speech at the opening congress, as did a few soldiers and a Wehrmacht chaplain named Father Kayser. The league issued an appeal signed by ninety-five German officers to the officers and men of the Wehrmacht.

The National Committee published a newspaper, *Freies Deutschland,* and arranged broadcasts over the Moscow radio to the German people and the Wehrmacht. Imprisoned army chaplains preached radio sermons. Sometimes General von Seydlitz addressed certain German commanders on the Eastern Front, and urged them to desert to the Russians. Both newspaper and the radio issued reports on the desertion of officers and troops and the acceptance of the deserters into the League of Officers of the National Committee. Even Marshal Paulus, taken prisoner at Stalingrad, spoke in August, 1944, over the Russian radio, and again in October, 1944, he spoke under the auspices of the National Committee against German continuation of Hitler's war.

The Nazi Government remained silent for a long time about the National Committee and the League of Officers. Not till the summer of 1944 was it publicly announced in Germany that a court martial had sentenced General von Seydlitz to death *in absentia.*

The Russians claimed that all this political warfare (in which neither Britain nor America engaged) paid handsome dividends. Demoralization of German troops at many points was reported. Among civilians in Germany, however, only a small number of people were influenced by the National Committee and its broadcasts.

The effect of these organizations on the German Army may have been very powerful. It is known that a part of the Officers' Corps in Germany, out of hostility against Great Britain, were inclined to a military coalition with Russia even in 1941. It can be assumed that these same circles today are thinking about a post-war alliance with the Soviet Union. The officers in the League of Officers and in the National Committee are obviously inclined in that direction.

According to reports from the Soviet Union, the National Committee carried out a great program of political propaganda among the German war prisoners. The National Committee sent speakers and teachers to all prison camps. Prisoners considered politically malleable concentrated on problems involved in rebuilding Germany. The prison camps maintained contact with the kolkhoses, from which they received supplies and land for cultivation. They participated in the reconstruction of destroyed factories. There was contact between the different camps and delegates were chosen for inspection trips. Some men were trained for communal administration and police work, as well as agricultural and industrial administration. These men, thoroughly sifted, form part of Russia's Army of Occupation in Germany.

The ultimate use to which these organizations will be put depends, to a great extent, on Allied plans for Germany and how they work out. Stalin himself, in many speeches, has made his own approach to the problem plain. He has disavowed any Russian aim to 'destroy Germany' because it is impossible, and asserted that the primary task is to destroy the 'Hitlerite State and its inspirers.' The Nazi war criminals and their assistants are, of course, to receive fitting punishment.

On the question of German frontiers, there are a number of indications of Russian plans. The Czechs, for one thing, have been informed through Ambassador Bogmolov, that the Soviet Government favors a pre-Munich frontier for Czechoslovakia. At the same time, the Russians dryly pointed out that since the Soviet Union did not participate in the Munich Agreement, it never considered itself obligated to defend the frontiers established by it.

Enough has been stated by the Russians, unofficially, to leave little doubt that they plan to help the Poles take parts of East Prussia, perhaps eastern Silesia and Pomerania. Although developed from an essentially nineteenth-century formula, it would be a very advantageous arrangement for Russia. Poland would have to depend permanently on Russian bayonets for protection against a vengeful Germany, since it was made obvious in this war that Britain and France could not aid the Poles effectively. It would deprive Germany of some good farmland, strategic positions, and considerable industrial assets.

On the whole, Moscow appeared to be planning for a Germany reduced in territory and obliged by treaty terms to pay heavy indemnities in kind to the Russians and perhaps to the other countries. Beyond this, there is little to go on. It seems improbable that the Soviet Government desires to split Germany up into small nations, although Litvinoff told me, in 1943, that he personally considered this a good idea. The Russians know that the future of Germany depends on one basic factor. If the Anglo-Soviet-American alliance holds together, then a small occupation force and powerful joint Allied control can easily and cheaply prevent Germany from becoming strong enough again to threaten even its weaker neighbors. If the three-power alliance becomes shaky or falls apart, then Britain and perhaps America can be expected to try to re-create a strong Germany to counterpoise Russia. But in such a contingency, the 'Freies Deutschland' Committee and other factors lead the Russians to believe that they are in an extremely favorable position to turn Germany the other way around.

In fact, steps were taken to make sure that the population of Germany, which forms the largest unit of the two hundred-odd million inhabitants of central and western Europe, would not be irrevocably hostile to Russia. America and England had become committed, partly due to Russian efforts, to what amounted to a Carthaginian policy toward Germany. Russia, on the other hand, had made few commitments, and as the last shots were fired the Soviet attitude toward the German people seemed to be marked by moderation. It seemed to some that Moscow was bidding boldly against London and Washington for German good-will. Ilya Ehrenbourg, whom the Kremlin had allowed to function as the spokesman of hatred against all things German, was publicly rebuked by the influential Party functionary, Alexandrov, for having gone too far. Königsberg newspapers under Russian control published pictures of Red Army men plowing Prussian peasants' fields. Russian soldiers, unlike those of England and the United States, were not bound by an ironclad regulation forbidding fraternization with the German people. As a consequence, any plan to weld Germany into an anti-Soviet spearhead would have to cope with the effects of the prior Russian campaign for the favor of millions of Germans.

Thus, at every turn, Moscow has followed an able, three-dimensional policy; based on a thorough analysis of events and trends in other countries, and playing skillfully on the intersecting national and class planes that form the structure of contemporary Europe. This policy, coupled with Russia's military might, brought the Soviet Union at the end of World War II to a position of supremacy in more than half of Europe, and to the status of a serious contender for the complete domination of the Continent.

VI

The Future of the European Revolution

THE TWENTIETH CENTURY is dominated by the conflict between two great principles of social organization, the principle of collectivism and the principle of individualism. In no country is either to be found unmixed with the other. In Russia, as we have seen, the collectivist revolution of October, 1917, was gradually modified by the return of individualist institutions. In America, a number of collectivist measures have gradually become accepted as part of the pattern of national existence. It would seem that both principles have a justification and continue to exist because they are necessary for some purpose.

Someone once remarked that Republicans are people who believe that if you make sure that the upper five per cent of the American people make an adequate living, everybody else will get an adequate income. Democrats reverse the formula and start with the ninety-five per cent. The difference between individualism and collectivism might be stated in the same way. Individualists believe that if you make sure that people are free to do as they please, then their material needs will be satisfied. Collectivists hold that if you make sure that the material needs of people are satisfied, then and only then can they really be free. Despite a number of complexities, it seems safe to say that historically both sides have made good their claims only partially.

Both principles will undoubtedly continue to exist and breed those institutions necessary for their furtherance. In the abstract, it may or may not be possible, by basing the organization of society on one principle only, to satisfy the other. At present, however, it seems certain that both principles will have to be invoked in order to fashion a complete, stable, satisfactory form of social organization.

In the two major wars of the twentieth century, the struggle between these two principles has played a great part. At present, one might almost say that the problem of maintaining future peace rests to a great extent on the problem of harmonizing these two principles, making them work together side by side in nations and in the world. If another devastating conflict arises, it is very apt to be the result of the extreme protagonists of either principle attempting to destroy the institutions of the other.

The two great dynamos of these principles, despite historical modifications that have occurred, remain Russia and America, which seem likely to be, during the next generation, at least, the two greatest powers in the world. The relations among these two and England will determine the future. The great arena in which the relations of these powers will be worked out will probably be, as it has been in the past, Continental Europe.

As we have seen, Continental Europe is in the middle of a collectivist revolution which had, as it were, an official beginning in Soviet Russia. Ever since the nations of Europe have been changing from nineteenth-century systems of capitalist, individualist enterprise to some degree of collectivist organization.

These changes came about in different ways and met different fates in various countries. In Sweden, profound modifications of society occurred without the use of force on either side. In Spain, the republic voted in very mild social reforms, whereupon the landowners, the Church, and other vested interests staged a counter-revolution that caused a bloody civil war. The reaction won out and put a devastated nation back to a point even farther than the one from which it started.

After this war, a series of revolutions may take place in Europe. Certainly there will be disorders and civil strife. After the earthquake of war, one may expect the restoration of stability to take place through a series of lesser shocks as the old surface is re-established or a new one formed. However, an examination of the European Revolution has shown us that National Socialism, war, and bombings have already accomplished most of what was achieved by the insurrection and dictatorship of the proletariat in Russia, namely, breaking both the resistance to change of the owning classes and their power to make such resistance effective.

As a consequence, Communists all over Europe are thinking along lines utterly different from those most people in America are apt to attribute to them. Most of them are wondering if it is at all necessary, or ever will be, to have an insurrection and a dictatorship of the proletariat. Obviously, if mines and heavy industry in France can be nationalized democratically by a right of center government in the presence of large numbers of Anglo-American troops, if business in France can be regulated and controlled to the degree necessary for effective economic planning, then why the bloodshed and sacrifice of revolution?

Furthermore, many of them know that neither they nor anyone else like the dictatorship of the proletariat *per se*. It is accepted or desired because it is regarded as a necessity, the *sine qua non* of even a fairly good economic and social order. If war has changed class relationships to such a degree that it is no longer necessary, it would verge on insanity to plunge nations into bloody conflict, destroy liberties, and inaugurate a period of economic suffering and hardship for the sake of applying an anachronistic idea.

Other left-wing Marxists analyze the situation somewhat differently. The aim of socialism, some say, is not socialism *per se,* but a state of affairs in which the greatest number of people will be able to live the best possible lives, where equitable distribution of wealth and income will be assured. If capitalists, or whoever else is in control of political and economic power, recognize the necessity for collectivist measures in order to achieve this general end and are willing to sacrifice their own personal interests to the necessary degree, then it is quite conceivable that a change to some form of collectivist society can come without a violent liberty-destroying revolution.

Still others prefer to express the same idea in different terms. Prosperity, they argue, is directly proportional to national income. National income grows with the increase of capital investments. Annual capital investments can be increased by conscious planning on the part of private employers, with or without the assistance of the State. If they are willing to do this and at the same time encourage or assure equitable distribution of commodities, then the welfare of the greatest number can be achieved almost fully without formal socialism.

Equally far-reaching changes have taken place in the viewpoint of the other side. Among large sections of what was the owning class of the Continent and among numbers of the owning class in England, the opinion has begun to prevail that a collective economy is extremely efficient and apparently has a better chance of avoiding economic crises and unemployment than does an unregulated free economy. The recognition of something of this nature has been responsible for many modifications of free enterprise everywhere, including those democratically instituted by the New Deal in the United States. These have worked out satisfactorily, by and large, and such a New Deal development as the Securities Exchange Commission, at first denounced as pure Bolshevism, is now generally admitted, even by conservative business men, to be a sound and useful institution.

On the Continent, things have gone much farther in this direction. Many business men and employers have begun to understand the full extent of the issues involved. These men may borrow willingly, even thankfully, many fundamental concepts and central methods from Soviet economy and from the European Revolution in general. They may even add a few of their own. These new seeds would thus take root and germinate without either the insurrection or the period of dictatorship that took place in Russia. In this way, too, civil war and bloody reaction, such as took place in Spain, would be avoided.

As has been pointed out, an important factor in modern society is the increasing power and dominance of the managerial class. Industry, in Europe, has been operated to a great extent by high-salaried managers. All other things being equal, these managers will not care if the factories, mines, and mills they run belong to the State or to a collection of impersonal stockholders. Moreover, they have become extremely conscious of the necessity for planning, and might welcome state control or nationalization because of its efficiency and the fact that it makes superior planning possible.

The collective revolution is today a bilateral affair. The Soviet Union, copyright holder, so to speak, of the revolutionary credo, started out a quarter of a century ago with grandiose plans to change radically the social and economic habit patterns of the world. During the years that followed, the Russians modified their ideas, watered down their extremism, eliminated those points of their program found to be impractical, and readopted many of the capitalistic institutions they had at first abolished. They did this because they discovered that those institutions worked.

On the other hand, the so-called capitalist countries modified their system in the direction of planned, collectivist economy because they found it worked; such modifications were also necessary because of the catastrophic crisis into which more or less unregulated free enterprise got itself during the late twenties and early thirties all over the Western world. As a result, today, economic and social differences between the Soviet Union and Great Britain are much less significant than they were twenty-five years ago, and the compromises have been mutual.

This is the pattern of the synthesis, the solution of the European Revolution, and I believe that far-sighted men on both sides realize it well. There is nothing new in this process of synthesis. Europe has had many revolutions, and every time a synthesis has taken place. In the France of Robespierre, in Cromwell's England, in the early days of the Reformation — in each case the most extreme stage of the revolution was reached during the early days or months or years. Old institutions and ideas were attacked simply because they were old, without sufficient examination of their merits. Revolutionaries and conservatives fought each other mercilessly on every issue. Then, over a period of years, a balance was gradually re-established. Ideas spread, sometimes by wars, by hypodermic injection, sometimes by a process of social osmosis. Institutions which served a useful purpose were restored in the revolutionary countries, and continued to operate in those countries untouched by the revolution. On the other hand, institutions which had outlived their usefulness were divested of power, or disappeared on both sides of the revolutionary line. By a series of compromises equilibrium was restored, and this process, like the similar one described by the second law of thermodynamics, proved to be irreversible. The changes brought about by these revolutions and subsequent syntheses — compromises — remained.

The social systems of Britain and France, vastly different just after the Paris Commune, merged gradually during the subsequent century until they had become quite similar at the beginning of the twentieth. This synthesis went on in England without the use of force, because the British people, often including the aristocracy, learned a lesson from the vitality of revolutionary France; they convinced themselves that certain changes were not only practicable but virtually necessary.

Similar compromises, similar syntheses, are going on today in Europe. They have been prodded on, accelerated, and stimulated by the war. The lines of development are merging so rapidly that it seems likely to me that within a generation an equilibrium will have been attained as steady, indeed, I hope a great deal steadier, than that which obtained in western Europe at the beginning of this century among the nations which had been in opposing camps during the revolutionary wars of the previous century.

I have dealt on these forces at such length because Americans, in particular, are so apt to pay them little heed or to misunderstand their nature and direction. Such understanding is vital as the background for the international co-operation that is so necessary to the future of the civilized world. Before discussing that future, it seems to me necessary to give a more concrete picture of the Continent in which those forces have been at work.

To achieve an understanding of Europe and its Revolution, and particularly of the difference between that continent as it is at present and the American continent untouched by actual warfare, it is not necessary to know every detail or every variation on a similar situation. Besides, such an account would require the efforts of the historian who works best long after the events have happened. Recent events in Italy, Yugoslavia, and Greece are perhaps more illustrative of the basic revolutionary trends about which I have been writing than the countries I describe, but Balkan confusion and complexity render conclusion today uncertain and controversial. I have chosen to sketch the events that took place in a handful of northern European countries that I know well, dwelling particularly on a problem or situation that can be seen clearly in one place, and is repeated, often in more violent and distorted form, all over the Continent.

PART
TWO

The Chemistry of Defeat

VII

Sweden

★ I. OBSERVATION POINT ★

EARLY IN NOVEMBER, 1943, I arrived in Stockholm and found myself, along with about a hundred and twenty-five other correspondents of every nationality, engaged in watching, from the best observation point in Europe, the European conflict move slowly toward an end. In the feverish atmosphere of this neutral exchange center, political intrigue reached an amazing degree of complexity, and at every turn one found numbers of spies, suspicions, blonde agents, amateur military and political experts anxious to turn a dishonest penny, and vendors of photographs of everything from pornography to secret military installations.

Our Stockholm Legation, headed by Minister Herschel Johnson, was one of the largest and one of the best in the United States Foreign Service. Its able, energetic personnel was efficiently guided without being smothered, and as a result it did some remarkably good work at collecting information and making more active contributions toward winning the war. It was also an indispensable boon to myself and the other American correspondents.

To observers of the European scene Sweden offered much. Not only was its foreign policy, with the degree it blew hot or cold on the Allies and the Axis, an effective index as to how the war was going, but its internal workings were a guide to post-war trends. Here, in one of the most civilized democracies in the world, one could watch the politics of the future taking shape under difficult circumstances, but without the distortions produced by the war's worst ravages. Sweden, too, was probably the largest asylum in Europe, and the Swedes were proud of the humanitarian work they were doing in organizing exchanges of prisoners and rehabilitating the two hundred thousand refugees that had poured into Sweden from every direction.

Across the narrow Öresund, in little boats, frequently swimming, came fugitives from Gestapo torture in Denmark. Across the icy mountains, on skis and sometimes on hands and knees, harried Norwegian patriots arrived to find rest and sanctuary. From Finland, Poland, Germany, France, Holland, and Austria men and women were heaved onto the dry land of Sweden out of the boiling chaos of war. In luxurious contrast, at the modern, well-equipped Bromma Airport, planes were arriving daily from Oslo, Helsinki, Copenhagen, and Berlin, bringing officials, agents, businessmen, and diplomats, Nazi and neutral.

These men and women knew what was happening on the Axis side of the war. They knew, if they would tell and often they would, that the Axis was losing the war and in what way. From them, too, one received mixed impressions of prevailing moods that at worst had the merit of forcing one to revise preconceptions, and at best gave one a flash of insight into what might be a significant current of opinion or feeling. Particularly, from the large numbers of Germans in Sweden one could get some idea of what was happening behind the steel wall of the Third Reich and the attitudes of all kinds of Germans.

Shortly after my arrival in Stockholm, I met a German who had been engaged in anti-Nazi activity for nearly a decade. After coming to Sweden in 1934 from a Nazi concentration camp, he continued his work, first with a left-wing Social Democratic group and subsequently with the Communists. After the outbreak of the war, his activities, which included illegal excursions into Germany, constituted an awkward violation of the carefully guarded Swedish neutrality. He was arrested and spent two years in a Swedish jail.

After his release, he promptly went back into action, but by this time the Swedish authorities were convinced that Germany was going to lose and interference by the police became negligible. He made frequent trips and maintained continuous contacts with the occupied countries by mail and through seamen. He was an extremely well-informed, courageous, and thoroughly sincere anti-Nazi German. The position of men like him was peculiarly painful, since his beliefs had made him an exile from his country at the same time that he suffered from the tendency of the civilized world to hate that country as a whole. His attitude toward the postwar period was one of subdued and wistful hopefulness. 'We Germans will have to change ourselves completely,' he once said to me, shaking his head sadly. *'Wir passen einfach nicht in die heutige Welt.* We must change our outlook on life, and we will. We will become good citizens of the world without ceasing to be Germans. But it will take a long time.'

Among the Nazi Germans, businessmen and the like, a thoroughgoing, unredeemed cynicism had begun to prevail which became increasingly corrosive as the end approached. Most of them were uncomfortable and did not express themselves too freely in public, but occasionally one got indications of their thoughts. At the swank Cecil, I once watched the jovial German Minister, Hans Thomsen, engaged in a loud, laughing conversation with two companions as all three dined luxuriously on steak and smörgasbord and drank copious quantities of Epernay. At the table next to me, two solemn-faced, worried-looking German businessmen who had just arrived dined modestly and quietly. 'What's our Minister so happy about?' I heard one of them mutter. 'Maybe he has a new job with Amgot,' the other replied, with unsmiling bitterness.

In the town of Mälmo I once entered into conversation with a thin, nervous German businessman just arrived from Hamburg. He could not get over the good things to be bought in Mälmo without coupons. I watched him consume éclairs and later drinking beer with preternatural relish. In the bar of the hotel, he began to ply me with questions about Germany's position in the world and the way the war was going outside. When I told him of the relative tonnage of bombs dropped on Germany and England, he shook his head and muttered, 'Ja, I was afraid it was so.'

He then gave me a fairly accurate picture of conditions in Germany and told me that the bombs had done a lot of damage, but had not stopped the factories from running. The people, however, had lost everything they owned and, as a consequence, were going Communist. The war was becoming national, a people's war. After a slight pause, he looked away from me and then back and asked: 'Tell me . . . are we, that is . . . do people hate us?'

I said that the Germans were pretty universally hated in many countries.

'But people will forget, won't they?' he said.

I told him that in Russia I had found the people still talking of the barbarism of the French in 1812 and that I was convinced that people would remember the German invasion even longer.

'Ja, I was afraid it was so,' he said.

He then stepped over to the counter and bought a German newspaper, apparently in an attempt to buck himself up against the realities he was hearing. He finally put it down and ordered more beer. A few laughing Swedes entered, and his face twitched badly and he shook his head in irritation.

'We must win,' he said suddenly in a low voice, looking at his glass.

I said nothing.

He looked up at me and repeated louder, 'We've *got* to win.' He raised his voice and struck the table with his hands lightly to emphasize his words. 'We MUST win.' I still said nothing. The German's face registered no animosity, simply blind, desperate resolution. His face twitched. He hammered his fists on the table and raised his voice till it cracked — '*We must win!*'

People at the other tables looked around. The German got hold of himself. 'Excuse me, please,' he said. 'I am speaking too loudly. I shall return immediately.' And with that he rose and walked with dignity through the door toward the cloakroom and men's room.

I waited nearly two hours, until it was time to go to the station to catch my train, but the German did not come back.

The advantages of neutrality were easy to find in Stockholm. Although blockaded and supposedly suffering from a shortage of coal and petroleum products, the country seemed amazingly prosperous. At night, Stockholm was ablaze with light. I found that Swedes ate better than Englishmen, better than many Americans, and certainly better than anyone else in Continental Europe. Taxis were more plentiful in Stockholm than in Washington. Houses were well-heated, and hot water during the winter was almost universal.

The greatest drawback of Swedish neutrality was psychological. A well-fed, smug complacency seemed to ooze from some of the more prosperous Swedes. Not uncommonly they reasoned: 'War is a stupid affair. Swedes are not stupid and are not in the war. Other people are in the war. So, you see . . .'

The Swedes I met always seemed to be at a meal, going to one, or coming from one. The ritual consumption of mounds of smörgasbord and other dainties did not seem to have been affected much by the war and the blockade. Members of the Swedish upper classes tricked themselves out in evening clothes at the slightest pretext and were continually taking their hats off to one another in the streets. After bomb-scarred, tightly rationed England, Stockholm was actually shocking. At first glance, it seemed a sensual, comfortable Babylon nourished by the misery that surrounded it.

Yet certainly Sweden could hardly be blamed for its sanity. A coalition government dominated by Social Democrats had kept the country out of the war and planned its economy so well that normal life went on almost as before the war, except for increased taxes. Statistically, living standards fell by roughly ten per cent. The country's vast forests furnished solid and liquid fuel; textiles, cloth, shoes, and even beefsteaks and marmalade were plentiful. Rationing was complicated and awkward at first, but everyone got enough.

A number of interesting and progressive cultural institutions were functioning with great success. More than one hundred and eighty Swedish towns and cities had their *Folksparken* (people's parks), owned and operated by trade unions and workers' organizations. In these parks moderately priced dance halls, restaurants, and shooting galleries made sufficient profits to be used as subsidies for almost daily theatrical and musical performances of high quality and at prices below those of the local cinema houses. Sweden's finest artists and musicians performed every summer for more than seven million people in these 'people's parks.'

However, powerful cartels and a strong-minded financial oligarchy were forceful influences in Swedish affairs. Typical, too, was the Post-War Planning Commission under the able chairmanship of the internationally famous economist, Gunnar Myrdal. In this industrious body, economists and state officials sat down with the country's biggest bankers and industrialists as well as the representatives of trade unions, co-operatives, and workers' organizations. Sweden would undoubtedly run into many knotty problems in the future and was attempting to solve them well in advance.

In her foreign policy, at every juncture, Sweden judiciously did whatever seemed necessary to avoid a disastrous entry into the war. In 1940, in flagrant violation of neutrality, German troops were given transit facilities through Swedish territory to Norway and Finland. After El Alamein and Stalingrad, a series of measures were instituted that culminated in the virtual cessation of Swedish-German trade, a cessation that was likewise a violation, at least in spirit, of signed agreements. In a word, Sweden's policy was determined by Europe's great powers — in direct proportion to their military might and in inverse proportion to their distance from Sweden. Similar policies had kept the country out of war for one hundred and thirty years and had fostered a relatively high standard of living, with a reign of reason and moderation in its internal affairs and relations with the rest of the world.

If the success of this policy tended to insulate some Swedes and make them almost oblivious to the war and the world, others were acutely concerned with events abroad. Stockholm financiers followed the situation in the Axis countries very closely. During the summer of 1944, Finnish bonds were being sold at a discount of eighteen to twenty per cent and German bonds at about forty-five per cent. Transactions in the latter were small and a single heavy buyer would have upset the market. The financial circles were worried and with good reason. By the end of 1944, they had more money tied up in Finland than was the case during the Winter War of 1939-40, and their heavy investments in Germany and on the Continent had prospects that were anything but favorable.

A major Swedish problem during 1944 was the situation created by its ball-bearing exports to Germany. The powerful Swedish firm S.K.F. (Svenska Kullagerfabriken) was shipping large quantities of vital ball-bearings to Germany, to be used in German planes and tanks. S.K.F. would have been perfectly willing to send an equal amount to Britain, but transportation was unavailable, and only a relatively insignificant quantity of small-type aviation ball-bearings were shipped by plane and motor boat.

Besides their exports to Germany, S.K.F. had three ball-bearing plants in the Reich itself working at full speed for the German Army. However, even before the war the German Government had so severely regulated these S.K.F. Schweinfurt and Berlin plants that they had become virtually the property of the German State. Formally, however, S.K.F. still owned the plants.

Early in the winter of 1944, as part of its campaign to undermine the strength of the Luftwaffe, the American Eighth Air Force, at considerable cost, had badly damaged several of Germany's ball-bearing plants. The damage to the Schweinfurt S.K.F. plant was not nearly so great as S.K.F officials implied in their conversations with foreigners. They obviously hoped that their exaggerations would reach the American Air Force Command and persuade it that it would not be worth while to raid the plants again. They did not succeed. Ball-bearings had by then become a major issue, and world attention was also focused on the continuous stream of Swedish exports to Germany.

In the spring of 1944, America and Britain launched powerful drives to cut Swedish ball-bearing exports to Germany. Sweden had signed a trade agreement for 1944 with Germany which obligated her to send large quantities of this vital commodity. Though fully informed, neither Britain nor America had registered a complaint at the time the agreement was signed. Now, however, a special envoy, Stanton Griffis, was flown into Stockholm to get the Swedes to break or modify the agreement, and at least to stop sending aviation ball-bearings. Upon arriving, Griffis, a fifty-seven-year-old banker and, currently, president of Paramount, coolly announced that he would stay one week, by which time, doubtless, the matter would be settled to the satisfaction of everybody except the Germans. The German press featured his arrival prominently and described his business methods as 'pure bolshevism.'

During the negotiations I visited the S.K.F. ball-bearing plant in Gothenburg and was much impressed by the efficiency of the plant and the high caliber of the management, technical personnel, and the workers. Griffis, too, must have taken away a sharp impression of the fifty-seven-year-old Harald Hamberg, who had been the director of the S.K.F. Schweinfurt plant for seventeen years. The combined razor-edge wit, mental agility, and business acumen of the latter was apparently not anticipated by Griffis, who had to stay fully six weeks before securing a satisfactory agreement.

The negotiations were protracted and tough. The Swedes held out solidly and obstinately against accepting the Anglo-American requests. They pointed out that the agreement with Germany was made in mid-January with the tacit consent of Washington and

London, and that Sweden was not in the habit of breaking her international agreements. 'This war,' they argued, ' is being fought, in some degree, to establish the sanctity of international agreements. Sweden has one on ball-bearings with Germany and it is sheer hypocrisy for the Allies to try to force us to break it.'

At length they were persuaded to modify it, at any rate. S.K.F. finally consented to a substantial reduction of their exports to Germany of those types of ball-bearings used by the Luftwaffe. In return, they received a generous monetary compensation from the Allies. It was reported to be more than half the sum that the S.K.F. would have received from Germany for the sale of the ball-bearings they agreed to withhold.

Nearly all the raw materials S.K.F. uses are obtained in Sweden. They get their eighty-one thousand tons of high-quality charcoal-smelted chrome steel they use annually from their own plant at Hofors. A problem arises from the fact that approximately three-quarters of their production is for the export market. Germany has been a large buyer. Now Germany is liquidated as a market and, after the war, will probably not be permitted to make airplanes and other machines that require high-quality ball-bearings.

The future of this large industry becomes then a matter of some concern and is typical of the kind of difficulty that will be faced by many European businesses after the war. When I left, the Russians had not expressed any desire to buy Swedish ball-bearings. They had announced their willingness to purchase ball-bearing factories. This left Mr. Hamberg and his colleagues in a rather awkward position. Their discomfort was, however, somewhat mitigated by the current boom. They had declared a twenty-four per cent dividend for 1943, and 1944 would hardly lag behind, since they not only had markets in which to sell, but could get one country to pay them for not selling to another.

★ 2. WEATHERVANE ★

IN 1944, as Germany's position deteriorated, the Swedes proceeded to whittle down their relations with the Germans at a spectacular rate. An object lesson in effective international tactics within the legal limits of neutrality was the astonishing series of governmental measures passed during August, which first restricted, then reduced, and finally virtually terminated, all Swedish-German shipping.

As in every country, the Swedish Government was able to exercise a restraining hand on wartime shipping by means of a State War Insurance Board, a government agency under the Ministry of Supply. This board announced that it would no longer underwrite Swedish ships going to German North Sea ports. Normally, some two-thirds of Swedish iron ore went to these ports. Thus this measure, combined with the shortage of German shipping, reduced Swedish iron-ore exports to Germany to the mere trickle entering through Baltic ports. This ore, then, had to be transported on the overstrained German railroad system to the Rhineland blast furnaces where it was needed. German war economy did not collapse because of the lack of Swedish high-quality iron ore, but its loss to the Reich was probably even a greater blow than the loss of Turkish chrome or Iberian wolfram.

A few days after this announcement, the S.W.I.B. declared that in future it would not underwrite Swedish shipping to Königsberg and all ports east of it. On July 17, 1944, the heavy Allied raid on Stettin was reported to have done great damage to Stettin shipping, and a few days later the S.W.I.B. discontinued underwriting shipping to Stettin. These measures caused some inconvenience to Sweden, which depended exclusively for coal and coke on Germany. German coal and coke exports had, to a great extent, been shipped from the North Sea ports and were now, therefore, seriously curtailed. But Sweden had substantial coal stockpiles and could get through the following winter without additional imports.

The Germans could make no reprisals because nothing the Swedes had done was technically unneutral. They had simply taken their ships out of dangerous waters. The only move the Germans might have undertaken would have been to impound Swedish ships then lying in German ports. This was a very large number — nearly half of Sweden's Baltic total — four hundred thousand tons. The presence of so many Swedish ships in German ports resulted from bombings which delayed loadings and unloadings. If Germany had taken this step, however, it would have been an unfriendly act toward Sweden and might easily have led to political complications and even war.

A few weeks later, another Swedish measure excluded all German ships from East Coast ports. This, too, was a serious blow to Germany. Swedish ports were filled with hundreds of good ships with skilled seamen and officers ready to sail them, but until the end of the war they would not put to sea. The result is that when peace does come, Sweden will have the tremendous advantage of being able to transport her own goods in her own ships.

In September, Sweden held one of the few free elections witnessed in Europe during the last five years. Since tangible public expressions of national opinion were scarce, it was closely watched, not only for itself, but as a possible indication of what Europeans might be thinking without having the means to record their thoughts. Seventy per cent of Sweden's 4,306,000 eligible voters appeared at the polls to elect representatives for the Riksdag. The Social Democrats lost nineteen seats and their absolute majority. The Communists added twelve new seats to their three old ones. The Farmers' Party gained eight seats, and the Rightists lost three. From the standpoint of Sweden's immediate future, this was nothing sensational, since, for all practical purposes, the Social Democrats retained their unquestioned domination of Sweden's political life.

Perhaps the most interesting feature of the results was the striking Communist gains. Why, in Sweden, where workingmen have probably Europe's highest standard of living, where war privations had been minimized (mainly high taxes and the unavailability of certain luxury commodities), where the Social democrats for years had supplied the country with able leadership — why this quantitatively small, but significant, swing leftward?

Most qualified observers agreed that this had little to do with the Soviet Union's prestige. The Soviet Union is more of a liability than an asset to Sweden's Communist Party because of the wide-spread traditional anti-Russian complex in Sweden. The chief causes probably were the freezing of wages and the popular feeling that the Government had not taken as strong a stand as it should have toward Germany. Another factor was that Communists had been the only significant party which had neither been in the coalition government nor had been given any responsibilities, and could therefore criticize without responsibility, capitalizing on the things the Government had failed to do.

Sailing a month or so before the elections, I met a typical young Swedish office employee. We had several long talks. He was com-pletely unpolitical, was interested in sailing and food, and as far as I could see, nothing else. I was, therefore, greatly astonished when, some two weeks before the elections, he announced to me one day, 'You know, I am going to vote Communist.'

'Really?' I said.

'Yes, and I will tell you why,' he said. 'I like sailing, but taxes are getting so high and prices are rising so fast that I am going to have to sell my boat this fall. Now the Communists are for higher wages, lower prices, and lower taxes.'

This Swede was one of thousands who voted Communist in the September elections for the simple reason that the Social Demo-cratic Party in Sweden gave the Communists the opportunity of irresponsible criticism.

Many well-informed people in Stockholm who had intimate connections with Denmark, Norway, and Germany agreed that the swing leftward in these three countries was far more pronounced than in Sweden. All pointed out that this was not caused by Mos-cow's political agitation or Comintern strong-arm politics. Indeed, such activities were virtually impossible in Germany and the occu-pied countries. As one put it, 'A leftward swing would make itself felt in Denmark even if Moscow were still the seat of the Tsarist Government.' Some went further and stated that the revolutionary swing leftward in 1917, 1918, and 1919 was more extreme than the current leftward swing, because now the Soviet Union tended to exercise a moderating influence.

Despite a traditional bias against Russia, most Swedish politicians and leaders recognized that the establishment of good Swedish-Russian political and economic relations after the war was Sweden's most important problem. Many opportunities to increase Swedish-Russian trade were pointed out by Swedish businessmen. An obvious example was the possibility of substantial exports of Swedish iron ore to Russia as soon as shipping from Lulea to Leningrad was safe. The heavily industrialized Leningrad district had always received iron ore from the Urals and Don Basin, both of which involved rail hauls of more than one thousand miles. High-grade Swedish ore was available at about six hundred sea miles from Leningrad and could supply Leningrad's blast furnaces more cheaply. Obtaining this market would relieve the Swedes of one of their worst headaches — where to sell their ore if the German market becomes unavailable.

The Swedish press reflected this desire for better relations with the Russians. The rightist magazine *Obs* on September 20 said: 'We must learn to know Russia. . . . We must recognize the possibility that our future, like the future of many other European nations, may be dependent upon Russia's policy. This depends not only on our good-will, but also upon how Russia treats Finland. . . . Among our six million population there are perhaps about six people who intimately know Russia . . . its social economic, technical position yesterday and today.'

Other articles in Swedish publications echoed these sentiments and frequently urged the Government to take more active measures against Germany. When the Norwegian refugee question became serious in December, 1944, many editorials urged breaking diplomatic relations with Germany.

The Swedes were also thinking a great deal about their position in the post-war world. Exemplary work was done by the Government's Post-War Planning Commission headed by Gunnar Myrdal. The commission was composed of twenty-one members, including representatives of the four big Swedish parties (the Social Democratic Labor Party, the Conservatives, the Farmers, and the Liberals). The Communists had not been included. As in the Swedish Riksdag, the Social Democrats had a voting majority in the commission. Management was well represented along with labor. Among the members were both the head of the Federation of Swedish Trade Unions and the president of the Employers' Association.

The Swedish Chamber of Commerce, the Swedish Export Federation, and the Swedish National Association of Manufacturers were represented along with the Swedish Farm Bureau and the Swedish Co-operatives. The two biggest trade unions also had seats in the commission, as did several of Sweden's more prominent industrial leaders and bankers.

The guiding principle for the commission's work was to attack specific, practical problems which might emerge during the reconversion period. Because of the unwieldy size of the commission and the great number of problems involved, it was decided to distribute the members into smaller delegations to study one or a group of problems and make proposals for their solution. These proposals were then put before the full commission, which determined what course to follow. In these discussions the commission followed the old Swedish custom of first trying to find the areas of agreements before starting to settle the controversial points. The spirit of co-operation was very strong and many decisions were accepted without a dissident voice.

During the first two months of its existence, the commission produced two important reports. The first concerned Sweden's postwar monetary and wage policy. During the war, costs of living had risen about forty per cent. Because of the wage-freeze policy which allowed only a partial compensation in wages for a corresponding rise in the cost-of-living index, the real wages of the workers had fallen by ten per cent. The commission decided that nominal wages should be kept at their present level. The rise in real wages aimed at was to be brought about by the fall in freight rates on imported goods and the return to ordinary types of fuel, instead of the high-priced wood and wood derivatives that were then being utilized. In carrying through this policy, the Swedish OPA had the difficult task of forcing down prices.

The commission's second report was on a public-works program in case of widespread unemployment. The commission unanimously agreed on the need for large-scale public works if private investment and export trade fell below the level necessary to keep full employment. Many of the projects (to the value of about eight hundred million Swedish crowns) had been worked out on blueprints and were being planned in detail. By these means Sweden hoped to be able to avoid such previous mistakes as too hasty inauguration of badly planned and uneconomic public works to cope with unforeseen outbreaks of unemployment.

The commission strongly stressed important principle of public-works policy. If public works were planned for periods of unemployment, these plans should not be considered apart from the long-range policy of the Government. If, for example, the Government should consider it advisable, from a social standpoint, to build special recreation places or erect buildings for the 'school luncheons,' these investments should be made during a depression.

At about the same time that the commission started its work, the Social Democratic Party put forward their program for post-war economic policy. Among the objectives were:

1. Full employment under the economic leadership of the government.

2. Housing as an important part of post-war economic policy. The housing standard to be increased.

3. The increased production of 'utility goods.'

4. The broadening of the social security program.

5. Shortening of working hours, but not primarily as a means of fighting unemployment.

6. Social and economic advantages for families with children.

7. Equal educational opportunities for all regardless of class, place, and income.

8. Equal standard of living and leveling out of class differences.

9. Socialization of insurance, creation of a government-owned commercial bank, and the direction of all investment activities by a public investment organization.

10. Improved foreign trade under government leadership.

11. Real estate in towns and cities to be gradually taken over by the municipalities.

12. Monopolies to be severely restricted.

13. Organization of 'joint production committees' to give workers a share in management.

Thus, sober Swedish economists, representing Government, labor, and management, charted a course for the little kingdom through the uncertain waters which lay ahead. And the course was unmistakably in the direction of a moderate, democratic collectivism.

VIII

Finland

★ I. BETTER TO DIE THAN NEGOTIATE ★

IN 1918, THE FINNS received their independence for the first time as a result of a fortunate coincidence. Russia was weak and the western European powers wanted a *cordon sanitaire* of small independent states around the Red Revolution. Making a virtue of necessity, Lenin declared Finland independent as an expression of national minorities' right of secession. The Finns guarded their independence stubbornly and took advantage of it. Within a decade they built up a clean, well-ordered country with a relatively high standard of living and very progressive social legislation. It became a stable, prosperous nation with one visible weakness — its foreign relations.

Finnish leaders failed to realize that Russia was bound to become strong again. Prominent trade-unionists, Social Democrats, agrarians, and industrialists, with very few exceptions, expressed ideas and pursued policies hostile to the Soviet Union. The anti-Russian bias, rooted both in Finnish history and fear of communism, went down through all the levels of the population. It was fostered in the schools, preached from the pulpits, and propagated in the press. The Finnish right extremists even nursed ideas of territorial conquest at Russian expense and aimed at spreading the domain of Finland at least to the White Sea and possibly to the Urals.

By 1939, Russia had become strong again, and it was inconceivable that Finland could continue to think as it had been thinking. Finnish intransigence, at length, led to armed conflict. In the Winter War, which began on December 1, 1939, the Finns fought bravely for three months, then buckled under the overwhelming weight of Russian manpower and armament.

During the next fifteen months, Russia squeezed the Finns and repeatedly attempted to interfere in the country's internal affairs. The Finns, meanwhile, began plotting with the Germans and in May, 1940, signed a secret agreement giving Germany transit rights through Finland. German troops entered Finland in increasing numbers and took up strategic positions. By June 22, 1941, when Germany attacked, Finland was mobilized and prepared. Four days later, with Marshal Mannerheim's order of the day ringing in their ears, Finnish troops crossed the Soviet frontier. Almost immediately, they found themselves at war with Britain, and relations with the United States became strained.

By November, 1941, the Finns had regained all their own territory and overrun some of Russia's. At this point the hard-pressed Russians offered Helsinki peace on the basis of Finland's 1939 frontiers and no indemnities. This offer was never publicized in Finland and was almost unknown elsewhere. It was flatly rejected by the Finnish Government. The war dragged on, the Finnish-Russian front remaining static through some thirty eventful months, during which it became obvious to the entire world, except censor-ridden Finland, that the Axis star was waning. Only in February, 1944, did the Finnish Government finally send an envoy, Doctor Juho Paasikivi, to Stockholm, to inquire about Russian peace terms. On March 29, the Russian conditions for peace included expulsion of the Germans, the reinstatement of the 1940 Russo-Finnish Agreement, the demobilization of the Finnish Army, the return of the Petsamo district (given to Finland by the peace treaties of 1920), and an indemnity of six hundred million dollars, to be paid in commodities over a five-year period. If these terms were accepted, Russia would give up its claim to lease the Hangoe district.

Just after Paasikivi's return from Stockholm, I arrived in Finland. The last time I had been there was in 1938, and I expected to find the country badly battered by its two wars; to find the hunger, rags, and apathy that prevailed throughout Axis Europe. Instead, I found Finland about as well-dressed, well-fed, and as hard at work as Britain. Bomb damage in Helsinki was less noticeable than in Liverpool. There were some serious commodity shortages and the black market thrived, but, by and large, the Finns were getting by. Foreign money was in great demand and black-market prices for Swedish crowns were ten times their nominal value.

Transactions, despite severe penalties, were numerous, since many Finns who spoke of fighting to the end were nevertheless preparing to leave for Sweden. Some forty thousand had applied for passports, though they were being granted only to children and an occasional mother. Many Finns felt confident and even elated. Their successful defense of favorable frontiers for two years, national stubbornness and censorship, had brought them to an estimation of their own strength which the real political and military situation did not justify.

On April 1, Russia's peace terms were given to President Ryti, Premier Linkomies, and Marshal Mannerheim, and the stage was set for an intricate political drama in a modern democracy, to be played to its conclusion against an international backdrop. Copies of the peace terms were distributed for the two hundred members of Parliament to take home with them over the Easter recess. Accompanying each copy was a memorandum by the economist, Bruno Suviranta, which, citing statistics of Finnish trade and national income, reached the conclusion that payment of the six hundred million-dollar indemnity in five years would be virtually impossible. Proponents of peace with Russia, if they had been given the opportunity, would have pointed out that Finland's war expenses amounted to four hundred million dollars annually, so that, at least theoretically, in peacetime the debt could have been paid off in eighteen months.

While Parliament was in recess, the Social Democratic Party, the largest in Finland with enough power to be almost decisive on any question, held district conventions throughout Finland to discuss the peace proposals. Vaino Tanner, party leader and boss of a carefully contrived and diligently tended political machine, a tough, able, hard-hitting individual, was against the acceptance of the proposals. An opposition, led by Jaasko Keto, kept attracting rank and file support to its position — that Finland should make peace immediately, at the best possible terms, provided that these guaranteed Finland freedom and independence. At one time it appeared that Keto's opposition had about half the membership of the party with it and was still growing. But censorship and the Tanner machine squelched it before it ripened into a serious threat.

At the secret session of Parliament on April 12, the Information

Chief of the General Staff reported that Finland was in no immediate military danger and that its ally, Germany, was in a serious but by no means critical position. Premier Linkomies then took up the cudgels. Time was working for Finland, he declared. The nation would be in its best bargaining position when the Soviet-German war ended, no matter what its outcome. Therefore, the Government had decided to reject the Russian proposals, which were, in any case, impossible to fulfill.

Heated discussion ensued among the parliamentary party groups, but the opposition could not muster enough strength for a showdown. In the evening, Parliament reassembled to hear each official party speaker support the government position. A technically unanimous verdict to accept the Government's decision was obtained. The Finnish people never even saw a word about all these events. On April 18, Soviet Ambassadress Kollontay received Finland's answer to the Russian proposals — a lengthy, tortuous document which meant 'No.'

In conversations with a score of Finland's political and industrial leaders, I found nearly all to be substantially in agreement with the position taken by Linkomies, Ryti, and Tanner. Russia could not be trusted. The conditions were impossible. Peace with Russia would mean war with Germany. Russia was becoming weaker every day, and, besides, Anglo-Saxon co-operation with Russia would not last long. 'The time is coming,' I was informed, 'when you will be profoundly grateful that we Finnish patriots stood firm as a bulwark against bolshevism at a time when all other bulwarks were crumbling, because you will want to use our bulwark against bolshevism yourselves.'

I talked to landlords, small peasants, landless peasants, and migrant agricultural laborers, and got the same answer virtually everywhere. Finland should not make peace unless the terms were reasonable. What were reasonable terms? 'Well, the 1939 frontiers should be a basis of negotiation, but we fought hard and should get something for all our struggles.'

I was told that there were a handful of Communists who would like to make peace with Russia at unfavorable terms because they admired the Russian system and were working for it. I was assured that they had no influence, which was probably true, as Finland's active Communists had long been in jail.

Leaders of the A.K.S., the numerically small but by no means insignificant organization which, with the I.K.L. (outspoken Finnish Nazis), represented the extreme right wing, informed me that as far as they were concerned, the only basis for peace negotiations were the present frontiers, which would leave Petrozoavodsk and part of Soviet Karelia in Finnish hands. The only problem for Finland, as they saw it, was to get the most defensible frontiers, so that when England and America declared war on Russia in a few months, Finland could do the most for herself and the anti-Bolshevik cause. The stubborn intransigence of most Finns reflected the lines from the country's great epic, *The Kalevala:*

> Just this much will they get from me,
> What the axe gets from the rock,
> A stump from slippery ice,
> Or death from an empty room.

In conversations with such leaders and statesmen as Premier Ryti, Foreign Minister Sir Henryk Ramsay, and Vaino Tanner, I found that war between the Anglo-Saxon powers and Russia was regarded as an imminent probability. All were frightened of the Bolshevik menace, and hoped either to avert a Finnish catastrophe by holding out till a general peace conference or by putting up a desperate resistance against a weakened Russia, no matter how the general war went.

The most reasonable estimate of the situation, I found, prevailed among a large number of the industrial and rural workers, who made up about forty per cent of the Finnish population, and one or two independent figures like Juho Paasikivi, who, at seventy-seven, had the most impressive personality of all to whom I talked. After having returned from his talks with Molotov, he was rather pessimistic. Anxious to promote peace, Paasikivi had then the difficult task of trying to influence his countrymen to a more reasonable estimate of their situation and to get Russia to moderate some of the harsher demands (that is, the indemnity, which Paasikivi thought could not possibly be paid). He had gone to Moscow without plenipotentiary powers, and his three talks with Molotov had been neither pleasant nor successful. He had found the Russian Minister confident but not arrogant, and firm in the position he had taken. Paasikivi had thought that if he could get the Russians to soften their terms somewhat, they would have a fair chance of acceptance by Finland. He had not succeeded, and thought there was a strong chance of a coup in Finland by the pro-German minority.

'I believe that the peace has already been lost,' he said to me, toward the conclusion of our talk, 'and that small nations are going to get trampled on after this war. Furthermore, there will be a great war within twenty years between Russia and an Anglo-Saxon-led coalition. And I do not think it is mostly Russia's fault. Their policies in Finland have been like your policies in Latin America and like England's policies in any one of a dozen countries from Malay to Ireland. Perhaps, if Finland were a great power, we would do the same things. I hope not. Anyhow, these things are being done today by all the great powers and they will reap the harvest in another war, perhaps before I am dead.'

One of the most impressive speeches I remember hearing was made by Paasikivi. Repeating to me what he had, probably, told Molotov — a description of what the results would be if Russia overran Finland — Paasikivi stood up, shook a bony, freckled forefinger in the air, and said, 'We will shoot from behind every stone and tree, we will go on shooting for fifty years. We are not Czechs. We are not Dutchmen. We will fight tooth and nail behind every rock and over the ice of every lake. I will not fight for long. I am old. But others will carry on.'

I left Paasikivi with the feeling that he was a great leader in a small country.

In spite of heavy pressure from Sweden (the Swedes were more anxious than anyone to get Finland out of the war), negotiations with Russia were not resumed, and early in June, the Russians attacked in force. Within three weeks the Mannerheim Line was pierced and Viborg taken. The Finns suffered some fifteen thousand casualties, and their military position became untenable. The Finns, as a whole, remained adamant and determined to fight, although it was obvious that even with German aid they could not last long. The mood of the Finns at this time could be summed up by a remark made by a woman whose brother had fallen in the Winter War, and whose husband was fighting in the Viborg sector:

'We Finns are real heroes. Anybody can fight and die for something, but we fight and die for nothing. That's real heroism.'

Mannerheim and the High Command began to feel that a collapse was imminent. On June 18, it was decided to form an interim government headed by Ramsay (who had been for peace for some time, but was too weak to make his influence felt), to make peace and then resign in favor of a new one more suitable to the circumstances. On the morning of June 19, the Finnish Government sent the Swedish Foreign Office the text of a request addressed to the Russians, asking what the terms would be for an armistice. Later in the same day, the Finnish High Command reconsidered and asked the Government to hold up the release of the request to Russia. The Swedish Ministry received no order to release the request until the evening of the twenty-first and the Russians did not get it until the morning of the twenty-second. The formation of the Ramsay Government was now impeded by sudden last-minute difficulties largely originating with the younger generals in the High Command, who still thought the Finnish Army might hold.

But meanwhile, either on the evening of the twenty-first or on the morning of the twenty-second, some traitor in either the Government or the High Command informed the Germans of the Finnish bid for peace. Berlin reacted promptly, and within a few hours Ribbentrop was on his way to Helsinki. Two hours before his arrival in Helsinki on the twenty-second, the German Minister informed the Finnish Foreign Office that he was coming. On the previous day, German troops had begun to arrive in Finland, to be followed on the next three days by a sufficient number of armored units, equipment, and aviation to give Finland the impression that a peace government would mean converting their country into a raging battleground of Finnish, Russian, and German forces.

On the twenty-third, the Russian reply to the Finnish inquiry about armistice terms was delivered. It simply stated that when the Finnish Government had decided, in principle, to capitulate, and a statement to this effect, signed by President Ryti and Foreign Minister Ramsay, was received, the Soviet Government would welcome a Finnish delegation to Moscow to discuss terms.

Not more than a dozen men in Finland knew the contents of the

Russian message, but a rumor was spread around Helsinki, partly by German agents, that the Russians were insisting upon an unconditional surrender and complete occupation of the country. German propaganda and Finnish imagination enlarged and embellished this depressing vision of the future into a delirious nightmare. Many, possibly most, Finns fully believed that peace with Russia would mean unconditional surrender, total occupation by the Red Army, followed by the loss of the last shred of Finnish independence, the deportation of all able-bodied men to Siberia and the herding of women into collective farms. On the other hand, a large number of Finns were in favor of peace with Russia at any cost.

In this atmosphere of fog, hysteria, and mirage, Ribbentrop worked feverishly. He waved his thin arms around wildly and gave the taciturn Finns a demonstration of the Nazi capacity for sustained frenetic volubility. He cursed, raved, and threatened the Finns with a German coup and civil war if they made a move for peace. He coaxed, and reassured them with promises of extensive military aid and a very special place in the New Order. Astutely, he exploited President Ryti's psychotic Russophobia, Tanner's overmastering desire to retain his power, and the weakness and indecision of Premier Linkomies and Foreign Minister Ramsay. In two days the ex-champagne salesman's torrential oratory washed away the last traces of their prudence, their intelligence, and their reluctance to yield up Finland's last chance for peace.

On June 24, in the presence of Generals Dietl and Jodl, every important member of the Finnish Government except Mannerheim agreed to fight to the bitter end with Germany. A letter written in the first person and signed by President Ryti was dispatched to Hitler. In this letter, wreathed in flowery phrases about the defense of European civilization against Asiatic bolshevism, was Ryti's commitment, not only to keep Finland in the war as long as Germany, but to prevent any group in the country from opening negotiations with Russia as long as Finland was requesting and receiving military aid from Germany.

In addition to the letter, a secret protocol was signed by Ramsay and von Ribbentrop. Under it, Germany agreed to send 'immediately' five hundred planes, four hundred tanks, and four hundred guns (mostly anti-tank guns which the Finns needed desperately), with crews, and between five and eight divisions, two of them mechanized. The Finns undertook to recruit five new divisions which the Germans were to clothe, equip, and train, and agreed not to make a separate peace. They also undertook, if and when possible, to join Germany's offensive and not to stop on or near pre-war Russian frontiers.

The text of the letter was known to most of Parliament. The contents of the protocol were known to about a dozen men in the Government. Four days after the agreement had been reached, the Finnish people knew nothing except that discussions between Ribbentrop, Ryti, and Ramsay had taken place and that the German Government had agreed to furnish military assistance requested by the Finnish Government. About Finland's commitments not a word was printed or broadcast.

The opposition was in a condition of strangled desperation. Parliamentary groups discussed the agreement with Germany in what should have been preparation for a vote, but it was obvious that a majority, now including Tanner and the Social Democratic members of the Government, were against it. Backed by the High Command, who now thought that they had the military situation under control because of the arrival of German troops, Ryti, Linkomies, and Ramsay insisted upon making the agreement operative without referring it to Parliament.

They produced several legal authorities to prove that this would be constitutional. The opposition produced several legal authorities of the opposite opinion.

From June 25 to June 27 in parliamentary group meetings, the Swedish party voted fifteen to two against the agreement and the Social Democrats voted thirty-six against, twenty-six for, and twenty abstaining. Under the Finnish system, in which parliamentary groups voted *en bloc*, this would have meant a clear defeat for the agreement, as the Swedes and Social Democrats together had a definite majority of the seats. On June 27, Ryti, Linkomies, and Ramsay forced a vote in the Government, not on the agreement itself, but on whether or not to submit the agreement to Parliament. In view of the group meeting results, however, this was, in effect, a vote on the agreement. Ten members of the Government voted for it, and five Social Democrats and one progressive against. On the same day, Ribbentrop flew back to Germany, his mission accomplished. With a majority of a democratic Parliament against it, German occupation and a Quisling Government had in effect been arranged. Not a shot had been fired, there had been no serious resistance. The German Minister had not even suffered the embarrassment of having to bulldoze an aged Marshal or import a Minister from Berlin as a new Premier. At a time when the whole world regarded the German cause as lost, Finland had been set to work in the best interests of Germany and the Germans had paid the minimum price.

The people of Finland had never been oversympathetic to the Germans, although they had tolerated their presence. After the publication of the Finnish-German communiqué on June 28, the people reacted sharply to the seizure of their country by the Germans. Large numbers of Finns gathered in the Helsinki railyards, where long trains of primitive boxcars were drawing up and units of German infantry were being entrained for the front. Although many talked to the Germans, it was not a friendly or enthusiastic atmosphere. It was felt that the Government was responsible for their unwelcome presence in the capital.

The Finns also blamed the Linkomies Government for the break with America. Feeling toward America remained very friendly, possibly because its relations with all the other great powers were such a source of torment to the country. There was, however, some resentment at Roosevelt's remark that 'American Foreign Policy is not for sale at $189,000.' The Finns felt that the fact that they had tried to pay their debts should not, even under difficult circumstances, be thrown back at them as a reproach. One evening I was sitting drinking with three Information Bureau officials. I passed around a bar of Swedish chocolate, a delicacy which most Finns had not seen for years. 'Mr. Scott,' said one of them as he chewed his piece, 'do you think the Finnish Information Bureau can be bought for one bar of Swedish chocolate?'

The atmosphere in Helsinki became tense. The longing for peace was general and resentment against the Germans was universal. Awareness of the fact that the Finnish people had been hoodwinked by their own Government became widespread. Everything pointed to an ominous future. Yet numbers of Finns continued to make their usual long weekend trips into the country. At war, their front collapsing, their Government suspect, German troops everywhere in the capital, a *coup d'état,* civil war, or both hourly possibilities, nearly all the leaders of both the group in power and the opposition spent long weekends in the country, drinking bootleg brandy at nine hundred marks a bottle and taking *saunas* (Finnish baths).

On June 30, Washington announced its decision to break off diplomatic relations with Finland. Chargé d'Affaires Edmond Gullion burned his codes and confidential material and prepared to leave. The only non-Axis diplomat in Helsinki for the past three months, he had probably been under instructions to remain aloof from the diplomatic and social life of the capital. However, he was expected to keep himself well-informed, and some quarters had probably hoped that he would be able to influence Finnish leaders and prevent them from falling into Ribbentrop's trap. In my opinion, Gullion did a remarkable job of keeping himself informed without violating his instructions. Of course, he could not influence the Finns much, one way or the other.

It took about a week for all arrangements to be made. I spent a great deal of time talking to Germans of all kinds who, though far from deserting their views, were nevertheless anxious to explain and justify themselves to an American. German leaders still figured they were good for a year of slow retreat on all fronts. Meanwhile, they hoped to drive a wedge between Russia and the Anglo-Saxon powers. They thought it more likely that they could stem the Russian advance from the east than the drive from the west, particularly since it seemed possible that the Russians might stop, of themselves, at the line of the Oder. It would not take much military strength and they could reinforce their western line, while gaining credit with a large number of 'sensible people' in England and America for keeping the Russians out of central Europe. Patience and determination would pull Germany through the war, impoverished, bled, but still the dominating power in central Europe, which America and England would inevitably support and arm Germany to ward off the Russian menace.

Germany was anxious to keep Finland in the war and to secure as much publicity as possible within Finland and throughout the world for Finnish heroism, vindictive Russian barbarism, and German gallantry and loyalty. When I left for Stockholm a week later with Gullion and eighty-nine of the few remaining Allied nationals, Finland was being slowly cracked in a colossal vise. She was utterly helpless. If she rolled about a bit, it only served to increase the crushing pressure from one or another of the powers that held her in a death-grip.

★ 2. REBIRTH IN DEFEAT ★

ALL THROUGH THE SUMMER of 1944, conditions in Finland worsened. Their defensive positions had been destroyed, the economy of the country was deteriorating, and the population became more and more bitter. The Germans were not only unable to deliver the pledged reinforcements to Finland, but actually had to withdraw most of their troops. Food became scarcer, hoarding increased, and inflation became a serious problem. Even with censorship, it became clear to the Finns that Germany faced collapse.

Early in August, seventy-seven-year-old Marshal Mannerheim stepped in. President Ryti resigned and returned to his job as Governor of the Bank of Finland. Mannerheim became both President and Premier of a new Government and the change was legalized by a special act of the Finnish Diet. The new Government made it known that they would work for an immediate peace with Russia and it became known to the world as the 'Peace Government.' After innumerable delays, a Finnish delegation signed the armistice conditions in Moscow on September 19.

The terms provided for the Finns to retire beyond the 1940 frontier according to a strict schedule, disarm all German military forces in Finland by September 15 and turn them over to the Soviet High Command as prisoners of war. Finland was obliged to give the Russians a number of important air bases, the Peninsula of Porkkala (only a few miles from Helsinki) as a naval base, the entire Petsamo district, a substantial portion of Finland's merchant shipping tonnage and all of Finland's military matériel. Finland was to release all Soviet prisoners of war in Finland, while the Russians undertook to send all Finnish prisoners of war in Russia back home. Finland was to pay three hundred million dollars indemnity over a period of six years, release its own political prisoners, suppress all Fascist organizations, and nullify all discriminating pro-Fascist legislation. A Soviet Control Commission was to check the fulfillment of the armistice terms on the spot.

All during August in Stockholm, peace rumors had been plentiful and speculation and curiosity about the fate of Finland widespread. With Edmond Gullion and Robert McClintock, both second secretaries in the American Legation in Stockholm and both formerly Chargés d'Affaires in Finland, I was invited to attend a luncheon given by the aged but still mentally agile Ambassadress Kollontay. Vladimir Semenoff, a hard-headed ex-professor of philosophy, the counselor of the Soviet Legation in Stockholm, was also present. Our hosts were irritatingly uncommunicative about preliminary peace discussions which we knew were going on. The Russians, however, emphasized one aspect of their intentions which struck me as genuine and unequivocal. They wanted peace, and they insisted on a friendly Finland, but under no circumstances would they want to see restored the old Tsarist frontier which included Finland in the Russian Empire.

On September 25, a few days after the Soviet Control Commission arrived, I returned to Finland. At the airport in Helsinki I saw Russian flyers and planes instead of the German aviators and Messerschmitts I had seen on my previous visit. The Germans had cleared out of Finland quickly and almost completely. In Helsinki the windows were still boarded up, but it seemed to me that there was a more cheerful look on the faces of the people in the street. They had peace, and it superseded every other consideration. In the market-place there was a queue of some four hundred men and women waiting to buy potatoes from a railroad car at 2.50 Finnish marks a kilo, ten kilos to a customer, and no ration coupons. This was in marked contrast to many other parts of Europe, such as Norway, where potatoes were severely rationed and almost unobtainable. Even in defeat, I found Finland comparatively well-off.

Before October 1, I found many of the Finnish leaders pessimistic and anxiously awaiting the arrival of General Andrei Zhdanov, Stalin's heir-apparent, and the man believed by most Finns to be responsible for the Soviet attack against Finland in 1939. Afterward, of course, when none of the anticipated horrors had materialized, a great deal of the dread was dissipated.

On October 12, I went to see former President Ryti, who seemed much more certain of himself and his problems as Governor of the Bank than in his former position of responsibility.

From Ryti I gathered that ousting Germany from the country's finances would create no outstanding difficulties. The German debt to Finland was comparatively small and German loans to any Finnish business organizations other than the Petsamo nickel mines were insignificant. In Finland foreign-owned shares and securities had to be registered in such a way as to make ownership easy to check. The Germans had not rooted into Finnish economic life by means of daughter organizations to anything like the extent they had in Norway and Denmark, or even in neutral Sweden. All German assets in Finland were already blocked and the financial readjustment was proceeding smoothly.

From Ryti I learned the interesting fact that Finland had, during the previous twelve months, exported large quantities of standardized wooden houses for devastated German areas and large quantities of plywood tents. The Finns had created a whole new industry in response to the German demand for these products. This fact was also extremely interesting to the Russians, who within a fortnight were suggesting the creation of many new industries to manufacture commodities needed by Russia.

Ryti also anticipated bad years for Finland between 1945 and 1947 when statistical indexes showed that many Finnish industries (paper and wood products, particularly) would reach the bottom of their production curve. In these trying times, he said, Finland would want and could easily service an American credit of about two hundred and fifty million dollars. In the next two years he anticipated that Finland would pass a capital-levy tax of fifteen per cent on all assets movable and immovable.

Typical, too, was the attitude of Wahlforss, the President of Finland's Association of Manufacturers, who the last time I had seen him had been talking about dying on the barbed wire of the front lines rather than capitulate to Russia. He was now Chairman of Finland's Economic Commission to treat with the Russians on the payment of the indemnity. He was now moderately sanguine about the Finnish future. One of his greatest worries was coal. According to him, Finnish industry had enough coal to keep going for three or four months. If it did not receive enough to make up its annual coal consumption figure of one million tons a year, industry would have to shut down and widespread unemployment and chaos would result. If Finland could avoid any serious growth of unemployment, he anticipated no great political or social disturbances.

'It depends,' he concluded, 'in great measure on what Russia wants. I sometimes have serious misgivings. Perhaps the Russians don't want us to organize our economy; perhaps they would prefer Finland to be harassed by unemployment, poverty, and social upheaval, because in that case the country would unquestionably go Communist in a few weeks. In such an event Russia could, with no difficulty whatsoever, take over Finland. Generally speaking, however, I don't believe that the Russians want to, or will attempt to carry out such a plan. I believe that the Russians desire and will work for an independent though weak Finland.'

Fear among many had become alleviated. Businessmen who had prepared to leave for Sweden, and had even sent their families on ahead, had decided to remain. They no longer expected Finland to be bolshevized and businessmen to be tried as war criminals. To their surprise many of them were even getting good orders and their business prospects appeared hopeful. They no longer feared Russia, but some of their anxieties had now been turned on the 'native Reds' and the possibility that they might get control of the situation.

Finland still faced economic and financial difficulties of all sorts. The wood and paper industry was operating far below its capacity because of a lack of manpower, the poor conditions of the forests, and bad marketing arrangements. Several paper mills were idle because of this last reason despite the fact that all of Europe was experiencing a severe paper shortage.

Finnish currency was in bad shape. The black-market price for Swedish crowns in Finland was then between one hundred and one hundred and twenty Finnish marks, as opposed to an official rate of eleven. The Ministry of Finance was considering the devaluation of the mark by about fifty per cent, which would mean raising the official rate to about eighteen Finnish marks per Swedish crown. This proposed devaluation would increase the tendency to inflation and would react heavily on all bank depositors.

The 1943 income tax had been increased by twenty per cent, partly due in 1944 and partly in 1945. The income tax of 1945 was to be increased by thirty-five per cent and collected from the beginning of 1945 as a sort of advance payment. It also seemed probable that an 'economic situation tax' (*konjunktursskatten*) would be levied.

The Government needed 2,300,000,000 marks for interest payments in 1945. Before the war, notes in circulation amounted to somewhat more than 2,000,000,000. At the end of September 1944, it was 14,300,000,000 and increasing steadily.

Civilian consumption in Finland was reduced but adequate. Clothes and consumers' gas were the most critical items. The city of Helsinki had enough coal to furnish some gas daily for some six months. Gas in most other centers was not available. There was a crucial shortage of living quarters. The combined statistical result of population increase, evacuations, demolition, and reconstruction indicated a total housing shortage for Finland of fifty-two thousand dwellings. In the year of 1938, when building was intensive, about eight thousand dwellings had been erected. At that rate it would require between six and seven years to meet the demand. But in addition to the present demand there would be a further 'normal' demand for about five thousand dwellings a year. This meant that if as many of the same type of dwellings as were built in 1938 continued to be built during the post-war years, it would take from fifteen to seventeen years to meet the requirements.

The living-space calculum in Finland was made at one room for a member of the family. In Magnitogorsk behind the Urals, when I was there in the middle nineteen-thirties, the calculum made was in the neighborhood of three square meters of floor space per person or, roughly, one room for a family, and housing conditions in Moscow and some other cities were much worse than in

Magnitogorsk. In other words, according to this index the housing standard in Finland was considerably better after five years of war than it was in a large city of the Soviet Union at the time of greatest Soviet prosperity. Of course, it must be said that the Finns had been accustomed to much higher standards than the Russians, but it must also be borne in mind that to an increasing extent direct statistical comparisons between Russia and her western neighbors cannot be overlooked.

This point was driven home to me one day when I went for a walk with one of the newly arrived Russians. We walked down to the market-place on the Esplanade. Here several hundred Finnish housewives were buying, without coupons and at reasonable prices, rabbits, pheasants, fresh and salt fish, a vast assortment of fruits and vegetables, buttermilk, and odd items such as mustard. The eyes of the Russian opened as wide as saucers. 'What the hell is this — did they win the war or lose it?' he said. 'In Moscow you can't touch this stuff at these prices without coupons!'

The same remark must be made here with regard to housing. Finnish standards have undoubtedly been higher; but to a member of the Russian Control Commission, just arrived from a victorious country to a vanquished one, from one of the world's great nations industrially and agriculturally to a small defeated neighbor, direct statistical comparisons were unavoidable, humiliating, and challenging.

The political situation in Finland, like the economic situation, was difficult and unstable. Finland was going through a major metamorphosis presided over by the aged Marshal Mannerheim, and very probably no one else in Finland could have done the job. No one else could successfully have commanded the young officers of the Finnish Army to give up a war which had been so expensive and for a long time so successful. Mannerheim's Government was subjected to continuous criticism by die-hards like Vaino Tanner, who considered the Government was too pro-Russian, and by extreme leftists, almost all of whom had been in jail until the amnesty provided for by the armistice terms.

It sounds paradoxical, but it is nevertheless true that Finnish politics were dominated by fear. Finnish bravery, heroism, even foolhardiness, displayed so prominently during the Winter War, were in part, expressions of fear — fear of the Russians, fear of a renewal of the civil war in Finland, fear of further excesses from the Lapua rightists. A large section of the population was sure the Russians would murder all decent people mercilessly as soon as the Red Army set foot in Finland. After the armistice Finland drifted away from a fear of Russian intervention and occupation to a fear of indigenous radicalism, aggravated by unemployment. Fear was a motive force among the leftists as well as the rightists. Among the masses of Finns, memories of 1918 were still vivid. Most workers by 1939 had reached a fairly high standard of living. They desired a return to 'normal' times and wanted social improvements, but no social upheaval.

So general was this fear of upheaval that the main argument used by the Social Democratic Party opposition against Tanner was that his reactionary policies bred bitterness, radicalism, and upheaval. Thus Social Democratic oppositionaries like Vuori were often motivated, not by any progressive, let alone revolutionary, ideas, but rather by a division of opinion with Tanner over the methods for preventing bitterness and social conflict.

Nowhere in Finland did I find or hear of a single person who wanted a revolution, or even the establishment of Soviet power without a revolution if that were possible. I talked with a number of recently released prisoners of the extreme left, among them Hertta Kuusinen, Mauri Ryömä, and Hella Vuolijoki. They resented bitterly having served long terms in jail for the expression of ideas which were now generally recognized in their country as having been correct. They stated that there had never been full democracy in Finland and that the Left had always been suppressed. They felt that the only program on which they could get full agreement was the general program of the United Nations — the struggle against fascism for full democracy. They added that the rich in Finland had started the war and should be made to pay for it. None of them thought that a Soviet régime in Finland was either desirable or necessary.

The first left organization to appear or reappear was the Society for Friendship between the Soviet Union and Finland. This society had been organized in 1940 by Ryömä and within a short time had some sixty thousand members. With the outbreak of hostilities between the two countries, the society was suppressed and most of its leaders jailed. In October, 1944, the organization re-formed under the leadership of Doctor Helo, one of the Sixlings and for a long time State Controller of the city of Helsinki. The Honorary President of the organization was Paasikivi, and within a fortnight thousands of people all over the country had joined, some of them Right-wing industrialists, some middle class, many workers.

At the general meeting of the society on October 16, Doctor Helo, the keynoter of the program of the society, advocated friendship and understanding between the Soviet Union and Finland. He made an attack on Finland's previous leaders, who had failed to achieve friendship and understanding with the Soviet Union. He praised democracy. (Corollary: Russia is also a democracy.) 'Finland has become a smaller Finland, but we must make it a better Finland.' Those responsible for Finland's criminal policy must be called to account.

Around such a program, not only the extreme Left, but also most of the city dwellers and many of the peasants of Finland could be united.

The Sixlings were a curious group. Most of them came from solid middle-class families, and had been successful men. By advocating friendship with Russia in 1941, they had fallen foul of the Fascist-minded Finnish police and had been jailed, although they were members of the Diet and should have had immunity. They all came out of prison bitter and well to the left of the Communist Party to which none of them belonged.

To the right of the Sixlings were a number of previous oppositionaries never jailed. Messrs. Voionmaa, Kekkonen, Erkko, Pekkala, Andersson, Kilpi, and Mrs. Kilpi. Most of these were in opposition to Tanner within the Social Democratic Party. Kekkonen was an Agrarian, Erkko Independent. All were eminently respectable, instinctively anti-Communist and somewhat confused.

The Social Democratic Party had been in the throes of a crisis for months. Vaino Tanner, leader of the party, hung on to his power stubbornly. I talked to him twice on this trip to Finland. He was cool, clear, and forceful. He said: 'There are two groups in the party leadership. One believes in the fulfillment to the letter by the Finns of the terms of the Soviet-Finnish armistice. The second advocates licking the ass of the Russians. I belong to the former group.' As I write, Tanner is still at liberty and fairly powerful.

By early October, some two hundred Russians were in Finland. They made up the Control Commission. Most of them went around in Red Army dress uniforms and behaved politely but coolly toward the Finns. Despite a few hitches, the provisions of the armistice with respect to expelling the Germans were being efficiently carried out. Arrangements for returns of Russian and Finnish prisoners to their respective countries were made. In Helsinki the rectitude of the Russians and their willingness to pay promptly whatever prices were asked for accommodations had made a favorable impression. Zhdanov had done a lot toward allaying Finnish fears by stepping out of his plane at the Helsinki Airport, grinning at the Guard of Honor of Finnish soldiers standing at attention, and calling out in Finnish 'Hyvas paivaa, pojat,' meaning 'Good day, boys.' The surprised Finnish soldiers had slowly returned the grin and the greeting. The story of this incident was printed in all the papers and repeated widely among the people.

One thing which the Russians did which aroused the ire of some Finns was to invite Finnish laborers to go to work on Russian construction jobs in Porkkala at a wage roughly twice the prevalent one for similar jobs on the Finnish side of the frontier. There were a few other minor causes of grumbling, but basically day-to-day household reactions between the Finns and the Control Commission were good.

It was impossible to see Zhdanov, who was very busy. The other members of the Control Commission, including its chief, Pavel Orlov, were available and willing to talk. They were very definite and emphatic on several points. There would be no bolshevization of Finland. They felt that the Finns were honestly attempting to fulfill the armistice conditions and were anxious to bury the hatchet and end the decades of ill-feeling between the two countries.

The Russian economic policy toward Finland required, among other things, American credits to make it function smoothly. The Russian economic mission in Helsinki informed the Finns that they did not want Finnish wood products as indemnity payments. They wanted ships, machinery, and manufactured goods — none of which

Finland had ever made in quantity. The Russians had prepared a plan for the construction of new factories in Finland to make these items. When the Finnish delegates asked where they were to get credits and equipment for these plants, the Russians shrugged and said: 'Go to your good friends the Americans.'

This plan would amount, in effect, to the rapid industrialization of Finland on American credits, while the products of Finnish industry would go to Russia in payment of war indemnity for five or six years. It would be a form of indirect American aid to Russian reconstruction, out of which Finland would get industrialization. Eventually this plan would benefit Finland, raise the country's productivity and standard of living. But for five or ten years it would mean to the Finns hard work on short rations. For it seemed fairly clear that the Russians would use prices of commodities taken from Finland as a handle with which to keep Finnish living standards from rising awkwardly higher than those across the frontier in Russia.

The Finns, meanwhile, had carried out the tremendous changes demanded by the situation. With impressive alacrity they had disbanded some four hundred and twenty pro-Fascist organizations. They had interned more than five hundred Germans and taken several thousand prisoners. Though censorship was still tough, pro-Allied and pro-Russian news was getting a fair hearing for the first time in years.

I went back to Stockholm in October. In Finland the reorientation process continued apparently unmarred by any serious difficulty. On November 17, the Paasikivi Government was formed. It included one Communist, Minister Urho Leino, left Social Democrat Mauno Pekkala as Assistant Prime Minister, and Helo, a Sixling, as Minister of Finance. Seven of the Ministers were members of the Society for Friendship between Finland and the Soviet Union. Premier Paasikivi defined the new program in a statement. 'Its purpose, in the first place, is to work for the best understanding with our neighbor, the Soviet Union, and at the same time to fulfill conscientiously the provisions of the armistice treaty. Good economic and cultural relations with Sweden and the other Nordic countries will naturally be maintained and developed. Moreover, we have so many economic and political problems resulting from the war, such as the resettlement of the evacuated population, unemployment situation, and the question of supply, that there will be more than enough of work. For that reason no other declaration of program is needed than a promise to contribute to the best of our ability toward the solution of these difficult problems. The Communist Party, like the other political parties, will be allowed to operate according to the valid laws of the country, and Finland will take good care of its democratic social order, which is based on Finland's political independence and right to self-determination.'

General elections in March, 1945, changed the composition of Finland's Parliament radically, expressed the drastic change in the Finnish political climate which had taken place since the signing of the armistice — a swing to the left. But neither the new Parliament nor the new Government formed in April undertook radical measures. It was clear that, although defeated, Finland would survive as an independent country and within a few years would have a relative economic prosperity restored.

It was clear that this would be done without any Soviet revolution in Finland, but, at the same time, that many economic and social changes of a leftward character would come about in the country, in a democratic fashion. Finland had been an advanced Social Democratic country before 1939, with model social legislation, a considerable degree of economic planning, and a measure of economic collectivism. That these things would develop even further after the war, no one in Finland doubted, though the *rentier* and employer classes regretted it. In no way, however, did these people show signs of resorting to force in an attempt to block this development. Thus, defeated Finland, having lost some two per cent of its population in killed, more than one per cent of whose living population were war invalids, a country impoverished and depleted, seemed likely to go over to modified collectivism without further bloodshed and disorder.

By the end of 1944, the armistice conditions were apparently being fulfilled to the satisfaction of Russia. Operations were still being carried on against the handful of German troops that remained on Finnish soil. The British Control Commission arrived in Helsinki to observe events and report to its Government. Other diplomats went back to the Finnish capital. Sweden extended a credit of 150,000,000 crowns and began shipping quantities of food, consumers' goods, and, most important of all, coal. But for reasons that were utterly incomprehensible, the United States had not yet sent a single diplomat or military observer to Helsinki, nor in any way attempted to get independent information about the situation in Finland.

This lack of interest irritated the Russians, who interpreted it as meaning that America no longer recognized Finland as an independent country. It bitterly disappointed the Finns, who felt that America was not at all concerned about their country and certainly was not going to help it, now that it was friendly to Russia and fighting Germany. The Swedes raised eyebrows as they observed that, during the period when Finland was at war with Russia, America had maintained diplomatic relations with Finland and, during the Winter War, had encouraged the Finns with substantial supplies, but now that Finland was fighting Germany and rapidly orienting itself on a policy friendly to Russia, not so much as an American vice-consul had turned up in Helsinki.

Among Americans there has always been a tendency to regard all policies toward Finland as polarized either in the direction of maintaining Finland as a bulwark of Western civilization against Eastern barbarism or ceding it over to Russia and forgetting about it with didactic finality. A serviceable American attitude would lie somewhere between these extremes. The Finns are now engaged in trying to rectify some of the mistakes they made in the past by taking it for granted that Russia would always remain weak. The Russian attack on Finland in 1939 was, undoubtedly, an aggression in violation of many ideals and beliefs which we now profess, and inexcusable on moral or diplomatic grounds. It was justifiable only in terms of Russian military exigencies (much as the German attack on the Sudetenland might be so defended). But the Russians are now trying to rectify what many of them, unofficially, recognize as their immoderate conduct in the past.

It is not for us to condemn or condone either country's national policy. In 1939, Finland was placed in a dire predicament from which it is now only slowly emerging. The only realistic policy for America is to give the Finnish people the support and encouragement they deserve as long as this support does not take on the aspect of 'saving the poor little Finns from the Bolshevik Bear,' or is not used to create the impression that America is building up Finland as a bulwark against Russia.

A great number of Finns have come to believe in the possibility of a future Finland, lying within the political, geographic, and economic orbit of the Soviet Union, but still preserving close, even intimate, ties with America and Great Britain. Such a future for Finland would express the interests and aspirations of the vast majority of the Finnish people, guarantee them peace and a maximum of freedom, independence, and self-expression. It is to the interest of the United States and Great Britain to foster in every way the realization of such a plan for Finland.

IX

Denmark

THE GERMANS took Denmark on April 9, 1940, at the cost of one German admitted killed. Thirteen Danes were also reported to have been killed in whatever actions took place. The Danes might have resisted, as did the Norwegians or the Greeks, but they did not. The King capitulated, the Cabinet under protest 'acknowledged the protection of Germany,' and the German occupation became a fact.

Until 1943, occupied Denmark was ruled under what was, nominally, a Danish Government. Under Socialist Prime Minister Stauning, the first Government lasted till May, 1942, as the Germans spared the Danes their worst excesses and pretended to treat them as 'friendly partners.' The Nazis felt that it might be profitable to hold Denmark up as a model of what might be expected by countries willing to take their proper place in the New Europe.

The conquerors managed to wring a number of concessions from the Danish Government, the most important of which was the signing of the anti-Comintern Pact by Foreign Minister Scavenius on November 25, 1941. At the same time the Danish Nazis managed to scrape together some eighteen hundred volunteers to form the 'Danish Free Corps,' which was promptly dispatched to the Eastern Front and ultimately cut to pieces at Lake Ilmen.

At first, the strongest anti-German notes were struck by the Young Conservatives, led by, among others, the Minister of Trade, John Christmas Moeller, later to become Foreign Minister. After June, 1941, the Communists became active. The Young Conservatives formed a working alliance with the Danish Communist Party, which was small, but well-organized and disciplined. The Young Conservatives were as popular in Denmark as the Social Democrats and much more active. They were willing to risk their lives in the struggle against the invaders. They co-operated magnificently in the illegal organizations and increased their prestige in Denmark steadily.

In May, 1942, as the Stauning Government was unable to cope with the innumerable problems that besieged it, a new one was formed under Prime Minister Bühl, a Social Democrat. It lasted about six months as signs multiplied to indicate that the passive capitulation of the first day had not been the final expression of the national character. The Germans at length became impatient at what was now flagrant unwillingness to co-operate and sent to Denmark a Nazi Commissioner, Doctor Best, a man of about forty, blond, pale, who affected an impersonal manner and an attitude of cold objectivity.

Doctor Best's first act was to demand the resignation of the Government which, of course, complied. The Danish Nazis were too hopelessly weak and incompetent to be of any use, and Best could find no suitable individuals to recommend for posts in a new government. Finally he compromised on a government headed by Scavenius, who had often made concessions to Berlin and had paid lip service to the 'New Order.'

The uninspired character of the Scavenius Government apparently affected Fritz Clausen, the leader of the Danish Nazis, with a sudden delusion of grandeur and popularity. Somehow he persuaded Best to approve a general election. As a result, an overwhelming vote of confidence was delivered by the electorate for the Young Conservatives and the Social Democrats. In disgust, the Germans cut off their subsidy of the Danish Nazis and Clausen departed for a more suitable abode in a German psychopathic hospital.

During the ten months of the Scavenius administration the war turned against Germany — El Alamein, Stalingrad, Tunisia. Legal plundering of Denmark by financial manipulation began and reached considerable proportions. The Danes were forced to slaughter a large part of their livestock to be sent as meat to the Germany Army. The behavior of German occupation troops became domineering and disrespectful. Many of the Danish people regarded Scavenius as a traitor. As a result, the people no longer felt obliged to obey King Christian's order of April 9 not to commit hostile acts against the Germans. In the fall of 1942, active sabotage began, with the King's tacit approval. Ships, factories, and railroads were affected. By the summer of 1943, Danish sabotage had become a serious problem to the German authorities.

In London, Moeller, the representative of the Danish Freedom Council, concluded an agreement with the R.A.F., whereby Danish towns would be spared if patriots would attack factories regularly and effectively. This gave a tremendous impetus to the Danish resistance movement, the activities of which were directed and coordinated by the Danish Freedom Council. Its general staff of engineers and experts proceeded to develop the technique of sabotage scientifically. It soon reached such a level of efficiency as to have a really important bearing on the over-all national economy, whereas in a country like Norway it remained, until 1944, relatively ineffective.

The underground council issued a program calling for general elections as soon as Denmark was liberated and punishment of war criminals and collaborationists, but concentrated its main efforts on sabotage.

In August, 1942, after German military transit rights through Sweden were withdrawn by the Swedish Government, a crisis developed in Denmark. The Danish railroad system had become extremely important to the Germans for the shipment of supplies and munitions to Norway. The Freedom Council made the most of the situation and, concentrating on the essential Jutland Railroad, proceeded to hamper transportation seriously by a series of skillful operations.

Riots occurred over the entire country as the Germans struck out wildly at evasive and omnipresent saboteurs. German countermeasures were impeded by the fact that the great majority of the police were still Danes and insisted stubbornly on a rigorous observance of the laws of their country. Apprehension of the culprits by the Germans was extremely rare. In August, 1943, the Germans demanded that the Government of the country they had hoped to keep friendly declare martial law, promulgate a strict curfew, institute the death penalty for acts of sabotage, and hand over saboteurs to be tried by Germans. The Scavenius Government answered with its resignation. German troops occupied key positions in the country; the King was interned; and a military administration was imposed upon the country.

From August, 1943, on, there was no government in Denmark. The Germans plundered the resources of the country openly while every aspect of resistance was intensified, often to the point of active, open fighting. The operations of the groups directed by the Freedom Council became bolder and more spectacular as the patriots were encouraged by success.

In December, one Friday afternoon, at 11:32, a telephone rang in the Fredericksberg Police Headquarters. Over it came a quiet voice, saying, 'At noon the Sören Wistoft plant will be blown up.' The speaker then hung up. Immediately, a fleet of patrol cars and ambulances were dispatched to the factory, a large one, making important machinery for the Germans. Two blocks away from their destination, the cars were halted by two shattering explosions. Débris rocketed skyward and rained down upon the streets. At the very same moment that the telephone call had been made, twenty men, armed with revolvers, had entered the plant and shouted warnings to all the workers to go to the air-raid shelters. Though the two factory buildings were blown to bits, not a single worker was injured.

Seething with indignation, General von Hanneken, the German Commander-in-Chief in Denmark, demanded that the Danish police take severe measures, including the search of every man in certain specified areas of Denmark. He was informed that this was impossible, as Danish law afforded no precedent for mass roundups.

Incensed beyond bounds, the Germans reacted in their usual style of quick, violent punishment of anyone on whom they could lay their hands. A German court-martial sentenced the youthful Axel Petersen to death for espionage and sabotage. He was the ninth of his countrymen executed by the Germans. Later, three more Danish patriots were taken for an examination by the Germans to Dagmarhus in Copenhagen. On the way back to Vestre Faengsale they 'attempted to jump from the police car.' German guards shot them to death.

After this widely publicized incident, the tempo of Danish resistance was accelerated. Treatment of the Danes rapidly became another instance of the brutal pattern of German domination in the rest of Europe. The editors of the Copenhagen newspapers were summoned before Doctor Best. Maintaining the matter-of-fact manner that had been so unrewarding, he informed them: 'Heads will roll till the sabotage comes to an end.' The implication of the statement was plain. Sabotage would not and could not be halted. The Germans would begin in Denmark what had long been their custom in France, Norway, and Poland — mass executions of innocent hostages, according to the heinous 'principle of collective responsibility.'

Dispensing with the pretext of a legal Danish government, the Germans substituted a reign of lawlessness and depredation. About five hundred of Denmark's six thousand Jews were arrested. Helped by the rest of the Danish people, the others went into hiding and later escaped to Sweden, where about five thousand were living in 1944. About five hundred were sent to a settlement in Bohemia. More than one hundred and seventy-five Communists were sent to a camp near Danzig. By the end of 1944, Sweden had received sixteen thousand refugees from Denmark, including numbers who had fled to it from other countries.

At the beginning of 1943, the number of troops in Denmark had increased to one hundred thousand. It fell off again, due to demands made by the fighting fronts, until by the beginning of 1944 it was down to seventy-five thousand. Most of them were in Jutland constructing and manning fortifications. Thousands of families were evacuated from their homes to make room for the German troops and many of the homes destroyed to clear territory for fortifications.

In addition, several thousand Danes were conscripted for labor both in the country itself and in Germany. In November, 1944, twenty-five thousand were demanded for the Jutland fortifications and about twenty thousand were recruited. At Randers alone three thousand Danes were put to work. German defense preparations were being stepped up everywhere. At Thisted, the submarine and hydroplane station was enlarged. The airfields were fortified at Rye and Aalborg, while coastal fortifications were hurried at Esbjerg, Fano, Sondervig, Thyboron, and Hansted. In Esbjerg, the Germans mined the harbor and part of the town. A great part of the burden was borne by the Danes. German hands were now extended to pluck whatever was of value in Denmark. They continued, of course, to pay for everything — with a 'clearing.' As a result of this improvement to its commerce, Danish currency issue, which had amounted to about three hundred to four hundred million crowns in 1939, had reached about four billion crowns in January, 1945. Inflation was proportional. German indebtedness to Denmark had reached the impossible total of six billion crowns.

Meanwhile, the Danish Freedom Council continued its resourceful direction of resistance, aided by industrious figures in the Allied capitals. In London, Moeller supplied fresh encouragements to the movement. In Moscow, the representative of the Council was Thomas Doessing, former director of Denmark's libraries, who was accredited to the Narkomindel as a Minister. The representative in Washington was Henrik de Kaufmann, an able, patriotic Dane. He participated in the disposition of Denmark's substantial merchant fleet of some eight hundred thousand tons (about half of which was sunk in the service of the Allies) and the utilization of Greenland's revenue, most of which comes from the sale of kryolite to the United States and much of which was used to finance the work of the Council.

The complacent belief that peaceful, prosperous, stable Denmark would never be dragged into the European battleground had yielded to a nation-wide resurgence of patriotism. Almost forgotten patriotic songs were revived and sung night after night by tens of thousands at open-air meetings all over the country. Under this stimulus the Freedom Council had developed into a tightly knit unbreakable organization. The most active elements continued to be the Young Conservatives and the Communists. Both had become more powerful as a result of their courageous and self-sacrificing activities against the Germans. By their far-sighted decision to collaborate with the Communists, the Young Conservatives had forestalled the unchecked swing of the youth toward Communist allegiance which was so notable a phenomenon in Poland and Norway.

In doing so, however, they had undoubtedly alienated some of the old conservative industrialists and others who still had nightmares about Bolshevik revolutions and thought that the Communists were the most dangerous element in Europe. I talked to one of these individuals in Stockholm, who said: 'We should adopt passive tactics in Denmark now and wait until the Allies invade and drive the Germans out. We are going to need all our ammunition to deal with our twenty thousand well-organized and Moscow-led Communists as soon as the Germans are out. These Communists would be even worse than the Nazis if they got the upper hand.'

Such sentiments were held by a small minority of Danes and most of them were outside the country. At home, systematically by its deeds the Freedom Council had won the undisputed leadership of the people of Denmark. Uniting as it did the forces from the extreme left, the right, and in-between, it could and did appeal for and receive the support of all circles of the population. Unlike some similar resistance movements, the Council had made itself successfully representative of the entire population.

With such power behind it, Danish sabotage never slackened its momentum. Bands of as much as one hundred men participated in a single operation. The Council issued its own communiqués, reporting successes achieved in destroying military installations and capturing arms, ammunition, and other useful equipment from the Germans to be used against them. Its courts condemned informers and traitors and the long arm of the Danish underground carried out the sentences. Often, the executions were audaciously planned to cause a maximum of embarrassment to the German authorities. In one case the bodies of two notorious collaborators were left swinging from a tree in the city park of Copenhagen, to be viewed by the population.

To an increasing degree, during 1944, the Freedom Council worked through the Danish police force. The most daring saboteurs, the 'administrators of patriotic justice' who executed the sentences against the informers, often wore police uniforms, and were enabled thereby, not only to function more effectively, but to hinder German reprisals and confuse the Gestapo. In March, 1944, the German military command ordered the Danish police to give them greater assistance in apprehending saboteurs. The police consented, but saboteurs remained as elusive as formerly. In June, harassed by fresh outbreaks, the Germans demanded that the Danish police force guard the factories. The Nazis received a formal acquiescence, but more factories were damaged and blown up than before.

The conflict was brought to a head by a short-lived general

strike. In September, 1944, the Germans were compelled to disband the Danish police force *en masse.* Some two thousand Danish policemen were deported to Germany. Several thousand went underground to continue their activity without the protection of their uniforms. The Germans permitted the organization on each city block of a watch corps consisting of four or five men who wore arm bands and carried truncheons. All other police functions, traffic direction, registration of travelers, and criminal investigations, were suspended indefinitely. This, of course, made German exploitation and control of Denmark much more difficult.

All plans to make Denmark the show piece of the New Order were abandoned as the country developed, instead, into a model of effective resistance. The Germans freely proceeded with mass roundups of suspects on the streets, martial law for troublesome districts, and incessant, indiscriminate raids on houses and offices. With such extravagant efforts they finally did succeed in capturing many of the leaders of the Danish underground. Sabotage, however, was not diminished, and it was no secret to the Germans that the resistance forces had stored away copious quantities of arms for use on the day of Allied invasion or German withdrawal. Sensing imminent danger, in the fall of 1944 the Germans withdrew many of their administrative offices from Copenhagen and other large cities to small localities where they could be more easily protected.

Inside Denmark, a Danish underground government had been designated, headed by ex-Prime Minister Bühl. The members lived in Denmark and spurned opportunities to go to Sweden to form a government in exile. Nearly all European resistance movements sooner or later were faced with the same dilemma. A government abroad was in a better position to remain intact, take care of foreign relations, and plan for the future. On the other hand, it tended to lose touch with the quickly changing moods and trends of the people at home under oppression. The laudable choice of the Danes had disadvantages. The Freedom Council, vital and effective during the war, had little time to plan for the economic, social, or political welfare of Denmark in the future.

One Danish group which was actively conspiring was the extreme right. One of the most industrious of its members was Colonel Knudsen, Chief of the Danish Police Force in Sweden, consisting of some two thousand youths being trained in Swedish camps for the job of maintaining order in Denmark after the war. Knudsen and some of his followers believed that their main job was not to apprehend and bring to justice Denmark's Quislings, but to suppress Communist revolts and deal with 'semi-criminal elements in the labor movement,' whom they expected to be overbearing, arrogant and dangerous because of their participation in the resistance movement during the war.

In Denmark the Germans had made concerted efforts to create friendly relations, to enlist the voluntary participation and co-operation of the Danish people in the Nazi New Order. They had failed miserably. Not only did they fail to subjugate Denmark, but they succeeded in uniting nearly all the diverse groups of the Danish people together in the tremendously strong movement headed by the Freedom Council. Conservatives, particularly the young ones, some of whom had discredited themselves during the late thirties by emulating the heel-clicking, heiling German Nazis across the border, found it necessary, for the sake of patriotic pride and prestige, to prove their solidarity with their own people and themselves by loyal participation in the common movement of resistance against the Germans.

All felt that the overwhelming immediate task was to fight the Germans; post-war problems could be settled after the war had been won. But on one point almost all agreed: collaboration between the left and the right, which had been forced upon the Danish people by the German occupation, must not be allowed to vanish after the war. The Conservatives conceded that a post-war election would probably place five to fifteen Communists in the Parliament. The left admitted that many of the outstanding patriots and leaders of the Danish Liberation Movement were Conservatives. Except for a few die-hards on both sides no one doubted that all important economic and social problems could be solved by negotiation, collaboration, and mutual compromise, which would result in a gradual, ordered leftward movement in the country after the war.

X

Norway

LATE IN NOVEMBER, 1943, the Oslo Gestapo, using the same technique that was employed in the case of the Reichstag fire, cracked down on Norway's anti-Nazi students. The 'fire' was reported in one of the University buildings. Little damage was done, as lectures were held in this building the next day, but Gestapo Chieftain Wilhelm Rediess arrested some fifteen hundred students and members of the faculty — all that the Gestapo could catch. Only a handful of Norwegian anti-Nazi Party members remained at liberty. Some seventeen hundred students evaded the police net and escaped into Sweden.

In Sweden, Denmark, and even in Finland reaction was immediate and sharp. Indignant editorials demanded that whatever action possible be taken to make the Germans retract their announced decision to send the arrested students to Germany. Students demonstrated in Stockholm and delegations visited the Government. Even the Finnish press disapproved vigorously.

Many failed to understand the motives behind the drastic German action. Norway was relatively peaceful. There was no anti-German guerrilla warfare as in Poland, Greece, or Yugoslavia, and attacks on German troops were rare. Battered German divisions brought from the Russian front were fed and rested in Norway before returning. Norway's important electro-chemical industry was working fairly well producing molybdenum, aluminum, and other important products for Germany. Norwegian fishermen were getting about forty per cent of the normal catch, most of which was frozen in the huge plants built by the Germans along Norway's coast, which put up and sent to Germany hundreds of tons of fish daily. The most important sabotage done in Norway had been carried out by parachute troops from England; that done by the Norwegians themselves had been relatively harmless. What made the burly, coarse-featured Rediess attempt to arrest the entire student body of Norway? Was it, perhaps, nothing deeper than the sadistic stupidity native to Gestapo officials? Or did German policy require the elimination of the future leaders of Norway? Or may not the Nazis have feared that the students were finally preparing really important action?

The invasion of Norway, in April, 1940, had been motivated chiefly by Germany's desire to forestall similar action by Great Britain; to acquire bases for aerial and naval attack on England and on Allied shipping; to acquire the vital non-ferrous metals produced in important quantities in Norway; and, in general, to integrate Norway into the economy of the New Order. The German attack had found the people unarmed, bewildered, and confused by the traitorous actions of a few hundred well-placed Quislings. For a few hours the Germans had held Oslo with nothing but a band playing 'Roll Out the Barrel.' When the country was under control and the British Expeditionary Force had been repelled, the Germans proceeded, in their treatment of the Norwegian people, to reverse Clausewitz's famous maxim that war is a continuation of politics.

During the first period of occupation, the Germans worked on the assumption that the war would be short. They busied themselves with technical problems and made attempts to humor the capricious Norwegians. But after the autumn of 1940, when it became clear that the war would be a long affair, the German authorities, working directly and also through the Quislings, proceeded to attempt to hammer a rugged, irregular Norway into its square hole in Nazi Europe.

About 70,000 Norwegians, many of them seamen, fled abroad, and some 9000 were deported to Germany. Into Norway came some 200,000 German troops (the number fell in 1943 to about 140,000 and was increased again in 1944 to roughly 250,000 when Rendulic's defeated army fled across the border from Finland), about 50,000 German civilians of all kinds, about 60,000 war prisoners, mostly Russian, and a few thousand Czech, Polish, French, Slovak, and Serbian forced laborers.

Currency depreciated because there was so little to purchase. A macabre method was used by the Germans to take excess money from the people. Thousands of Norwegians whose relatives had been sent to the Oranienburg concentration camp in Germany received notices to pay monthly sums for the support of the prisoners. If the prisoner survived his sentence, he was freed in Germany and his family had to pay his passage back to Norway. Many received printed forms informing them that their husbands or brothers had 'died' in Oranienburg. This notice was shortly followed by another stating that the ashes of the deceased prisoner could be obtained for seventy-five crowns.

German economic exploitation of Norway was extremely successful. Besides essential war materials, Germany got the important export channel through Narvik for the shipment of vital Swedish iron ore. From Norway itself Germany received ample quantities of sulphur, copper, ferro-alloys, molybdenum, and vanadium, all of which were desperately needed and for some of which Norway was the chief German source of supply. The annual thirty thousand tons of aluminum taken out of Norway by Germany was so highly prized that the Germans even supplied the industry such of their own raw materials as the production of this metal required. Germany also got large quantities of herring oil (useful as a lubricant) and dynamite, and was able to have manufactured in Norway the materials needed for fortification projects in that country.

Through the so-called 'Norwegian' commercial agreements with Sweden, industry was supplied with the necessary semi-processed and processed goods (particularly iron and steel) which the Germans bought through Norwegian firms without using valuable Swedish currency. Norwegian industry had its permanent envoys in Stockholm and London, in order, among other things, to acquire raw materials and machinery in exchange for the small amount of Norwegian fish which the Germans did not take for their own consumption either in Germany or Norway. A typical strand in the infinitely complex web of German-Norwegian (in reality German-German) trade routed through Sweden was the sale of a large part of the aluminum produced for the Germans in Norway by Norwegian middlemen to Swedish consumers in payment for deliveries of Swedish machinery to the essential war industries in Norway.

Strategically, the Germans made good use of Norway, building important air and submarine bases, often with Norwegian labor.

For many months the greater part of Germany's fleet was sheltered in Norwegian fjords over which the shadow of German defeat was already visible. There was considerable difficulty, during 1943 and 1944, with the crews of German vessels, particularly submarines. One crew in Trondheim refused to go to sea and threw its officers overboard. The leaders were shot and the rest were sent to German concentration camps for insubordination cases in Alta, Kvenangen, and Kirkenes, where, among others, some three thousand German deserters were confined. Several of these deserters escaped to Sweden, where they were only too ready to talk, so that in Stockholm we had a fairly clear idea of what was going on.

The Norwegian population recovered from the initial stupor of invasion rapidly. Resistance grew and was met by ruthless Gestapo repression. Throughout the country manifestations of strong anti-German sentiment occurred mostly in 'passive' forms. In February, 1942, the Quisling régime decreed regulations requiring teachers to propagandize the New Order. The teachers refused and eleven hundred of them were arrested and sent to Arctic Kirkenes. Some two hundred illegal newspapers of all kinds were organized and widely distributed. Illegal groups urged the workers to 'slow down,' delayed production, hampered the administration, and secured valuable military information for use against the Germans.

The Gestapo cracked down brutally on the Norwegian underground. Hundreds were shot and about twenty thousand were imprisoned. Seven hundred of the fourteen hundred Jews in the country were deported to Poland, and the other half managed to flee to Sweden. The standard of living was stamped down to the subsistence level and beneath it. Food was strictly limited to a near-starvation diet. A Norwegian adult received an average of one pound of potatoes, half a pound of bread daily; a glass of milk, an ounce of fat, and two and a half pounds of dried fish every twenty days, and virtually nothing else. Nerves trembled under the constant menace of the Gestapo and life was made drab by severe regulations.

Under these circumstances many, particularly the younger Norwegians, grew restive with the desire to undertake a more active struggle against the Germans. Meetings, leaflets, and 'passive resistance' were all very well, but they wanted to start a shooting war, or at least intensify sabotage and begin 'knocking off' German sentries and Quislings. But, until 1944, the Norwegian Government in Exile ordered the postponement of active resistance pending the hoped-for Allied invasion. The Norwegian underground was disciplined, and obeyed. The Norwegian Government in Exile reasoned that, in order to get the maximum military benefit from Norway, delay was advisable. Thinking in terms of military expedience, the Government, like those of many other countries, lost authority over and leadership of many people in the 'home front'—those who stayed in Norway and lived in the thick of the struggle.

Among those who gained in authority and leadership were the Communists, who previously had been very weak. Because of their experience in underground activities, the Communists were skillful tacticians, while many well-meaning non-Communist beginners made blunders and got themselves arrested through inexperience. Then the Communists were excellently disciplined and demanded the maximum of sacrifice from themselves; it was a standing rule that Communists should not flee to Sweden even when the Germans were on their trail. Moreover, they constantly urged active fighting. For more than a year Communist illegal papers called for guerrilla warfare. As early as December, 1943, *Avantgarden* stated: 'The time has now come for active guerrilla warfare. Recent events in our country show clearly what awaits us. The only language which can be understood is war with weapons in our hands.' The Communists did not actually start the guerrilla warfare, as that would have been an open breach of discipline (besides which they did not have enough arms), but they constantly urged it and showed in every way that they were prepared to participate in it, and, if called upon, to lead it themselves.

Abroad, heated discussions were going on among Norwegians. Many refugee Norwegian trade-unionists and leaders joined the Seaman's Union, which became a sort of funnel for trade-union activity among Norwegians in Sweden. Many parties, including the Communists, were represented at its meetings. Even such problems were threshed out as the vexing one of the disposition of several thousand children fathered in Norway during the previous three years by German soldiers. A draft was made, outlining measures necessary to keep those children from suffering social ostracism because of their origin. In the book *S.S. Lebensborn,* which appeared later in Norway, signed by the notorious Rediess, the solution proposed for the same problem was that the children be brought up in special Nazi schools to be the new *Herrenvolk* of Norway.

The question of post-war organization in Norway was debated at length in *émigré* groups. Many thought the old Government would go back immediately after the German collapse and run the country for several months until new elections could be organized. But certain 'home front' groups insisted that 'home front' representatives be included in the Government immediately. These questions were likewise being discussed in Norway by groups of all parties.

What did most Norwegians want? First, to punish the Quislings. Then, everyone, including the Communists, wanted the King back again. All agreed that no 'revolution' was necessary or desirable in Norway. All agreed that Norway must be organized in such a way as to ensure permanent full employment. All agreed that wages, which had been frozen tight since the invasion, should be readjusted to increased living costs.

Here unanimity ended. When I asked how many Norwegians in Norway must be shot, a government official said about two hundred — Quisling leaders, police officials who tortured Norwegians, and a few dozen spies who served the Germans. These were to be shot according to due process of law, he assured me. This was the official government line. Other Norwegians wanted a few days open season on Quislings. In one Swedish lumber camp where Norwegians were working, a Norwegian official, urging the government policy, said that any lynch mobs would be severely punished by the Government. A burly Norwegian enquired, 'How severely?'

Some Norwegians both at home and abroad urged that the Germans be forced to reconstruct Norway after the war, but important groups, for instance, the clandestine newspaper *Fri Fagbevegelse* (organ of Norwegian trade unions), pointed out the dangers of basing Norway's post-war economy on reparations, came out for post-war co-operation between the German and Norwegian working classes, and asserted that Norway should be rebuilt by Norwegians. The sharpest disagreements concerned the composition of the Government. The closer one got to Norway, the less popular became the Government in Exile (not the King, who was popular everywhere, but the Government itself), and old guard Labor Party leaders. The 'home front' accused the Labor Party of playing favorites in allocating jobs and economic support. The Government was fully cognizant of these facts and promised to resign within a reasonable time after the German collapse, but many suspected that the Government would not resign until it was forced to. Indeed, few governments ever have.

In May, 1944, the Germans began to make preparations for the evacuation of Norway. This was obviously necessitated by the signs of imminent Finnish capitulation and the consequent weakening of Germany's entire northern flank. Heavy coastal artillery which had been brought to Norway from the Maginot Line was shipped back again to where it came from. Construction jobs involving an outlay of between three hundred and five hundred million Norwegian crowns (many of them more than half-completed) were halted and in some cases the machinery and the equipment shipped back to Germany. This did not involve a serious financial loss to the Germans, as the money for the construction had all been furnished by Norwegian banks at the point of German revolvers. The cessation of the construction work, however, did mean that the Germans had given up the hope of further developing Norway's immense waterpower and non-ferrous metallurgical resources for Hitler's New Order.

These signs of evacuation caused considerable speculation in Sweden. Was Sweden to participate in the occupation of Norway in case the Germans withdrew voluntarily?

The question had already been considered in 1940, when Sweden was approached by the Norwegian Government on June 3 with the suggestion that Swedish troops occupy the Narvik area which would then become a neutral zone, south of which the Germans, and north of which the Norwegians, would be in control. It was later revealed that the Swedes had accepted the idea in principle because both the Germans and the British wanted it — both for their own reasons. The British had given up the idea of regaining southern Norwegian positions and the German positions at Narvik were

their weakest. On June 7, the matter was still not definitely decided, when the Germans learned that Haakon and his Government were leaving northern Norway for Britain because their military resources were inadequate. The Germans, therefore, dropped
the matter of Swedish neutralization of Narvik.

Had some such plan been undertaken in 1940, Norway might
have been spared many trials, but it fell through. Sweden was
forced to limit herself to extensive and much-appreciated relief
work in Norway. This relief work was made possible by the persistence of Swedes in a chronic dispute with Anglo-American
blockade officials. London and Washington had agreed to prevent,
whenever possible, the export of all commodities, including food,
to areas under German occupation. The Swedes had to fight for
Anglo-American permission every time they sent a shipment of
food to Norway.

One of the best known leaders in this relief work was fifty-five-
year-old Pastor Axel Emmanuel Webe, of the Swedish Church in
Oslo. Pastor Webe was the chairman and the moving spirit of the
Oslo Branch of the Swedish-Norwegian Aid Society. The Swedish
voluntary organization began its activities modestly in 1942 by
feeding thirty children in the Swedish Consulate in Oslo. Money
came from voluntary donations by Swedes of all classes. In 1943-
44, some twenty-six million crowns were collected. Pastor Webe
organized the distribution and sometimes the feeding of children
in his church, other churches, and in schools. The German occupation authorities did not object to this feeding of children, but the
Norwegian Quislings tried to bore into the society in order to gain
prestige. During 1944, 108,000 undernourished youngsters throughout Norway got one Swedish meal daily, mostly in churches and
school buildings.

In thirty Norwegian towns fourteen thousand children, medically
certified as undernourished, got a daily dinner consisting of hot
soup and a good meat dish. In Oslo these dinners were served in
Pastor Webe's church under his supervision. Ninety-four thousand
school-children received, each day, a breakfast consisting mainly of
a generous portion of cereal. This gruel was made with sweetened
condensed milk and served with a portion of synthetic honey or
fish preserves which was spread on bread and eaten with the gruel
or sometimes taken home.

Pastor Webe and the Swedish-Norwegian Aid Society did not limit their activities simply to food distribution. Webe found that many Norwegian children were unable to go to school, or even to food centers for the Swedish meals, because they lacked shoes. A special appeal was made and many thousands of shoes were collected in Sweden and sent to Norway in spite of the strict shoe rationing in Sweden. Pastor Webe's church, as such, did not organize the shipment or distribution of food and clothing for Norwegian children, but it strongly supported the society.

As 1944 brought one Allied victory after another, the tortured Norwegian people, hoping week after week for invasion, became more active. The Germans intensified terrorist measures against them and sometimes won fleeting, brutal victories, one of which occurred in Oslo, early in 1944.

Up and down the broad, slush-covered stone steps of the Diechmanske Library countless men and women hurried one February afternoon. From all over Oslo they came past the sinister Gestapo prison, Möllergade 19, past the Swedish Church to the central library of the Norwegian capital where many books were still available, where, too, conference, class, and study rooms were open to Norwegians.

On that particular afternoon of February 23, into the library one by one came a group of editors of the illegal press and other underground functionaries to attend a conference. The library conference rooms seemed an ideal place for such a meeting. But on the library steps slouched a Gestapo informer, who noticed the entry of several Norwegians suspected of anti-German activities. An alarm was raised and within an hour a heavily armed detail of Gestapo men burst into the conference room and arrested some thirty of the most important underground workers in Norway, representatives of all parties.

It was the heaviest blow the Norwegian underground had suffered. The arrested were hurried off to Gestapo detention rooms. Instead of enforcing the usual cooling-off period before the grilling started, the dull-witted, sadistic Wilhelm Rediess decided on an innovation. The cooling-off period weakened some people, but men of courage and high ideals used it to steel themselves. Rediess knew he had in his hands the flower of the Norwegian underground. He gave the word and the interrogations began immediately.

After a preliminary beating inflicted with sticks, lengths of pipe, and whips, the Gestapo's newer instruments were brought into play. Wide, heavy metal cuffs were put around the wrists and knees of the prisoners. A large wing nut ran through a hole in each cuff and was attached to an inner cuff like a brake shoe inside a wheel. When the wing nut turned, the shoe pressed hard against the wrist or knee. When a length of pipe was inserted in the wing nut for leverage, the shoe pressed inward, crushing bones like walnuts in a cracker. This process could be made to last as long as forty-eight hours. When the victim fainted, cold water in the face and another turn on the screw revived him. Rediess was determined to locate and seize every illegal printing plant and editor in Norway.

But he was unsuccessful. For a week or so eight of the eleven principal Oslo illegal newspapers suspended publication. But by March 1, all had resumed publication, their editorial staffs had been filled out with reserves and new recruits, emergency printing plants were functioning, and distribution was normal. Each copy was read by hundreds, reprinted in local provincial illegal papers, and read at illegal meetings. By the middle of 1944, as many illegal papers were published as legal papers before the occupation (nearly three hundred). The editions were much smaller, but the wide circulation of each copy made up for the difference.

The collapse of Germany's Finnish position in the fall of 1944 changed Norway's situation radically. Late in October, Berlin reports stated that Finnmark would be evacuated without any serious resistance. Berlin stated that the Russians were using twelve divisions, supported by tanks and aircraft, operating against the German rear guards, while the main German forces had already reached the new front, presumably Lyngenfjord. Thus the Germans wrote off some ten per cent of Norway's territory. They wrote it off and also made every attempt to wipe it out. Everything they could lay their hands on was destroyed. Individual farmhouses far away from the coast or from roads were systematically razed as were all towns and villages. This wanton destruction did not appreciably hold up the Russians. It did drive nearly one hundred thousand Norwegian civilians from their homes into the woods to freeze to death, or to German concentration camps south of Narvik to starve.

Into Russian-occupied Kirkenes were sent official representatives of the Norwegian Government in Exile in London, whose relations with Moscow were cordial. General Staffens and Justice Minister Wold arrived with Press Attaché Schieve as representatives of the Government. Foreign Minister Lie traveled from London to Moscow in early November and was assured by the Russian leaders that the Soviet occupation of Norwegian territory was temporary, that the re-establishment of Norwegian civilian authority in the occupied area would be facilitated in every way. The Russians also promised that every consideration would be observed with regard to the Norwegian civilians in liberated districts. They gave full authority to the Norwegian civilian administration, and even re-opened the Kirkenes church. This behavior was not at all surprising, as Russian-Norwegian relations had been good even prior to World War I, when the two countries had had a common frontier.

In Sweden some ten thousand Norwegian youths, who had been trained for eighteen months as 'policemen' in special camps organized by the Norwegian Government, prepared to travel to Kirkenes to help liberate their country. The term 'police troops' was used as a concession to Swedish neutrality. Actually the men were thoroughly trained and well-equipped commandos spoiling for a chance to do battle with the Germans. There was some talk of permitting these troops to proceed across the Swedish-Norwegian frontier into the part of Norway still occupied by the Germans. But after due consideration, the Swedish Government decided against this course, as it would have been a flagrant violation of Swedish neutrality — as flagrant in fact as the German transit traffic in 1940. But the tail of the writhing Nazi monster was still free, though its fangs and claws were heavily engaged on three fronts. The Swedes were concerned about the lashings of that tail and were taking no chances.

The liberation of Norwegian territory by the Red Army and the imminence of the German collapse let loose a flurry of political activity and intrigue among Norwegians both in England and in Sweden. The Norwegian home front continued to work solidly and well, increasingly influenced by the left, though the Communists were still not represented on the central executive committee of the home front in Oslo. The long duration of the war, the impatience of the youth, the increasingly heavy toll of life and property among patriots, had persuaded the majority that active resistance would mean little more in the way of sacrifice and be much more effective. Well-informed Norwegians maintained that the government representatives in Stockholm had been employing arbitrary, unfair methods. The home front leaders who desired active sabotage and guerrilla warfare were systematically isolated. Information about the home front wishes was deliberately withheld from the London Government. Trade unions were accused of being government tools because they feared left-wing socialism.

As a result many bourgeois intellectuals and workers were forced to side with the Communists. Not only this, but the wishes of the Government itself — namely, *status quo* in post-war politics — were partly circumvented, since through enforced contacts with Communists many learned to admire them and sympathize with their political aims. In Stockholm, this reached such a pitch that a third group of 'neutrals' emerged, attempting to seek influence above the heads of the Norwegian London Government, in the hopes of saving Norway from the 'increasing danger of Communism and leftist Socialism' caused by the Government's arbitrary methods.

These opposition forces were instrumental in causing a late change in government policy, to more direct sabotage against the munition factories and lines of communication. In the execution of this policy there were a number of examples of confusion because of lack of centralized co-ordination. One case occurred when the pro-government illegal newspaper *Fri Fagbevegelse* of October 7 said: 'We have an excellent sample from well-known free newspapers of how not to behave when we disapprove of something. The newspaper brands as traitors those acting as factory guards. We wrote to this newspaper at the end of July that for tactical reasons, which cannot be explained, factory guards should not be boycotted. We advise workers to be on guard against those trying to provoke disunity.' The newspaper under attack was one of those under the influence of Communists not admitted into the Government's Home Front Central Council. Its editors had not been told that the factory guards should not be boycotted because they helped saboteurs.

Dissatisfaction against the Government ran high in Norway

until June, 1943, when the Government promised to resign as soon as Norway was free. During 1944, the situation improved, but still at the end of the year there were heated disputes. Underground members accused the Government of refraining from sabotage because it was heavily influenced by shipowners and Norwegian industrialists, who did not want their plants destroyed. That the London Government was in part influenced by shipowners was particularly obvious because of the fact that Norway's immense merchant marine was the main Norwegian asset put at the disposal of the Allies. That, after five years' war, the Norwegians in London were badly out of touch with their fellow countrymen at home was equally obvious. These points were frequently aired in the Norwegian illegal press.

The opposition illegal newspaper *Norge* of September 26, 1944, emphasized editorially that the Government should be reinforced immediately by the inclusion of strong representation from the home front, and that it was necessary to hold elections directly upon liberation. On October 22, *Norge* said: "Nygaardsvold group deserves honour for continuing the fight for us abroad, but they have performed their task and must hand over the power to others. The Government's first act must be to hand in its resignation.'

To record the state of mind of some Norwegians, I asked one of the departing 'police troopers' to write something for me about Norway. He wrote, in part:

'In all our police cantonments, study circles have been founded, to help us develop ourselves along a socialistic line. With socialism as a political and economic work-line, they try theoretically to solve the many post-war problems which the people and the country will be faced with after the liberation. The interest in these study circles is spreading, and one can really say that the socialistically interested youth is in the majority among the Norwegian police forces. They continue with their studies unaffected by the factional conflicts within Norwegian circles in England, Sweden, and at home.

'The general idea is that a great tug-of-war is taking place between the government party and the Communist movement, but there is another equally important and politically active group — the reactionary faction in which the Norwegian capitalists and others are powerful mainsprings. This organization — it can really be called so — is acting in conflict with the government circles and naturally also in conflict with the Communists. This reactionary faction has in its egoism even tried its utmost to vindicate its interests and in order to revenge itself on the circles — to which this egoism has been obvious and who have tried to push the capitalists' faction somewhat aside in the fight for liberation — the capitalists have gone too far, namely, to treachery.'

The general opinion is that in an eventual election after the liberation of the country, Det Norske Arbeiderparti (Norwegian Labor Party) — the party of the Government — will share its seventy-two mandates in the Storting with the Communists.

Everyone seemed to have read King Haakon's speech to his people, unreservedly praising the Russians and the Red Army, and everywhere his thoughts were echoed. Astonished at the frequency with which I met opinions of this kind among Norwegians in Sweden, I took a poll of as representative a group as I could get and asked all what they thought of the Soviet occupation of Norwegian territory. Out of more than a score, only one was worried that the Russians would stay too long and would interfere with Norway's internal affairs. Several others had expressed dissatisfaction with the fact that the Russians had only taken Kirkenes and had not gone on around the coast to Hemmerfest, Tromsö, Narvik, and farther south before winter set in.

The great successes of the Soviet Union, based on technocratic socialism, have given the Norwegian workers and many of the Norwegian middle class and intellectuals great confidence in the rapid peaceful socialization of a free Norway. The Norwegian people, like many other European peoples, were swinging leftward.

XI

Germany

★   I. TOKENS OF DEFEAT   ★

AFTER D-DAY and particularly after the German collapse in France, conditions inside Germany deteriorated rapidly. Naturally, this situation was reflected in the behavior of the hundreds of German diplomats, businessmen, journalists, agents, refugees, and travelers that were to be met in Sweden. German Legation officials and correspondents, never given to talk to Allied correspondents, became completely close-mouthed unless the risk of being overheard or having the conversation reported was at absolute zero. Except for the refugees, other Germans, too, only conversed about important matters against their better judgment. When this occurred, it was extremely revelatory, since it meant that the talker was yielding to the ever-present human need for giving vent to his gravest concerns. The anxiety of some Germans to express their points of view and to witness reactions was so great that it often succeeded in bursting the bonds of prudence.

The German citizens in Sweden had, of course, good reason to be prudent. Among them were numerous agents of various German intelligence and police organizations; the Gestapo, the Sicherheitedienst, the Abwehr. Some of these agencies worked openly, others under such elaborate façades as the well-equipped premises of the Deutsches Wissenschaftliches Institut. Prior to the establishment of this 'scientific institute,' the same premises had housed the Deutscher Akademischer austauchdienst, the main purpose of which was to form and develop contacts among Swedish university and student circles. This organization also arranged for exchanges of school-children between Germany and Sweden. It was, at first, under the supervision of the notorious Doctor H. Kappner, who apparently performed to the satisfaction of his Berlin superiors and was rewarded with the secretaryship of a legation for his services. In 1941, after his departure, an S.S. officer arrived to preside over the intricacies of 'academic exchange' between Germany and Sweden, and branches of this bureau blossomed forth in many of the larger Swedish towns.

Most of the German agents were engaged in spying on their own people and they also devoted a large part of their energy to spying on the spies of other countries. From what I observed in Sweden, I would say that most spies spend nearly all their time spying on other spies and reporting on what the spies of other countries have been reporting about the spies of their own country or those of a third power. These reports were reflected back and forth from each other like the images in a hall of mirrors — until reality dwindled to the merest shadow of itself. Nevertheless, all the major powers contributed their quota of spies and agents to the Stockholm beehive and they all managed to keep very busy.

Whereas in Turkey and elsewhere responsible German officials began deserting to the Allied side at quite an early stage, no large-scale defections took place in Stockholm. The inclination was there, and for more than a year a number of Stockholm's German residents and visitors undoubtedly were anxious to desert the foundering ship. A few did. One of the first was the Oxford-educated Doctor Ertel, who was married to a Swedish professor of Russian literature in the University of Stockholm and had himself been a teacher of English at Heidelberg. The Nazis had sent him to Stockholm as a British expert, unaware of the fact that his sympathies had been pro-British for a long time.

In the spring of 1943, Doctor Ertel finally established contact with the Allies and prepared to desert. After he had ignored several warnings, his wife returned from the theater one night and found his body hanging from the chandelier. Many believed that he had at first been poisoned. His murderer was reputedly a Gestapo agent and pseudo-journalist named Winfred Martini, who subsequently returned to Berlin.

When, during the summer, many Germans in Stockholm began to vacillate between desire and fear, a whispered 'Remember Ertel' often tilted the scales. An additional restraining factor was the murder of two Gestapo agents by colleagues who considered them unreliable. A few more similar incidents were enough to intimidate the German colony and prevent actual desertions. It did not, however, inhibit many Stockholm Germans from establishing contact with the Allies secretly and furnishing them with much valuable information.

In every way the Germans were preparing as best they could for the calamity they knew was not far off. One of their major occupations in Stockholm was connected with the transfer of large quantities of cash, capital, and articles of value from Germany to Sweden, sometimes for their own use and sometimes for friends and colleagues in Germany. This had been going on for a long while, since many who had pinned their prospects on the success of the Nazi régime were cynical enough to invest in what might be termed political insurance policies. From April to June of 1944, a great intensification of these activities took place.

New methods were added to the old. A common one was the organization of bogus shipping and fishing companies. Large sums were forwarded to these concerns from Germany as payment for ships that were ordered but never actually delivered. It was estimated that millions of crowns had been sent to Sweden in this way during these three months alone. Jewel-smuggling flourished as it always does in European crises. Great quantities of precious stones arrived in Sweden by diplomatic pouch to be sold by several agents working in Sweden for Germans. The agents then banked the money either under the name of the German to whom the jewels belonged or in the name of a Swedish confederate. International blackmail was used to help swell the coffers of important German officials, among them Himmler himself, as they carefully laid up wealth in what they hoped would be their future sanctuary. It was known that in 1943 Himmler had personally intervened to save the life of a condemned German Jew. In return, relatives in Sweden banked some three million kroner in the name of the Jew, who, however, remained in Germany under Himmler's protection. There were numerous similar transactions, with variations according to the circumstances.

Some German officials did not bother with ingenious schemes, but confined their depredations quite bluntly to their own government. Thus, German Naval Attaché Paul von Wahlert and Assistant Naval Attaché Gotthard Walter Raehmel received from O.K.M. (German Naval Command) approximately one million kroner for expenses and entertainment during the period from April to July, 1944. They promptly salted it away to make it possible for them and certain comrades in O.K.M. to settle down to a comfortable post-bellum existence in Sweden.

Meanwhile, the prospect of imminent defeat also spurred on the activity of the two hundred German political refugees who lived in and around Stockholm, as well as a greater number from Austria, Hungary, and Czechoslovakia, of every political complexion and shade.

Early in 1944 I was invited to one of the meetings that took place frequently in this colony. In a bare room in Stockholm's Folketshus a score of earnest old-school Socialists gathered to discuss post-war problems, particularly those of Germany. These men and women were representatives of Social-Democratic Parties and trade-union organizations of several European countries. They were members of a group of democratic socialists in Stockholm who sometimes jocularly called themselves the 'Little International.' This irony had a touch of pathos in it, as these people, who had nearly all once been important figures, invariably suffered from the reduction in size that took place in exile. This feeling of having been pushed to one side by history and being dwarfed by impotence was now lifted slightly by their anticipation of a busy future.

Most of those in attendance were snowy-haired, rugged labor leaders who fought Naziism before Hitler came to power and had fled its advent in country after country. They were still fighting it as well as they could. Several had been back and forth illegally to Germany many times. Some had even made the hazardous trip after the war had begun, braving Gestapo terror to try and keep together the threads of the central European labor movement.

Among those active in the 'Little International' and other refugee political groups were Vice-President Ernst Paul, Secretary of the Sudeten German Social Democratic Party, thirty-year-old Secretary Willy Brandt (writer and German Youth Leader who fled to Norway in 1933, became a leading Norwegian labor movement functionary, and then fled to Sweden in 1941 from a German prison in Norway), Martin Tranmael, a leader of the Norwegian Labor

Party, and the meticulous Hungarian, Wilhelm Boehm, who was the War Minister in Bela Kun's revolutionary Hungarian Government and had left to become the *émigré* leader of the Hungarian Social Democrats. A number of prominent and rank and file Austrians, Poles, Frenchmen, Danes, and Czechs made up the total.

Most of the 'Little International' groups had been functioning since July, 1942, each national group meeting separately and then all meeting together. Two commissions had been formed to thresh out a program on post-war economic, social, and cultural problems. All groups held in common a belief in internationalism and some variety of Marxism. Important meetings were closed by singing the *Internationale* — no longer the Soviet national anthem. Most of them accepted as axiomatic that the producers should inherit the earth, that international trade unions should play a vital rôle in the post-war world and be directly represented on any international governing body or league of nations. Nearly all believed in achieving their aims through democratic methods.

Resolutions were passed in favor of the most important points in their post-war program, which included:

1. The Four Freedoms.

2. Socialization — 'extended social control of economy in order to prevent crises, create order, and efficiency and obtain the greatest possible social and economic equality. Society, by means of its democratic organs and free associations, would take over or regulate the most important branches of production, finance and distribution (the German group unanimously demanded, for their country, the nationalization of heavy industry).

3. National and international economic planning.

4. The right of national self-determination.

5. Effective international control of the armed forces of all nations until universal disarmament became practicable.

6. The nationalization of all armament industries as quickly as possible.

7. The maintenance of good relations with the Soviet Union.

8. The confiscation of war profits.

9. Effective international control of all colonies as yet unable to rule themselves.

10. To make the defeat of Naziism lasting, the strength of the

groups that supported it must be smashed. The economic power of the alliance between the Junkers, the generals, and heavy industry must be broken.

11. Intervention against democratic popular socialist movements in Europe should not be instigated. It would be contrary to the spirit of the Atlantic Charter and would strengthen reaction both in the countries that intervened and those that suffered intervention.

In discussions of the concrete realization of this program, one of the knottiest problems that confronted them was the disposal of the Arbeitsfront apparatus. Several leaders believed that since the organizations and material property were mostly stolen from the German trade unions, they should be taken over almost intact as nuclei for the reconstruction of these unions. These men believed that the unions would be indispensable in the task of getting German economy back on its feet. Others argued that the Arbeitsfront was permeated with Naziism and should be destroyed. The trade-union movement would then be built up around the tiny underground groups which were already working in German factories. This question, which involved a multitude of important political principles, since the structure of the unions would be intimately connected with its leadership, policies, and chances for immediate influence, was still under discussion in 1944.

Another subject of heated controversy was the question of relations with the Communists, who had recently proposed increased collaboration with the Social Democrats. Old-time Social Democrats feared the tendency of the Communists to use faction politics and seize control of any organization in which they were allowed. The majority, however, thought that it would be necessary to work with the Communists. Many pointed out that post-war Communists would probably stand on the right and not on the left wing of the labor movement in central Europe. They would be anxious to maintain production at all costs and to avoid social disturbances so that Germany would be able to deliver the machines and commodities necessary for Soviet reconstruction. Statements were cited from authoritative Communists in Stockholm to the effect that revolution in post-war Germany would be wholly undesirable. This meant, as one proponent of collaboration expressed it, that 'post-war Social Democrats might have the same position in relation to the Communists that the Communists had in relation to them after the last war. Then, for more than a decade, the Socialists were afraid that the Communists would arouse the masses to open class struggle. After this war, the position may well be reversed.'

Besides the 'Little International,' there were in Stockholm immigrant trade-union organizations of various national groups. In the German trade-union organization were some fifty political refugees who were all either enrolled in Swedish trade unions or former members of German trade unions. The last election for officers of this group was surprising. Fifty per cent of the vote was Social Democrat and the other half was divided evenly between the Communists and the Trotskyites.

In the spring of 1944, a united front organization made its début. The first meeting of the new German Kulturbund (League of Culture) took place in Borgarskolan. Doctor Max Hodann, formerly a practicing physician in Berlin and a fellow traveler, introduced the league as a non-political association of anti-Nazi Germans in Sweden. The meeting was attended by about eight hundred people, most of them German refugees. A few Swedes and Norwegians were also present.

Doctor Hodann inaugurated the league with a sober, judicious address in which he stated that the aims of the organization were to preserve and sustain the best elements of German culture and to bring together forces which would aid in the restoration of a democratic Germany. He urged the destruction of the Nazi legend that Germany was attacked, and sharply condemned the Herrentum of Germany. He declared that Germany had attacked its neighbors five times in the last eighty years. By inference, he placed the burden of the war guilt on the Reich and urged German participation in the reconstruction of the countries that had been ravaged by Germany in the present war.

Though Doctor Hodann left the league for a job in the British Legation, it nevertheless continued to function and do valuable work in bringing refugees of various political groups together. On such burning political problems of the moment as the Polish frontier and Moscow's attitude to post-war Germany, the league adopted no position whatsoever. The initiative in the organization unquestionably came from the Communists.

It was difficult to estimate how significant these trends were in relation to the total picture in Germany and to guess what influence these and similar refugee groups elsewhere would have in Germany when the war was over. A great deal depended on the policy of the Allies. The exiles of many of the occupied countries had tended to lose touch with the populations that actually suffered the ravages of war and the resistance groups that led them. The situation would be different in Germany, since, in the minds of those who would forsake Naziism as a political creed, a vacuum would be left which the programs of these groups could fill. If the pattern of German exile thought in Sweden were to become widespread in Germany, the composition might not be so vastly different from that of the Weimar Republic. The power of the labor groups would have increased, the Social Democrats would have moved quite a distance to the left, and the Communists would have swung some distance to the right.

★ 2. CRUMBLING WALLS ★

WHILE IN STOCKHOLM two very different kinds of Germans engaged in feverish activity in anticipation of Allied victory, inside Germany the carefully built Nazi economy was beginning to fall apart like an old house. Leaks and gaps appeared everywhere and no sooner was one mended than another required immediate attention. Shortages and insufficiencies of every kind had nearly reached the breaking point.

The shortage of oil, particularly of lubricating oil, had become critical. It meant that machinery and vital equipment of every kind would depreciate with abnormal rapidity. The overburdened railroad system creaked and groaned under the demands made upon it, coupled with the daily strafings and bombings of the Allies. Every possible locomotive and railroad car was pulled out of France and Belgium, but the need for more rolling stock could not be satisfied.

War factories of all kinds were hampered by shortages of metals. While the German armies were advancing, thousands of tons of scrap metal, including the priceless non-ferrous metals from shell-casings, fell daily into German hands. After Stalingrad and D-day, this precious battlefront crop was harvested by the Allies. The metal shortages were drastically intensified when Germany was unable to get chrome from Turkey, wolfram from Portugal, and nickel from Finland. Important non-ferrous metal sources in Russia had been lost in 1943, so that by the end of 1944 Germany's supply of these metals was perilously inadequate.

As every ounce of German energy became harnessed to the war effort, elementary necessities, such as shoes, clothes, and housing, became agonizingly scarce. Throughout Germany none of these could be bought and, as a result, money virtually lost its buying power. Articles like fountain pens, watches, and furniture were bartered for food. Used articles of clothing were exchanged at government barter stations.

With every nerve and sinew strained to meet production demands, Germany suffered a catastrophic shortage of labor power. The ten million foreign workers inside the Reich failed to compensate for the enormous drain on Teutonic manpower. To economize, many customary services were eliminated. Guests in hotels had to clean their own rooms, make their own beds, and frequently bring their own sheets. In the restaurants, customers not only served themselves, but often had to wash their own dishes.

The food situation demanded the closest kind of rationing and supervision. During the 1943-44 season the shortage of potatoes had been compensated for by increased bread rations. In 1944-45, the potato ration could not be increased because large quantities were being used for the manufacture of V-2 fuel alcohol. But the bread ration meanwhile had dropped from 5.33 pounds to 4.9 pounds. Nevertheless, the Germans were able to keep the individual consumption of calories in 1944-45 up to the same level as 1943-44, with the exception, of course, of regional shortages due to transport breakdowns. To further this, a greater number of German pigs had to be slaughtered, which was in any case necessitated by the shortage of pig feed. In 1943, the number of pigs in Germany had already been cut in half.

One factor that enabled the Germans to cope with their food difficulties was that the Nazis, having learned a lesson from the last war, had spared a sufficient number of agricultural workers from military duty to keep the farms in working order. Another was the introduction on a huge scale of collectivized kitchens, which were much more efficient than home kitchens. These collectivized kitchens used less fuel, saved work, and made it possible to cut the consumption of the more expensive foods, such as meat, and increase the consumption of potatoes and grain (a calorie of meat represents a much greater investment of land and labor than a calorie of grain or greens).

Tremendous attention was being paid in Germany to the development of ersatz materials. A good example was rubber. Concentrated efforts were made to develop sources of raw rubber to feed into the insatiable maw of the war industries. Production of Buna rubber in Germany suffered because of the bombings. But Germany had, by this time, another important source of rubber in the koksagyz plant developed by the Russians during the first five-year plan.

When the Germans entered the Ukraine, they found many fields planted with koksagyz and in 1942 they began transplanting it to various sites in Europe. Two heavily capitalized companies were formed for the development of vegetable rubber in the Reich. In August, 1942, regular transportation of koksagyz plants to Germany was organized and experimental culture of the plant had been instituted all over Europe. It was found to grow satisfactorily in Galicia and in 1943 many fields were planted. In Rumania in 1943, one hundred and fifty hectares of koksagyz matured with a yield that varied from fifty to one hundred and fifty kilograms of raw rubber per hectare. The Rumanian Government did everything possible to stimulate the development, even giving exemptions from military service to peasants who planted two acres of the koksagyz culture. In Bulgaria, Hungary, Latvia, Finland, and Denmark, koksagyz and other varieties of the plant were introduced and cultivated with considerable success.

As mountains of prime military material melted away on the

flaming Eastern Front and as the Allied air forces whittled down both the Luftwaffe and German productive capacity, the Nazi leaders tried desperately to pull the ragged edges of Germany together over its bleeding body by whipping the exhausted population into increased production. A large staff of industrious publicity agents and brass-throated Nazi ward-heelers reached into every home, factory, and office, cajoling, threatening, and nagging.

Campaigns were instituted against wasting coal, water, and time. These were popularized by widespread official ridicule of *Kohlenklau* and *Stundeklau* (coal-pinching and hour-pinching). Hans Landwehrmann, the Berlin painter and cartoonist who fathered the campaign, drew posters in Germanized Peter Arno style which depicted Germans shivering in wintry blasts because some thoughtless individual forgot to close a door or extinguish a fire. A drive was launched in the papers to encourage hitch-hiking on a national scale. Owners and operators of every vehicle including army cars were urged to pick up any pedestrians and never to waste space. Brigades of schoolboys and schoolgirls, members of the Hitler Youth, pasted up posters and made inflamed speeches threatening and shaming workers who loafed on the jobs. Newspapers wailed continuously about absenteeism and abjured the workers not to shirk their duty.

Spurred on by ceaseless campaigns, haunted by the fear of punishment if their production lagged, emotionally drugged by incessant fiery speeches demanding that every German increase his output by ten per cent every hour, many workers managed to sustain fatigue through long hours under the most difficult conditions, toiling in a kind of mindless delirium. According to German press claims which many neutral experts regarded as fairly accurate, the productivity of German workers actually went up in many factories. This spurt was hardly expected to be permanent, but for the time being Germany, nettled by air attacks and apprehensive of the Russian offensive, kept producing at a frenzied pace.

When the Germans were forced back to the Rhine, the Nazi authorities began to prepare for a *Volkskrieg.* On September 5, 1944, the Nazi press chief, Herman Sundermann, publicly proclaimed the adoption of 'the scorched-earth policy.' 'Not a single straw will be left for the enemy,' Sundermann asserted. 'No German mouth will inform him, no German hand will aid him; he will find every path completely destroyed, every street blocked. He will meet nothing but death, annihilation, hatred. He will bleed to death in the most awful way on every foot's breadth of German earth which belongs to us, and which the enemy wants to rob from us . . . a nation that in its soul has cut the words — rather death than slavery; a nation which with fanaticism made these words a clue to its whole fighting achievement. Such nations will never surrender. . . . The German nation trusts the German Army's resolute achievement in defensive fighting, which is becoming the more embittered the nearer the fronts advance to the home doors. But we want to prepare now to be able to obey the order whenever and wherever it is given. Every individual German must remember this duty, even if the order does not reach him. To be prepared.'

Mingled exhortations of every kind appeared in the press, to heroism, to patience, to confidence in German ingenuity and contempt for the enemy. On September 3, the *Völkischer Beobachter* published an appeal for those born in 1928 to volunteer. In an article entitled 'Nazis to the Bone,' in the same issue, the Youth Leader, Arthur Axmann, wrote: 'Never was the belief in victory in our young people stronger than in this period of heaviest burden on all fronts and on the home front. With unshakable belief in the Führer, the German youth marches into the sixth year of war. . . . It depends on you whether you will be the last of a race disregarded and despised by posterity or whether you will see the beginning of a new time more glorious than you could ever imagine.'

The same paper also ran a lengthy serial by Sundermann, in which he tried to prove that Germany was forced into the war. 'Germany's enemies are trying to settle the war before new German weapons and fresh powers can be used,' said the *Berliner Montagspost,* discussing the Finnish armistice. 'But we are firmly convinced that the weapon technical development in connection with the effects of total war achievement will make itself felt shortly and that this will show the enemy that today he exults too early.'

In an attempt to keep up falling spirits, some Nazi leaders even had recourse to humor. Official jokes appeared ridiculing every dereliction from the Nazi code. Although political jokes were not as common in the Europe of 1944 as they were in the late thirties, or even during the first World War, German miseries nevertheless found some relief in jest. As Jews, Irish, and others have adjusted to misfortune by means of humor, so, in their own ponderous style, did the Germans.

These were the current favorites of Berlin in 1944:

In Berlin, a *kleiner Mann* (Germany's name for the average man, the little fellow) had been bombed out of his home, went to the N.S.V., the organization for aid to those bombed out of their homes. He went into the building and found himself in a huge room having two exit doors over which were written, 'Partly Bombed Out' and 'Completely Bombed Out.' *Kleiner Mann* reflected that there was still something left of his house, so he entered the first door and found himself in another crowded room having two exits, over which were written 'Poor People' and 'Rich People.' Reflecting that he certainly was poor, *kleiner Mann* entered the first door to find himself in a third room whose two exits were marked 'Party Members' and 'Not Party Members.' Without hesitating, *kleiner Mann* went through the second door and found himself in the street. He shook his head and said, 'But WHAT organization.'

Hitler, Roosevelt, Stalin, and Churchill agreed to test the courage of their soldiers and one German, one American, one Russian, and one British soldier were placed together in front of two thousand guns which were fired simultaneously. The English, American, and Russian soldiers soiled their trousers, but not the German, to whom Hitler forthwith gave the Iron Cross with oak leaves and asked what his dearest wish was. The soldier answered, 'Enough to eat so that I can react like a human being.'

From Denmark: In a Danish factory one dark night a German sentry heard a noise and shouted in a frightened voice, 'Who goes there?' The answer was 'Saboteur Olsen.'

From Berlin: Once in a cinema when Hitler's picture came on the screen, a voice shouted, 'Who the devil is that?' Immediately the lights came on and a Gestapo guard shouted, 'Who was that?' Several voices answered, 'Don't you know either?'

From Berlin: Someone asked a Berliner when the war would be

over, and he said, 'When the British are eating rats and we are eating ersatz rats.'

From Berlin: Mrs. Germania felt bad and went to a stomach specialist, Doctor Churchill, who diagnosed undernourishment. 'Nonsense,' she replied, 'i have plenty to eat every day.' Then she went to the celebrated nerve specialist, F. D. R., who diagnosed a nervous collapse. 'My nerves are excellent,' said Mrs. Germania in a hurt tone; and then she went to see General Practitioner Stalin, who smiled, patted her on the back, and said, 'It is easy to see what's wrong with you; little Germany is on the way.'

Despite friction and difficulty of every kind, the German economic machinery continued to function. Throughout the Reich food was scarce, but everyone got enough to be able to continue working. Air-raid victims received special attention. Many were evacuated to quiet districts and given emergency tents or mass-produced bungalows. They received special rations of sugar, coffee, fats, clothing, and cigarettes. Travelers from Berlin in the fall of 1944 reported that since the heavy air raids had begun, Berliners had been getting an extra ration of two hundred and fifty grams of pork a month. Additional allowances of essentials had also been granted and small rations of such luxuries as cigarettes.

Deutsche Allgemeine Zeitung pointed out that to maintain food rations every last drop and morsel had to be squeezed from 'thousands of minor sources.' The fat supply had to be kept up at all costs. To this end 'a couple of tens of thousands' of tons more butter were necessary. Compulsory deliveries had to be increased, and if every German farm delivered one extra liter of milk every day, it would mean thirty-two thousand additional tons of butter. In turn, to realize this, the German diet had to be changed. More pork had to be eaten instead of veal. The chief difficulty in maintaining and increasing the pig stock was the poor potato crops. Sugar beets now had to replace potatoes, the newspaper explained, and added that the serious decline in the pig stock during the last few years had to be remedied immediately.

To ensure fair food rationing, it was essential for all individuals to make sacrifices and not to take advantage of such privileges as that of obtaining an extra liter of milk from some farm or other. Evacuees had to keep to town rations, although they resided in the country. It was further stressed that the most vital point in the whole supply policy was to see that armament workers obtained their rations so that production should be maintained. The rural as well as the urban population had to bear this constantly in mind. The war industries continued to produce at high speed. Moreover, despite everything, German industry even went on manufacturing for export. In Sweden one could buy fine quality German films, optical equipment, and machine tools. I talked with a paper manufacturer who had received a paper-rolling machine worth about twenty thousand dollars from a large German Rhineland factory in the fall of 1944. The machine contained many scarce non-ferrous metals and its workmanship and quality were excellent. The German machine-building industry likewise produced a remarkable assortment of special wartime devices for the German war effort. An extraordinary specimen was a machine in use in Hamburg in 1944 which scooped up bomb rubble, ground it, and transformed it into concrete which the machine then poured into forms from which issued one-story emergency dwellings. This huge mechanical monster crawled slowly through the devastated areas laying several immense barrack-like dwellings daily.

To save labor power, drastic simplifications and severe restrictions were the rule. The publicity business was virtually abolished, newspapers and magazines reduced to a tiny fraction of their prewar output, and a considerable portion of the country's schools were shut down until after the war. The only two forms of entertainment which survived were the radio and the cinema. A huge economy was effected by arbitrarily declaring all 1944 taxes equal to those of 1943. An immense saving of labor hours in the tax department, the post office, and other facilities accrued from this simple measure.

By the end of 1944, the entire consumers' goods industries had been virtually closed down, and such articles as household goods, clothes, and furniture were no longer manufactured for civilian use. Germans were urged to co-operate in a 'help-your-neighbor' plan calculated to make one electric iron and even one frying pan do for several families.

Another remarkable development was the dispersal of industry which took place during 1944. Large complicated factories were broken up into small units which were relocated in villages, small towns, and, in instances, in completely uninhabited districts. This created new transportation difficulties, but it made it nearly impossible to bomb German industry out of operation.

German economy continued to function basically because German men and women were still willing to work. Of course, they all had to work because of the relentless Gestapo supervision which made resistance, or even 'doubting,' suicidal. But there was more to it than that. Germans were probably still willing to fight for the following additional basic reasons:

1. The successful maintenance by the German authorities of a reasonable food supply even in the most heavily bombed German areas.

2. Fear of the Russians.

3. Fear of the reported extreme intentions of the United Nations if victorious.

4. Widely publicized and wildly exaggerated reports of disunity among the United Nations which raised German hopes of a negotiated peace.

5. Successful German defense action in Italy, East Prussia, and along the Rhine.

6. Hope of a stalemate as a result of the effectiveness of the V weapons.

★ 3. UNSUCCESSFUL OPPOSITION ★

A LTHOUGH GERMANY continued to function under the dictates of the Nazi tyranny, the sufferings and calamities did provoke an opposition. Political opposition in Germany has never been very successful, never sufficiently strong to modify the policies of the group in power or influence its action. When opposition became strong, it was suppressed. This was the fate of the Communists and, indeed, all those who opposed the Nazis when they took power. During the war, opposition in Germany followed the traditional pattern.

In 1933, perhaps fifty per cent of the German people supported Hitler and wanted to give him a chance to fulfill his promises. By 1937 or 1938, a modicum of success had probably increased the percentage. In the early part of the war, aided by military triumphs, Hitler probably had the support of a large majority of the German people. By 1944, the hardships and sufferings endured by both the civilian and military population had drastically altered the situation. Opposition of an active and passive kind had developed, chiefly in the following groups:

1. Dissatisfied Army officers   5. Left-wing trade-unionists.
   and soldiers.
2. Foreign workers.   6. Communists.
3. Catholics.   7. Monarchists.
4. Social Democrats.   8. Industrialists.

The common soldier of the Wehrmacht, when he became sufficiently disaffected, was prone to desertion rather than opposition. Many deserted to the Russians, frequently joining the Free Germany Committee in Moscow or becoming members of its armed forces estimated at two hundred thousand trained troops. Others ran away to neutral Sweden. Some went A.W.O.L. in Germany itself. German officials estimated in September, 1943, that this last category numbered about fifty-six thousand soldiers. It grew steadily, and by the end of 1944 it probably amounted to about two hundred thousand.

The only example, which I know, of organized anti-Nazi activity among the German troops was the circulation, in early 1944, of a pamphlet entitled *Ich Will Nicht Mehr*. It was probably printed and circulated by the Communists, but it bore no identifying marks whatsoever. Its effects on the soldiers, at this time sufficiently embittered and disgruntled, was considerable.

A rebellious force of tremendous potentiality was the twelve million foreign workers in Greater Germany. In the summer of 1944, it included some four million Russians (of which three hundred thousand were women), two and a half million French, one and a half million Poles, one million Italians, six hundred thousand Belgians, five hundred thousand Yugoslavs, four hundred thousand Dutch, three hundred thousand Czechs.

Nearly all of these were anti-Nazi in sentiment, but, with the exception of the Russians, they were not organized at all, not even sufficiently to bargain collectively with their Nazi overseers for better conditions. Consequently, the sporadic manifestations of opposition among other foreigners than the Russians were spontaneous, unplanned, and resulted in massacres. Several of these massacres occurred during the week of May 26 in Dresden, Berlin, Hamburg, and Osnabruck. Workers had demonstrated for permission to go to the air-raid shelters when the radio announced the approach of enemy planes and before the sirens actually blew, SS troops opened fire, killing several. In some cases the workers seized arms and retaliated. Blood was shed, but to no fruitful purpose. Machine-gun battles were even known to have occurred between foreign workers and police, but such clashes were no more a serious threat to the State than similar clashes are in America.

The activities of the German trade unions were a greater menace to the Nazis. Although the organizations were broken up when the Nazis took power, their members nevertheless continued to make contacts in the factories, in public places, and in homes. Organized groups were co-ordinated by the trade unions, but with no centralized connections. The Social Democrats engaged in similar activity. Its groups functioned and contacts were maintained. Although all this was on a very limited scale and casualties were high, it was, nevertheless, opposition, and it was organized in a definite direction.

The Catholic Church was in an extremely favorable position for the growth of opposition under its protection. Anti-Nazi Catholics were able to communicate with each other and make contacts because of the fact that the church functionaries, with some exceptions, had not been molested by the Nazis. They were permitted to hold services, see people at confessions, and circulate in their communities. They could always meet each other freely, something which frequently was not permitted to German generals.

The officers of the German Army were, obviously, the group in the most strategic position for effective opposition to Hitler's authority. Seven million German soldiers were under the command of the untutored ex-corporal, who now bore the title of Supreme Commander of all Germany's armed forces. Next in command was

Field Marshal von Keitel, who had been a Nazi Party member since 1934. A man of sixty-two, he was an egocentric, dandified pseudo-sportsman and addicted to Wagner as some people are to opium. He was Chief of the Supreme Command, and it was his task to co-ordinate the activities of the Army, the Navy, and the Air Force. German military men regarded Keitel as stupid, unimaginative, and foolhardy. He had been in favor of attacking Russia immediately at the end of the Polish campaign — thus out-Hitlering Hitler.

Under the authority of these two wool-gathering, rash tyros, a number of competent and highly trained military men chafed and nursed resentments. Among them were men like the professional soldier and tank expert, General Heinz Guderian, Chief of Staff. Like De Gaulle, Guderian had published a book emphasizing the military virtues of the tank. During the French campaign, the two tank enthusiasts clashed at Abbeville and Guderian's forces were temporarily halted by De Gaulle. When Guderian was stopped in front of Moscow, he indulged in some trenchant criticism of Hitler's supreme command. He was temporarily eclipsed, but was later brought back by Hitler and made General Inspector of the armored forces, a position which he held until after the assassination attempt, when he replaced Zetzler as Chief of Staff.

After Field Marshal Hermann Göring blustered himself out of power in the summer of 1944, the Luftwaffe was actually run by Erhard Milch. Fifty-four years old, Milch had been a member of the legendary Richthofen squadron, a stunt flyer, and had been employed for several years in the Ford plant at Detroit. He was reputed to be Jewish, which made his advent to the top of the difficult Luftwaffe hierarchy all the more remarkable. This was made possible by the death in accidents of such former colleagues of Göring's as General Udet, Colonel Moelders, Captain Balthasar, Lieutenant Colonel Pfandt, and General Walzburn. Milch was outspoken against war with Russia and stuck consistently to the opinion that Germany could not survive a war on two fronts. Unknown but powerful, Milch directed the Lutwaffe in its gigantic losing battle.

These two were typical. There were many other generals with grievances and serious differences of opinion with the Nazi leaders; each one of whom could have become the focus of powerful coalitions against the Party. Opposition of various degrees of intensity came from the other three groups; the monarchists, who no longer had any strong hold in German life; the industrialists, who had lost much of their power; and the Communists, who had suffered many reverses, but finally emerged in considerable strength. Until early in 1944, cells of opposition from these eight groups functioned more or less separately and rather ineffectually.

The Nazi authorities experienced some difficulty in handling opposition because air raids had caused a breakdown in the police-registration system. Devastation introduced chaos and anarchy into the tightly controlled pattern of German life. A traveler from Berlin gave me an interesting description of prevailing conditions.

'After the big November raids,' he told me, 'we were kept busy repairing broken windows and helping neighbors. Then a bombed-out family moved in on us. Then another. At first it was not so bad. To the kids in particular, it was like a picnic. There was a feeling of comradeship. We all felt heroic, and what with the extra bomb rations and cooking in common, we ate better than we had done for some time.

'Then one of our boarders got influenza and another began taking food from the cupboard arbitrarily. After the raids in December, the water supply went bad and my visitors started to stink. Maybe I did, too. At the same time a brother of one of the visitors got bombed out of West Berlin and joined us, bringing only the torn clothes on his back. Plates, cutlery, and clothes had to be shared. New arrivals had been smelling bad even before they reached us.

'Some of the guests had visitors who stayed late and talked a lot. It occurred to me that they might be doubters. Doubters were being arrested and, some say, shot in larger numbers than the press reported, and I was very worried. But the worst happened when the husband of a daughter of one of my guests came home from the Eastern Front on ten days' leave and decided to stay with us. The police records in our district had been destroyed, so he was safe enough in borrowed civvies. Nearly everyone looked like they were wearing borrowed clothes, anyhow. By this time the house was a hell of petty squabbles, bawling kids, and raw nerves. I got out.'

To cope with chaos, desertion, and opposition, the Nazis continually devised fresh schemes. Front-line soldiers and weary warworkers were officially patted on the back and told: 'Yes, boys, you are having a hard time and we know it, but you have got to go on.'

Official propaganda now thumped monotonously on a single note. War was a grim, ineluctable reality from which there was no escape. Struggling against it, refusing to face it, shirking, only made things worse for everyone. *Das Schwarze Korps* devoted its entire front page to a huge editorial entitled 'Say Yes to War.' It was somberly illustrated with dark-garbed, maudlinesque German soldiers. A new kind of stoicism rang from resounding articles designed to stiffen German spines to war by dwelling on German hatred of war. 'We have no reason to love war and we do not fight with the dizzy enthusiasm shown in 1870 and 1914. We love our work and know that war is a roaring cataract between us and the future. We hate it because it steals precious years, banishes our life aims to an unknown future, and upsets all our plans. But because of this we must say yes to it.'

Veritable barrages of similar propaganda covered Germany with a thick, dusty war atmosphere through which any other reality but that of war was not even visible. 'Anyone who tries to turn his back on war,' went one of the articles, 'or through weakness and fatigue does not accept war, serves to lengthen it and cuts off his nose to spite his face. Whatever one does, one cannot escape war. It is, therefore, best to put all effort into the fight.'

Daily, Germans were reminded that 'to eat or be eaten is the gruesome philosophy to which all life on earth must be subjected.' As a consolation for present sufferings, a mother's day editorial attempted to hearten the morose, ravaged readers by dwelling on the remote future: 'In a thousand years from now will our people have enough space to live a new life? That is what Germany is fighting for, and one day our children will see with their father's eyes the wide world which was closed to us.'

Civilian spying multiplied through Germany like a rank war weed. There were spies in every factory, church, office, government bureau, and school in the country — most of them terrorized amateurs. These acted as spies on their fellows and friends neither for money nor from patriotic motives. They were usually blackmailed and browbeaten into becoming informers and then threatened with exposure to the wrath of their fellows if they did not continue. In the spring of 1944, one could be found on every city block who was ready to sell his neighbor to the Gestapo for a pat on the back.

Many informers denounced their fellow workers and often their fellow informers, with such frequency that Gestapo offices and jails became clogged. Another Nazi growth had mushroomed into a serious nuisance and had to be trimmed. A rule was finally put through requiring denunciations for 'doubt,' listening to foreign broadcasts, and other 'crimes,' to be made by at least two Germans if the accused was a German. Himmler's spy system then continued to function efficiently.

All during 1944, press and propaganda bureaus worked overtime thinking up new ways of coloring, distorting, and inventing news. On several different occasions, for weeks at a time, Nazi papers ran wild with fabulous accounts from Tokyo of Japanese victories over United States naval and military forces in the Pacific. Ferocious attention was paid to such events as the dispute in Persia over Russian oil concessions and the unsuccessful insurrections in Slovakia and Warsaw. When everything else failed, worn-out Nazi propaganda marksmen trained their sights on the riddled Jewish target.

Amazing new strategical epithets made their way into the military lexicons. Nazi battles were now described in such phrases as 'elastic defense,' 'planned withdrawal,' and mysteriously effective 'front shortenings.' Gyrating wildly, a military commentator finally came up with the phrase 'elastic stability' to describe German tactics in France. The Allied and Rusian armies were verbally restricted to such dull occupations as 'unsuccessfully attempting to hinder the German retreat.'

To counteract the effect of the millions of leaflets dropped on Germany by the R.A.F., the Germans themselves dropped leaflets ostensibly printed by the Allies, with subtle Nazi propaganda. Copenhagen, at one time, was showered with leaflets ostensibly dropped by the Allied High Command urging the Danish populace, in the interests of Anglo-American-Russian victory, to welcome cordially the Negro troops which were to arrive shortly, along with

Tartar Red Army troops, as an army of occupation in Denmark.

I ran across a remarkable document in Stockholm. It was a full-size, perfectly counterfeited edition of *Life* magazine, dated July 5, 1943. The cover looked like the real thing. On the first page were advertisements for a brand of underwear and some general letters clipped from various issues of *Life.* On page 3 was a full-scale editorial entitled 'America's Purpose.' It asserted that American boys were now dying to make all men free and equal. The next six pages were devoted to genuine, well-printed photographs of the most bloody and violent episodes in the Detroit race riot. Although it was printed in English, there was no doubt that this and similar laboriously contrived publications were intended for German consumption.

But in spite of police, spies, propaganda, and the absence of Allied appeals for a German revolt, the opposition continued and grew stronger. In 1944, perhaps the first centralized organization of opposition was formed. It was known as the 'Berlin Center' and had members in all parts of the country and in most of the important administrative organizations like the Gestapo, the Reichswehr, the O.K.W., and O.K.M. (Supreme Army and Navy Commands).

The goal the Center had set itself was the creation of an alternative administration for Germany. It linked together the following groups:

1. Catholics.

2. Trade unions — mostly S.P.D., also Communists and S.A.P. (the Socialists Workers' Party was a group which split from the left wing of the Social Democratic Party).

3. Communists — though they had only two representatives in the central body of the Berlin Center, Communists were the strongest single group of the German underground.

4. Various unaffiliated anti-Nazis, mostly intellectuals, who held positions in government organizations.

5. The Goerdeler group, a young nationalist group, very strong in Leipzig. It was backed by the big industrialists and claimed to represent Schacht and similar people.

6. The Boy Scouts, an illegal organization of a completely unpolitical character. Chiefly, they urged revolt against long working hours and regimentation.

7. A small but tightly organized group of high Army and Navy officers.

The intense dissatisfaction that prevailed among large numbers of Army officers was utilized by the Berlin Center as much as possible. Causes of this dissatisfaction were numerous. German generals on the Eastern Front were enraged by the transfer of a great proportion of their reserves to France. They felt betrayed, and the stories which reached Stockholm indicated the seriousness of their disaffection. The widespread animus among the generals was well known to Hitler and those around him, who feared that an important concerted conspiracy was already under way. Immediately before the Allied invasion a very tense situation was created between Hitler and Himmler. Using internal security as a pretext, the Gestapo chieftain made the greatest difficulties for Reichswehr officers to get supplies, ammunition, and spare parts, particularly when their units were inside German territory. Himmler acted through his political connections and his power with the Führer. In this way S.S. units inside Germany were well supplied with enough munitions and equipment for the remote future, while the Reichswehr units had barely enough ammunition to fire one round each. The generals were infuriated and took the matter to Hitler, who sided with them on the issue, countermanded Himmler's edicts, and transferred supplies from the S.S. to the Reichswehr units.

In addition, Himmler had shown many signs of a desire to build himself up as Hitler's successor. It was very likely that Himmler was casting himself for the rôle of eventual negotiator with the Allies. Swedes, Turks, and other neutrals who talked to him spoke of his extreme politeness, gentleness, and humanitarianism. He took to giving gifts to children, feeding animals, and intervening in behalf of criminals. A Latvian newspaper, *Tevija,* stated that the chicken farm Jelgava Mitava had honored 'Balticum's protector Heinrich Himmler' with a gift of two hundred pedigreed chickens. On a previous visit, Himmler had displayed a flattering interest in Latvian chickens.

The Berlin Center also attempted to use the general dissatisfaction of Germany's industrialists as a lever with which to pry the Nazis loose from power. Besides feeling betrayed by Hitler, the man they helped launch, Rhineland industrialists saw their factories being systematically destroyed by Allied bombs while Nazi officials lopped off fat slices from their profits and usurped their powers. They were, consequently, for immediate peace at any terms. It was their sole chance of saving something from the wreckage. If the war continued, Germany would be economically ruined and the people would go overwhelmingly Communist.

If the industrialists had possessed daring and ingenuity, they could have banded together and taken effective steps. But they were afraid of competitors, of each other, and of the Gestapo. Moreover, they had no reason to believe that the Anglo-American attitude toward them would be at all friendly. They, therefore, groaned, sweated, and cursed, but did nothing decisive. One by one they were clipped off by the Gestapo, and by the end of 1944 a dozen of the most powerful Rhineland industrial magnates were lodged in jail.

In June and July, 1944, the activity of the Berlin Center reached a climax. I received my first concrete information about this organization from one of its members, a patriotic German of great courage named Adam von Trott zu Solz, who came to Stockholm in March, later in June. Along with six others he was hanged in September for conspiratorial activities in connection with the July 20 attempt on Hitler's life.

Von Trott was a tall, bald aristocrat of about thirty-five. He had one American grandparent and spoke perfect English. Although he had been anti-Nazi for a long time before the war, his sheer brilliance and scholarship kept him in his position as Gesandschaftsrat. During the early part of 1942, he had been one of the active organizers of the Berlin Center, specializing in work abroad. His duties at the Wilhelmstrasse involved frequent trips to Ankara, Lisbon, and Stockholm which enabled him 'legitimately' to see a variety of people under the guise of obtaining information. In Stockholm, von Trott's attempts to establish direct contact with Madame Kollontay or some other responsible person in the Soviet Legation were unsuccessful. The Russians said, in effect, that they saw no necessity for talking to him. Von Trott was informed that before any Anglo-American commitments could be made, his opposition group would have to do something tangible. In general, he was told, it was doubtful whether the unconditional surrender formula would be modified. This discouraged von Trott who pointed out that the opposition would think it pointless to run the formidable risks involved in a *coup d'état* if success would make no difference in the course of the war or the nature of the peace.

On June 26, I had a conversation with von Trott that lasted more than three hours. He was passionate, sincere, and precise. He enumerated the purposes and aims of the Berlin Center, which were:

1. Hitler must be overthrown, Nazi leaders arrested, and a new government set up whose first act would be to negotiate an armistice with the Allies.

2. All political prisoners in Germany must be amnested.

3. The Nazi Party and all its auxiliary organizations must be dissolved and all the Nazi criminals tried and punished.

4. All Nazi elements must be rooted out of the state administration, civil service, judiciary, and other public positions.

5. All Nazi legislation directed against the Jews and against the trade unions, the Social Democrat, and other democratic parties, must be immediately repealed.

6. Basic civil rights — freedom of speech, press, religion, congregational association — were to be re-established.

7. The free trade unions were to take over all arbeitsfront institutions and assume their former position in the economic life of the country.

8. German economy must immediately be converted from war to peace production and concentrated on the rehabilitation of devastated areas.

9. All property illegally taken by the Nazis, both inside and outside Germany, was to be returned as soon as possible.

10. War prisoners and foreign workers in Germany were to be sent back home.

11. The schools and cultural institutions of Germany were to be reorganized immediately along democratic lines, aiming at cooperation and friendship with the nations of Europe.

I pointed out that if the opposition had to sign an unconditional surrender, it would be impossible for the new government to do many of the things outlined because of occupation by foreign troops.

'These are things that we wanted to do,' von Trott said, 'and now I will tell you the assurances that the opposition would like to get from the Allied powers, because without these assurances it will be extremely difficult for us to get the support and co-operation inside Germany which we will need to do our job. In the first place, if our new Government is to be effective, it will have to have a chance to get started for a few weeks at least before the Allied occupation begins. Otherwise it will be regarded as a Quisling government by the German people and will have no authority.

'In the second place, we would like to be assured by the Allies that no territory which was German before 1936 will be taken away from Germany. This is in the spirit of the Atlantic Charter and is likewise necessary if we are to receive the support of the German people.

'In the third place, we would like to be assured that one point in the Moscow Agreement will be modified. We would want German war criminals apprehended in Germany to be tried in Germany and not brought back to the scene of their crimes, as such an extradition would destroy even the formal appearance of German sovereignty.

'In the fourth place, we would like to be assured that the German Army will be demobilized by the German High Command or by some other German organization and not simply sent home, as this would create tremendous and quite unnecessary internal problems for the German Government.

'If these guarantees can be given, or if it could be stated that the Allied Governments would include these principles in the terms of the unconditional surrender, then the German opposition can become an effective mass movement, the war can be shortened, and thousands, perhaps millions, of lives saved.'

It is probably unfortunate that von Trott did not inspire more confidence among officials who learned of his aims. He returned to Germany without receiving any of the assurances he desired. One reason was, of course, that his entire program was too pretentious and, in a sense, naïve.

Another prominent German anti-Nazi with whom I talked a month later was more realistic: 'Von Trott is naïve,' he said, 'as are most of his associates. If Germany survives this war with the loss of only East Prussia and the left bank of the Rhine, we will be

very fortunate; that is what most people in the opposition, most of
the upper middle class and aristocrats like von Trott, do not understand. They think that things will go back to where they were before the war. That is the essential weakness of the opposition.'

Whatever may have been the weakness of von Trott's position,
he was an honest, courageous German patriot, doing the best he
could to get his country out of the war with the minimum of loss.
In my opinion it might have been well worth while to treat more
seriously with von Trott and other members of the Berlin Center
before they were liquidated.

The precise details of what happened in Germany during July
will probably never be known. The following account, though
based on considerable information, is, of course, conjectural. A historical analogy might help to make the intricacies of the situation
clearer.

On December 1, 1934, Sergei Kirov, Communist Party Chief of
Leningrad and heir-apparent to Stalin, was assassinated in his office
in Leningrad by a young man called Nikolaev, who was immediately tried and shot, along with a number of others, as a political
assassin and the agent of a foreign power. Heinrich Yagoda was
the chief of the Russian Secret Police at the time of the assassination of Kirov and was in a position toward Stalin, very much like
that of Himmler toward Hitler. In 1937, Yagoda himself was
tried for treason. During the course of the proceedings it became
obvious that Yagoda had known of the preparation of the attempt
to assassinate Kirov in 1934 and had deliberately allowed Nikolaev
to remain at liberty, because Yagoda needed this assassination for
his own political purposes.

I believe very much the same thing happened in Germany in
July, 1944. Himmler believed that a powerful opposition was
growing up in Germany backed by imposing numbers of Germans.
Himmler, of course, knew a good deal of what was going on and
had his own agents in the organizations of the opposition. In many
cases, however, particularly with regard to the Army, the leaders
were men of such importance and power that Himmler could not
take action against them without some overt act having been perpetrated.

Himmler, therefore, allowed the preparations for the July attempt to be made, watched it grow, and perhaps guided it through one or more of his agents who worked within the leadership of the opposition. Himmler allowed it to happen because he figured that it would give him the necessary justification for taking over vast new powers, and supply him with an opportunity to liquidate a great number of the leaders of the opposition throughout the country. If the attempt were successful and Hitler actually was assassinated, it would enable Himmler to take over completely the administration of the entire country with scarcely a challenge.

These seem to be the facts. At about midnight of July 19, 1944, a bomb exploded in the council room of the Führer's headquarters. The bomb had been left in a briefcase under a table, close to where Hitler was sitting, by Colonel Count von Stauffenberg, a thirty-five-year-old Catholic who had lost an eye and an arm in the Tunisian campaign, and was then holding a position on Hitler's staff. A number of prominent militray men were wounded by the explosion, including one individual designated as Berger, who later died. It is probable that Berger was one of Hitler's doubles. Immediately after planting the bomb, Stauffenberg got into a courier plane, flew to Berlin, and proceeded to the military headquarters on Bendlerstrasse. Hours later, when the Gestapo arrived to arrest him, he committed suicide.

At one o'clock on the afternoon of the twenty-second, Hitler spoke over the radio and was followed by Admiral Dönitz, and later, Göring. In his speech Hitler appointed Himmler Commander-in-Chief of the reserve army. This legalized Himmler's control of the S.S. and all military units inside Germany.

In his speech, oddly, Hitler remarked that he had received either contusions *or* burns. It seems highly improbable that Hitler, nearly three days later, should not have known what happened to him. Moreover, judging from the photographs of the room, if anyone had been there and had escaped with nothing more than contusions *and* burns, it still would have been a miracle of the first order.

The obvious deduction is that Hitler was not in the room at the time of the explosion. His double, Berger, however, was in the room and was killed. Stauffenberg saw Berger, believed him to be Hitler, and rushed ahead to Berlin in order to supervise or participate in the new Government which was to seize power. This was exactly what Himmler wanted and he caught them all red-handed.

A well-informed eye-witness who was on Leipziger Platz in mid-afternoon, described the scene to me:

'Suddenly military cars rushed into the city. S.S. men and Gestapo men jumped from the cars. They had steel helmets, hand grenades, and guns with fixed bayonets. In a moment they had occupied Wilhelmstrasse, the Reichkanzelei, the Propaganda Ministry, and the buildings of the Army Command. All traffic was stopped. Machine guns were placed on all street corners. The district between the Anhalter Bahnhof and Unter den Linden was blockaded. Dense chains of S.S. men guarded the government buildings. Late in the afternoon, special S.S. units screamed into Bendlerstrasse and other places where the opposition was meeting "organizing the new Government" and caught the lot of them. In two places that I know of — in Köln and in an East Front German Army camp, the opposition on orders radioed from the Berlin Center actually seized local control and held some buildings for several hours.'

The chief result of the attempt was that Himmler had his great chance to liquidate the opposition leaders almost to a man. This he did and, probably for safety's sake, liquidated at the same time all those of his agents working inside the opposition who had helped organize the assassination attempt or kept their chief informed.

Goebbels also proceeded to make capital out of the assassination and it figured in speeches and broadcasts for many weeks.

Most of the German anti-Nazis in Stockholm with whom I talked were convinced that the Gestapo had been very active in staging the assassination. To begin with, it seemed improbable to them that uninfluenced assassins would have made the attempt with a bomb. It would have been much easier with a revolver; but, they reasoned, the propaganda value of a bomb attack on Hitler was much greater. Then, too, it was all so cleverly arranged: the population of Germany was told over the radio that the attempt had been made, but that, of course, Hitler was unscathed, whereas Stauffenberg and the leaders of the opposition were given many hours to work under the impression that Hitler had been killed.

This again seemed to indicate Gestapo control over the whole affair.

In the fortnight or so after this attempted assassination had been made, about thirty thousand members of the opposition were arrested and numbers of them shot. Furthermore, powerful independent spirits in the Army like General Beck, who might well have become a major leader in the anti-Nazi movement, were eliminated. Among the mass of the German people all opposition was stigmatized as tantamount to participation in a bomb attempt perpetrated by a terrorist organization in enemy pay.

Himmler's position was solidly buttressed. Exercising his new powers promptly, Himmler made a series of appointments favorable to himself. S.S. official von der Bach was made chief of the underground forces which were to continue fighting in those parts of Germany occupied by the Allies. Ernst Kaltenbruner, who succeeded Heydrich in Czechoslovakia after the latter's assassination, became Himmler's assistant.

By the end of 1944, abroad and in Germany, it was obvious that Himmler was running Germany. In addition to commanding the Volksturm and all German troops on German soil, an important group of Army commanders at the front were S.S. men who received their orders from Himmler. Goebbels, it can be conjectured, was not at all opposed to this new disposition of authority. Himmler would now take to himself the responsibility for military reverses as well as the atrocities of the Gestapo.

But Naziism remained more firmly in the saddle than before. The opposition had suffered a crushing defeat which precluded any kind of effective revolt until Allied arms had reduced Germany to rubble.

Opposition was crushed in Germany, hundreds of thousands of revolutionaries perished in concentration camps, but the German Revolution was not destroyed. It remained alive, and as Allied armies swept across the Reich, virtually the only forces they found which promised leadership for the future Germany were among the emaciated, jittery prisoners of Buchenwald, Dachau, and other concentration camps.

PART THREE

Victory Is Not Enough

XII

Peace and Unity

For several generations most people in Europe would probably have been happier if Europe had been unified. For a hundred years technical conditions, transport, and communications have been ripe for unification or federation, but every time someone tried to do the job, they tried along the big-frog-swallows-little-frog principle and instead of federation they got *festung*. They begot against themselves hostile coalitions, often led by extra-European powers, which crushed them. They also generated internal forces which negated the ideas they were trying to put across.

This happened several times each with Spain, France, Germany, as the center of gravity — the heartland — of Europe moved eastward. An important innovation this time is that the restoration of Europe is being done principally by three extra-Continental powers, with only secondary European participation. This is, perhaps, an expression of the fact that the Continent's center of power has moved out of Europe. Europe has become a mere peninsula on Eurasia, and the problem which presents itself today is federation of Eurasia or of the world.

One of the Nazi tenets, the economic unification of Europe, was basically popular, historically progressive, and won considerable support in many countries. Hitler might have succeeded had his tactics not been so inept and his understanding of the principles of federation so hopelessly inadequate. He failed, but the idea of economic unification and federation has penetrated deeply into the consciousness of millions of Europeans. We must lead, not follow, and certainly not try to hinder, this idea in our European policies or else some Marshal Tito or perhaps Mother Russia may conceive and deliver alone a unified Europe in a form which few Americans would like.

One of the main factors preventing unification in the past has been the fact that economic and national lines were always getting crossed. This difficulty can be overcome now by population exchanges, propaganda, and education. A European federation organized along the lines of Switzerland or the United States, a federation, the central authority of which would be stronger than any of the constituent units, would solve many of Europe's immediate problems. In broader terms, however, the problems and needs of Europe are intimately bound up with those of the nations of the world. If conflict should again disunite Europe, it is almost certain to affect millions throughout the world.

In every nation, the overwhelming majority of the people want peace. In any history book, the method by which peace can be secured may be found. The method is government. Since primeval times groups of people have been fighting each other and in every case these groups have continued to make war until they have been superseded and contained within a larger unit. Clans fought each other until they were united into tribes. Then wars raged between the tribes for whole eras until they destroyed each other or were subordinated by agreement or conquest within a larger unit. Later, the Greek city-states, bound together by many common ties, warred incessantly among themselves till Philip of Macedon and his son settled the disputes by conquering all the belligerents. Up to the last century, wars raged among the principalities and city-states of Italy and Germany until centralized national governments were formed in both countries and imposed a single rule and a single law on all.

During the last hundred years, nations have assaulted each other, with immense forces equipped with the implements of destruction developed from the achievements of modern science. More recently, giant coalitions and constellations of nations have extended the horrors of war to global proportions. Steadily these mass murders have become more devastating, more crippling, and even to those who do not suffer its worst effects, more expensive. It cost fifty thousand dollars to kill one man in World War I. According to as yet incomplete estimates, in World War II the production costs of a single death have been quadrupled. One hardly dares to imagine what another war would be like, if we are foolhardy enough or incompetent enough to allow it to happen.

Yet the way out is so astonishingly simple — law and government. It does not require a master to draft a blueprint for world peace. The great difficulty is to put it into effect. With a few exceptions like the American Civil War and the Taiping Rebellion, any region which has been unified by one law and one government has known an end to internal war.

To be effective a world government would have to acquire the same power over nations that Washington has over the forty-eight states or Moscow over the sixteen constituent republics of the Soviet Union. Unfortunately, none of the great powers will at present consent to be governed in this manner. Each insists on its own sovereignty to such an extent as to make an effective world government an impossibility. In the United States it is clearly because the citizens are not ready for it, have not been educated or had experience enough to make it seem feasible and necessary. There is no chance that their representatives in the Senate would ratify any such arrangement, and without such an arrangement, war will remain a constant, harrowing threat.

Till the political conceptions of mankind have matured and other conditions are ripe for the formation of world government, we must work along the lines of co-operation and friendship between sovereign states. The machinery for such collaboration has been worked out haltingly and tentatively at Dumbarton Oaks and San Francisco. The organization which began to take shape there was a grouping of 'peace-loving nations' for the purpose of: 'A. (1) To maintain international peace and security; and to that end to take effective collective measures for the prevention and removal of threats to the peace and the suppression of acts of aggression or other breaches of the peace, and to bring about by peaceful means the adjustment or settlement of international disputes which may lead to a breach of the peace; (2) to develop friendly relations among nations and to take other appropriate measures to strengthen universal peace; (3) to achieve international co-operation in the solution of international economic, social, and other humanitarian problems; and (4) to afford a center for harmonizing the actions of nations in the achievement of these common ends.'

The principles of this nascent world-state are, in part: 'B. (1) The organization is based on the principle of the sovereign equality of all peace-loving states. (2) All members of the organization undertake, in order to ensure to all of them the rights and benefits resulting from membership in the organization, to fulfill the obligations assumed by them in accordance with the Charter. (3) All members of the organization shall settle their disputes by peaceful means in such a manner that international peace and security are not endangered.'

The San Francisco Conference did much to extend and implement these principles. It has been argued, however, that world organizations along the lines followed at San Francisco are both gratuitous and fatuous. If the Big Three can get along, the argument runs, they can keep the peace perfectly well without an organization. If they fail to keep up their present good relations and start preparing for war, then no organization will be able to stop it. Within certain limits, the truth of this analysis is indisputable. But the great value of the new League will be educational, in habituating people to think in terms of global unity, in making the reasons for and the corrections to whatever failures occur obvious to all. Meanwhile, it looks very much as though the major questions of the future, of peace and war, will be left in the hands of the great powers. Decisions affecting the future of the civilized world will have to be made by them rather than by a federation or collective organization. What, specifically and concretely, must be done by America to help prevent the post-war period from becoming another pre-war period?

XIII

What to Do With Germany

THE FIRST CONCRETE PROBLEM of major proportions which the Allies face in Europe is the disposal of Germany. This problem is complicated by the fact that some Germans have already begun to take matters into their own hands. As long ago as November, 1944, as many as forty thousand well-armed German troops had gone underground behind the Allied lines and kept popping up as saboteurs, guerrillas, and spies. They operated in conjunction with thousands of French Vichyites and their apprehension and extermination were extremely difficult.

Germans have done and will continue to do the same thing in other countries and in their own. For a considerable time they can be expected to continue masquerading as Allied officers and soldiers and to go on fighting to the last ditch, as they were abjured to by Doctor Goebbels. They will put up a prolonged, stubborn, and skilled resistance which will have to be met by armed force for many months to come. Inside Germany, these guerrillas will be aided and supplied by the local population in many places. It is a mistake to assume that these partisan troops will only consist of die-hard Nazis. Allied occupation of Germany, especially if it is severe, will, like German occupation of other countries, tend to unite all the elements of the population, from left to right. The Schwarzwald-Sudet, the German Alps districts, and the towns ruined by bomb and shell will offer favorable terrain for operations.

Such guerrilla warfare is not without precedent in Germany. In the Ruhr, under French occupation, as late as 1923, violence broke out in one mine after another as angry unemployed workers stole explosives, blew up factories and industrial equipment, smuggled weapons and engaged in effective sabotage. The Hügel Caleum Ueberruhr Duisburg was blasted. Coal and transport trains were wrecked. Steamers were sunk in the Dortmund-Ems Canal.

This time it will be worse. In 1944, elaborate academies of

sabotage were organized in Berlin, Munich, Dortmund, Reichenberg, Linz, and Graz. The directors of these institutes were Himmler, Martin Borman, S.S. Generals Hoffman and von der Bach. An underground general staff was formed and special instructions were issued, 'Anweisung für klein und Partisanenkrieg.' Equipment, munitions, and foodstuffs were prepared as well as large quantities of counterfeit money. It was established that partisan policy would try to take advantage of differences between the Allies and do everything in its power to increase them.

I remember the expression on the face of a German diplomat in Stockholm in the fall of 1944. We were discussing the partisan movement in Russia and France and its effects. 'Yes,' he said, 'partisans are always considered heroes by their own people, while they are branded as bandits and criminals by others, but they fight bravely and effectively and so they will in Germany. You will see.'

Operations against these guerrillas will necessitate a large and dispersed Allied occupation force in Germany, numbering probably between two and four million combined British, Russian, American, and French troops. There is a good possibility that some two hundred thousand of the Russian occupation troops will be German war prisoners picked from among those who have spent the last two years or so being re-educated in Russian prison camps. These occupation troops will try to keep order and suppress the guerrillas. They will also be confronted, possibly from the very first day of occupation, by the armed risings of anti-Nazis anxious to settle old scores in the large centers of German population. In the Rhineland, for example, the skeleton workers' councils which were organized in many factories in the summer of 1944 made concrete plans for taking over mines and factories, deposing Nazi directors, and operating the plants.

The attitude of the Allied occupation forces toward such movements is a question of primary importance, which presumably has been the subject of study on the part of the Allied High Command. The activities of these workers' councils in deposing and suppressing Nazi executives and leaders will involve considerable disturbances. Numbers of Germans will probably have to be executed, as both Nazis and anti-Nazis may snipe at the occupation forces in order to accuse the other of having done so.

After the initial period of establishing order, many questions of basic policy will have to be decided long before the peace conference takes place. Numerous commitments have already been made in the personal utterances of Allied leaders and by official statements and agreements. Some rules for German conduct have also been established, such as the inter-Allied declaration against acts of disposal committed in territories under enemy occupation or control of January 5, 1943, which warned the Germans that all transfers of property and interests of any kind in German-occupied territory could later be declared invalid and suitable rectification made.

The leaders of Great Britain and America met in mid-Atlantic in the summer of 1941 and stated in the name of their countries that they would endeavor, with due respect for their existing obligations, to further the enjoyment by all states, great and small, victor or vanquished, of access, on equal terms, to the trade and to the raw material of the world, needed for their economic prosperity. They expressed the desire to bring about the fullest collaboration between all nations in the economic field, with the object of securing for all improved labor standards, economic advancement, and social security. They undertook to abstain from and prevent territorial changes that did not accord with the freely expressed wishes of the peoples concerned. They undertook to respect the right of all peoples to choose the form of government under which they should live.

In the House of Lords, in April, 1940, Viscount Halifax, British Secretary of State for Foreign Affairs, said: 'It is no part of our purpose to destroy Germany, to seek a vindictive peace or anything of the kind; but it is our purpose to see that liberty, so far as we can achieve it, be restored to peoples who have been deprived of it, and above all, we seek security for the world. And I cannot, I think, sum up our aim better than it was put by the noble lord opposite — to convince Germany that she is not entitled to exercise sovereignty above the moral law.'

In his broadcast on February 2, 1943, President Roosevelt said, 'To these panicky attempts to escape the consequences of their crimes we say — all the United Nations say — that the only terms on which we shall deal with any Axis government or any Axis factions are the terms proclaimed at Casablanca: "Unconditional surrender." In our uncompromising policy we mean no harm to the common people of Axis nations. But we do mean to impose punishment and retribution in full upon their guilty barbaric leaders.'

Similar statements were made by other important English and American leaders including Walter Nash, New Zealand Minister to the United States, Viscount Simon, Lord Chancellor, and Henry A. Wallace. A number of official statements have indicated that the duration of the period of military occupation must depend upon the rapidity with which the people of Germany, Japan, Italy, and their satellites give convincing proof that they have repudiated and abandoned the monstrous philosophy of superior race and conquest by force, and have wholeheartedly embraced the basic principles of peace and democracy. Furthermore, from the Anglo-American side it is fairly clear that great domestic difficulties will be encountered in trying to keep an army of occupation in Germany for longer than, let us say, five years. After this time, and even during this time, a great deal will depend on what the Germans themselves do. Thus, while most people in Germany had been led to believe by Goebbels's insidious propaganda that unconditional surrender meant nothing less than complete annihilation of the German people and nation, Allied leaders had made numerous assurances of reasonable magnanimity and there was every probability that they would be fulfilled.

It is difficult to determine exactly what most of the Germans want. In the first place, many of them simply do not know. There were small groups of left-wing workers and also small groups within the Army, and a few, strangely enough, among small-town Nazi leaders, who wanted to see Germany become a part of the Soviet Union because they believe the Russians would protect Germany from the wrath of the Anglo-Saxons. Others were more fearful of Russian vengeance. Some small groups, particularly in the Rhineland and in Bavaria, believed in the possibility of their provinces seceding from Germany, perhaps to become Dominions in the British Commonwealth. 'Endlich los von Preussen' were words not infrequently heard in the Rhineland during late 1944. But most Germans have been too overworked, unhappy, war-weary, and confused to think. They do not know.

It was difficult for many Germans, even those who had suffered the most under the Nazi régime, to imagine quite how their country looked to the rest of the world. In all the anti-Nazi groups both in and outside of Germany, the only two which I found that accepted the unconditional surrender of Germany as axiomatic in their political thinking were the Communist Party and the Socialist Workers' Party (S.A.P.). The refugees in Stockholm who had belonged to the latter party had issued a pamphlet called 'Post-War Politics of German Socialists.' It contained a detailed program and was much more realistic than many similar manifestoes.

It tended to accept the more inevitable and obvious consequences of defeat, reparations, the return of conquered territories, and the occupation of Germany by Allied troops. They consented to the idea that Germany should endure one-sided disarmament, but they expressed the wish that a distinction be drawn between an army and the force necessary to maintain internal order. As they saw it, it would be disastrous for both Germany and the United Nations if the Allies were guided by the policy that foreign officials must take over functions which could be performed in a better fashion by German anti-Nazis. They granted the justice of the demand that Germany compensate the world for the damage it had inflicted and make good on its theft. They were opposed to the idea that millions of German laborers should be deported for work in foreign countries. They held that the Versailles solution of the Polish Corridor was unsatisfactory, that Poland should have access to the sea and Germany an unbroken eastern frontier. To bring this about, an exchange of German and Polish populations would be necessary. Internally they were for complete democracy and the destruction and punishment, not only of the Nazis, but the groups that supported them. They wanted the German labor movement to be the leading power in German reconstruction and were for the nationalization of key industries and state control and planning of business, prices, wages, and foreign trade.

This was, of course, a highly articulate group, with political experience, who had not known the worst stages of war-weariness and confusion. About the great mass of the German people, it was difficult to draw any conclusion as to their mentality except that it was confused. As far as the Germans went who did have any definite notions at all, they would probably want Germany to continue to be a united country. Most of them would also want a Socialist Germany or at least a left-wing Socialist Government.

Among the Allies, many general statements have been made, but few official pronouncements have been forthcoming on specific points. One widely publicized opinion was expressed by the leading Russian economist, E. Varga. In an unguarded article, he wrote that Russia wanted ten million Germans to work for ten years building up devastated areas. Most serious observers did not believe that this represented the official viewpoint of the Soviet Government. The Russians will probably let most Germans stay where they are, with the exception of recalcitrant prisoners, who will be assigned to arduous jobs like building canals in the far north.

The Russians, in my opinion, will insist that Allied military and economic control commissions maintain a constant check on Germany's economy. The Russians will aim at setting reparations and damages payment in such a way that, by dint of hard work, the Germans will be able to live on the lowest standard compatible with continued production. If the tempo of their work relaxes, they will be the first ones to take the consequences. The standard of living will fall, and they will suffer acutely. The products of German industry, above the bare minimum necessary to Germany itself, would go toward the reconstruction of devastated Europe. The Russians will desire political stability within Germany and a minimum of confusion and change. It is always much more difficult to control and direct factories and industries when a country is in a state of economic and social unrest and experimentation.

For security and protection against a recurrence of German aggression, the Russians will depend chiefly on their control commission and economic policy. They will also put some trust in the re-education of Germany, but with a slightly different twist from that which most people expect. In Stockholm in the summer of 1944, a Soviet official said to me: 'Many plans today have been made for post-war re-education in Germany in the interests of lasting peace. This is a fine thing. But there is another kind of re-education going on currently, perhaps more important. Millions of Germans are enduring such extreme discomfort and suffering that the German women of tomorrow may say to their sons and grandsons, "Never be a soldier." If I am correct, this current re-educational process will mean that in future for many decades, or forever, no rabble-rouser in high shiny jackboots shouting Wagnerian nonsense will again be able to raise an army of conquest.' This is hardly a political, let alone a revolutionary, point of view, but it is one to be met with frequently among contemporary Russians.

Parenthetically, the attitude of the Swedes is surprisingly similar to that of the Russians. In conversation with a prominent Swedish banker, I asked what he thought was the best way to organize Germany after the war. He said: 'The first thing necessary would be a strong German government acceptable to the German people and Anglo-Americans. I regret to state that such a government would almost have to be leftist Social Democratic. Given proper economic support, such a government could make German economy function and give the people food and shelter in reasonable quantities within a reasonable time.' Most bourgeois Swedes oppose the subdivision of Germany on principle, because it weakens central Europe and leaves it unprotected against the Russian Colossus. Most solid Swedish citizens with whom I talked thought reparations from Germany impracticable.

In discussing ultimate policies toward Germany, responsible quarters in Britain and America have acknowledged that the problem of Germany cannot be solved apart from the problem of Europe as a whole. Germany has, for many years, been the center of European economy. Its coal, iron, and industrial products have been indispensable to the industries of a dozen smaller countries. Its waterways are similarly necessary. The value of Lorraine iron ore, for example, derives in part from its excellent downstream river transportation facilities to the coal basin in the Ruhr. If Germany were completely annihilated economically, if the population of Germany were cut to one-third as it was during the Thirty Years' War, if Germany were turned back into a nation of peasants, the effect on neighboring countries like France, Belgium, Sweden, Czechoslovakia, Switzerland, would be serious if not disastrous. For some time, perhaps, this consideration stood in the way of a more active Allied war policy. If German economy were to be completely destroyed, then all of central Europe might become a place of mass unemployment, mass undernourishment, and perpetual political tension. Could this really be called a plan for peace?

In the Anglo-American world, a great deal of controversy has arisen on the question of Allied peace terms to Germany. *The Economist* (London) published several articles on the subject in the summer of 1944 advocating a 'reasonable peace.'

> Nothing coud be *worse* than a *severe* settlement that *is not maintained*. The most certain way of ensuring a short peace is first to give the German people a burning grievance and then to let them become strong. . . . Any peace that stops short of complete extermination has to be maintained if it is to endure. And maintenance, if there are any penal clauses, requires enforcement. There are not many examples in modern history of settlements that have, in fact, been enforced. Those that have lasted a reasonable time — pre-eminently the settlement of Vienna in 1815, which did not undergo a general revision for a whole century — have been those that were self-maintaining; that is, those that no large country seriously desired to upset. Those that required enforcement, such as Versailles, have been short-lived.
>
> It is quite clear that no self-maintaining peace — that is, a peace whose terms would be satisfactory to everybody, including the defeated countries — is quite possible. Peace after World War II will have to be enforced, and that is the crux of the matter.
>
> Only the three great powers — the United States, Britain, and Russia — can, in terms of industrial war potential and population, enforce peace against a recalcitrantly resurgent Germany if this should become necessary.
>
> For the first year or so it will be very easy (*a*) to keep the three major powers together in enforcing the peace agreed upon, (*b*) to persuade the people of the three major nations that the peace must be enforced. But after twenty years?

I remember very clearly a conversation I had on a railroad train going across the Polish Corridor in 1938. My companion was one of the more famous Anglo-Saxon foreign correspondents of the decade. 'Perhaps it is a crime to say so,' he said, 'but the plain fact is that the Germans *should* have Danzig and the Corridor, according to all the principles which we ourselves profess.' This man was, even at that time, moderately anti-Nazi, and this made a great impression on me. What will prevent other men, fifteen or twenty years after World War II, from making similar remarks about the territorial changes made now, if they are not made more or less self-maintaining, as *The Economist* calls it?

Another point which arises is this — if the three great powers agree on and implement a total disarmament of Germany, it will be quite unnecessary to deindustrialize the country. But if they cannot agree on disarming Germany, then there is no hope for a permanent peace at all, certainly no hope for any more complicated measures involving territorial sanctions and economic penalization of Germany.

These arguments were met with a storm of opposition. Indignant patriots from all walks of life protested that the trouble after the first World War was that a lenient peace was made with a supposedly democratic Germany. However, so innately evil were the German people that, as soon as an opportunity presented itself, they flung away their democratic masks and appeared once more as the barefaced aggressors they naturally are. They then urged extreme severity this time.

But what will result from extreme severity?

In 1918, for example, the armistice terms required the Germans to surrender five thousand locomotives, five thousand motor trucks, and one hundred and fifty thousand railroad cars to the Allies. Should such provisions be made this time? It would almost certainly prevent, not only the beginning of German reparations shipments to the victors, but would also involve widespread and serious famine in Germany.

Who should pay the costs of the army of occupation? The last time Germany paid them on paper, but actually they were paid by the Allies, who kept lending Germany money to pay the interest on their debts to the Allies which were never paid. If this time the Allies adopt the plan, which I believe to be the Russian plan — give the Germans tools, make them work hard and live on a very low standard of living for a number of years, and skim off all the economic surplus — then any additional expenses which the Germans would have to meet, occupation expenses, for example, would come directly out of the actual reparations payments to the victors. This consideration would make it seem desirable to maintain as cheaply as possible only a small mobile force, no matter who should pay for it. On the other hand, a small occupation force would permit the Nazi guerrillas and pro-Nazi elements to operate more or less freely.

Then there is the vexing question of the German market. After World War I, Britain desired the restoration as soon as possible of a vigorous German economic life as a market for British goods. However, a market means the ability to pay, and if the surplus of German production has to be taken as reparations, Germany will have nothing with which to pay for imports. Presumably, too, the control commission should allow only those imports absolutely necessary to maintain production and fulfill its obligations to the victors. The plain fact is, of course, that it will be a physical impossibility for the Germans to repay in full all the damage done in Russia, Britain, Poland, Denmark, Czechoslovakia, France, the Lowlands, and the Balkans. It will be even more impossible, therefore, for Germany to make exports over and above damage payments in order to finance imports of goods which Britain and America and perhaps other countries will desire to sell to Germany.

The Russian proposal for the reconstruction and industrialization of devastated nations by American and English exports is one solution to the problem, since by it a large market would be created for those Anglo-American industries most likely to be threatened by depression in the post-war period. On this and similar questions decisions will have to be reached, both when the armistice is signed and at the peace conference or conferences to follow. One obvious suggestion is that the peace conference be held only two or more years after the cessation of hostilities and that it be attended by representatives, not only of the victorious countries, but of the vanquished and neutral countries as well. A man like Gunnar Myrdal, the Swedish economist, free from undue prejudice, at once learned and original in his thinking, would be extremely useful at the peace table.

Some concrete planning had already been done. In London, the European Advisory Committee had been busy for many months. It had drafted and approved armistice terms for Germany in two versions, one to be signed by some German representative, the other a unilateral Allied declaration to the effect that organized

German resistance had ceased, and organized hostilities were ceasing. The brief, concise terms provided for occupation of all of Germany by the forces of Britain, the United States, Russia, and France. Allied prisoners in Germany were to be released immediately; German prisoners, particularly in Russia, 'after a certain time.' Germany was to pay substantial reparations in labor and in kind to Belgium, Holland, Czechoslovakia, Poland, and particularly Russia. Fascist organizations in Germany were to be destroyed and Nazi leaders and other war criminals turned over to courts of justice. German war industries were to be reconverted and the army demobilized. Protocols to the armistice provided for the formation of an independent Austria and Czechoslovakia, for the incorporation of parts of East Prussia, Pomerania, and Silesia into Poland, most of the west bank of the Rhine into France.

Beyond this it had been decided in principle that the policy of the Allied occupation forces in Germany would be determined in Berlin or some other center by a joint supreme Allied control commission. Germany was to be administered regionally by three (or four) group control commissions operating in the occupation zones of the Allied powers. The head of the American Group Control Commission was Robert Murphy, and of the British, Ivone Kirkpatrick. These control commissions already were organizing twelve departments corresponding with the German ministries, preparing to take over, along with the usable personnel and apparatus of the German ministries, the administration of Germany's railroads, finances, schools, press, army (demobilize it), and industry. Lower German civil servants would probably keep their jobs unless they had been active Nazis.

This was the machinery which was to disarm and control Germany for several years until, gradually, a German democratic administration won the confidence of the occupation authorities and began to resume the administration of Germany, still under Allied controls. This was the plan for Germany, and it had been drafted and approved by British, Americans, and Russians.

But on many vital points no policies had been determined on an official level. Who was to own and run thousands of European factories and other enterprises which had been stolen, bought, or built by the Nazis? The Hermann Göring Works had acquired industrial property from the North Cape to Salonika. Some of the former owners had been killed. Others had become collaborators and would be taken care of by their irate fellow countrymen. Many had fled. Few of the legitimate owners would be at hand on V-E day, and many of them never. In many German plants the workers were planning to take over and continue production. In some cases city or county councils would take over and run public utilities, perhaps other enterprises. What attitude were the group control commissions planning to take to these actions? Many were afraid that the problem had not even occurred to some members of the American Group Control Commission. The only expression of policy on the subject on a high level had come from Rome when Pope Pius XII said, 'Christian conscience cannot admit as right a social order that denies or renders impossible and useless in practice the natural right to ownership of commodities and means of production.'

Were the Big Three powers going to agree on this and other vital questions of principle? The Russians insisted that they were determined to reach agreement. They pointed to the four armistices already signed with Rumania, Finland, Bulgaria, and Hungary, in each of which the Russians had signed terms approved by the Allies, in the name of the Allies, although in all four countries victory had been won by the Red armies virtually single-handed.

A Russian friend in Stockholm said to me: 'We should like to get along with you in Germany. We are willing to make concessions. We do not suggest communism, or even socialism, in Germany. We want stability, production, order. But we cannot tolerate the re-creation of a powerful Germany once more to lay waste our cities and farms. If Germany is re-created as a military power, its armies will not be led by von Brauchitsch and von Beck. There are others. There are, for example, von Seydlitz and von Paulus.'

Again, the Russians were ready to change quickly if circumstances compelled it. The Free Germany Committee had its boots shined and its bag packed. Somewhere in Russia an estimated one hundred and fifty thousand German soldiers, selected from war prisoners, indoctrinated and armed, were ready to be used as the potential army of a potential 'Lublin Government' for Germany.

But the most important fact about the German problem is its

essentially secondary importance. Despite the complexity of the problems of armistice and peace terms for Germany, it is apparent that they are only incidental to the over-all problem of maintaining good relations among the Allies. If lasting economic and political co-operation between Britain, Russia, and America can be assured, then even inadequate peace terms can be made effective. International police and air forces, progressive universal disarmament, could be arranged, and the arrangements could be cheap and efficient. If, on the other hand, Anglo-American-Soviet relations are allowed to deteriorate, then no peace terms, however well-planned and implemented, will ensure Europe against another war, probably with Germany at the center of hostilities. Neither the territorial subdivision, the economic impoverishment, nor the physical destruction of Germany is the essential prerequisite for peace, but the maintenance and improvement of harmonious relations between the three strongest of all those nations that joined to defeat the German aggression.

XIV

Russia — The New Menace or the New Hope of Europe

B ESIDES THOSE MENTIONED in the last chapter, there is still another reason why the peace terms dictated to Germany are — in themselves, and not in what they signify — relatively unimportant. It is the fact that Germany will hardly ever again be in a position to challenge the world in a bid for European or world domination unless hostility between the great powers leads one of them to resurrect Germany and revive its military might. Even then, it is unlikely that a Teutonic war machine as formidable as that of 1914 or 1939 could be built, because both in population and resources Germany will never again be a really first-rate power.

The Anglo-Saxon powers fought World War II for a number of different reasons. Britain declared war formally in fulfillment of her treaty obligations to Poland. America participated in the war as a very active non-belligerent for months before being attacked by the Axis and forced into the war in December, 1941. The real issue at stake, however, was that neither country could allow an aggressive nation to become the master of the Continent of Europe. Britain could have made peace in the fall of 1939 and many times afterward, but it would have been at the cost of German domination and control of Europe which Britain could not afford. For one thing Germany would have possessed shipbuilding facilities, submarine and naval bases which would in a very short time have enabled them to launch a navy superior to that of Britain. This Britain could not tolerate. Neither could America.

In the eighteenth century, Britain fought a series of wars against Napoleon to prevent the domination of Europe by one power. Previously, it had fought the France of Louis XIV and the Spain of Philip II for the same reason. In the twentieth century both America and England fought two wars against Germany with more or less the same objective. By inference, Britain and probably America would fight again to prevent any new power from dominating the Continent in the future.

The nations which have sought to dominate the Continent of Europe have had one thing in common at the time of their attempts — large populations and great natural resources in contemporary terms. France, during the eighteenth and early nineteenth centuries was the most populous nation in Europe and had most of those resources necessary for her economy at the time. Germany toward the end of the nineteenth century outstripped France in population and in coal and iron production. What is the distribution now of these vital elements in national supremacy?

Population statistics are one of the variables in modern political equations which are more or less predictable. The results of wars alter birth and death rates to some degree, but certain basic trends exist which make it possible to forecast, with fair accuracy, the populations of the nations of Europe for several decades in advance. An authoritative study on this subject is *The Future Population of Europe and the Soviet Union* (League of Nations, Geneva, 1944). An exhaustive analysis in this book leads to certain conclusions which I shall attempt to summarize. The figures are based, not only on actual births, but on such considerations as the fact that the mothers who will be bearing children twenty-five years hence are now being born and their numbers are known. All references will be to the national boundaries of 1937.

The most striking conclusion of all is that in 1970 the Soviet Union will have a population of roughly 250,000,000, while all the countries of northwestern and central Europe — Britain, Ireland, France, Switzerland, Germany, the Low Countries, Scandinavia, Latvia, Lithuania, Estonia, Austria, Czechslovakia, Hungary — will have a population of 225,000,000. This is in sharp contrast to the situation in 1940, when the population of Russia was 40,000,000 less rather than 25,000,000 more than the combined population of the countries enumerated above. In other words, the net increase from 1940 to 1970 in the difference between the population of Russia and that of the aforementioned group will have been equal to the population of Germany.

In greater detail, the population of France will fall from 41,-000,000 in 1940 to 37,000,000 in 1970; the United Kingdom, from 47,000,000 in 1940 to 43,000,000 in 1970; Germany (frontiers of 1937) will have in 1970 roughly the 70,000,000 which formed her population in 1940; Italy's 38,000,000 in 1940 will have increased to 50,000,000 in 1970. The populations of the Balkan countries will increase substantially, while the Polish population will be augmented slightly from 39,000,000 in 1940 to 41,000,000 in 1970 (frontiers of 1937).

Not only is western Europe, including Germany, declining in absolute population compared to eastern and southern Europe, but another important factor is present. Life expectancy in western Europe is high, the birth rate low, which means that an increasingly large percentage of the population will fall into the old-age groups. By 1970 the population of Britain, France, and Germany will be topheavy with old men and women. In 1940 there were 20,000,000 over sixty-five years of age in northwestern and central Europe. By 1970 there will be 33,000,000. The number of old people in the Soviet Union will likewise increase — from 7,000,000 to 16,000,000 — but it will still be proportionately small.

The Soviet Union will outweigh Europe, not only in population, but even more so in terms of young men and women. In 1970 the Soviet Union will have an estimated 43,000,000 men between the ages of fifteen and thirty-four years, compared with 10,000,000 in Germany, 5,000,000 in France, 5,000,000 in England and Wales, and 6,300,000 in Poland. The men of the age group between fifteen and thirty-four constitute the prime military manpower reserve of a nation. Men between the ages of fifteen and sixty-four are generally regarded as forming the industrial and agricultural productive portion of the population. In this category in 1970 the Soviet Union will have 84,000,000 (as compared to 49,000,000 in 1940), more than the countries of central and northwestern Europe will have in the same group.

If one takes into consideration the fact that the 1937 frontiers no longer exist; that the Soviet Union has already pushed its frontiers into what were, in 1937, Poland, Rumania, and the Balkan States, and that it is generally agreed that Poland and a large part of the Balkan countries will be part of a Soviet sphere of influence, the conclusion is inevitable. The Soviet Union is overshadowing Europe. By 1970 no combination of European powers, even if all united in a common cause, will be in a position to offer serious opposition to the Soviet Union.

Russian superiority in natural resources is equally impressive. In 1943, I visited South Wales to do a story on coal mines. In the Tredegar Valley coal was being mined at the depth of a mile from veins with a thickness of two, three, and sometimes five feet. At the same time coal was being mined in the Ruhr Valley in Germany in mines of about the same depth from veins ten to fifteen feet thick. In the Kuzbes in central Siberia coal was being extracted from brand-new mines less than a mile deep from veins up to sixty feet thick.

Europe, outside the Soviet Union, produces annually a total of some 10,000,000 tons of petroleum. The Soviet Union in 1940 probably produced 40,000,000 tons and by 1970 will, in all likelihood, have doubled or trebled this figure, as Russia's total reserves are immense. Liquid oxygen is, apparently, going to be a tremendously important fuel in the future. Its production is almost entirely dependent on power. The great Siberian rivers have waterpower far in excess of all that is available in Europe outside the Soviet Union. In reserves of iron, copper, lead, nickel, in arable lands and in forests, the Soviet Union is richer than Europe and, by 1970, it may well have outdistanced central and western Europe in absolute production.

An additional point not to be forgotten is the fact that the Soviet Union is not a European but a Eurasian power, with good shipping ports in the Pacific Ocean on the one side and ports like Petsamo and Murmansk, which may be considered Atlantic ports, on the other. Another important consideration is the fact that several million Russians are already within the gates of western Europe. The Germans imported them from occupied territories in 1942 and 1943. They were found by Allied armies in France, in Italy, and even in Tunisia. Several travelers from Berlin in late 1944 told me that Russian was heard on the streets of the German capital more frequently than any other foreign language, and, in some sections of the city, as frequently as German.

In many respects the Soviet Union at the end of World War II stands in relation to the rest of Europe as Germany did in the middle of the nineteenth century, France in the early eighteenth century, or, to go even farther back, as did the Rome of Caesar's childhood. This estimate deals with the Soviet Union only in terms of its population and its geographic, economic, and administrative assets and liabilities in relation to Europe.

An element which cannot be overlooked in the analysis of Russia's position with relation to Europe in the post-World War II period is the fact that the Soviet Union, quite aside from its social ideology, prides itself on its racial heterogeneity. Whereas Germany was psychopathically race-minded, the Soviet Union, with a population of which just over fifty per cent is Great Russian, is proud of the fact that it is made up of many races and nationalities speaking many different languages. It is obviously easier, all other things being equal, to make friends and allies of other races and nationals, if one declares them to be equal and defends their rights, than if one publicizes their 'inferiority' and persecutes them as did the Nazis.

Moreover, the Soviet Union, like the United States of the last century, and like Britain today, is in a fair way to mastering the principles and practices of the commonwealth or federation. I have spent some time in the minor republics of the Soviet Union and, contrary to popular assumption abroad, these republics have very considerable autonomy in questions of local importance -- language, national culture, educational systems, national economy. Even on questions of defense and foreign policy, these nations are shortly to receive at least a degree of formal autonomy with the organizing of Commissariats of Defense and Foreign Affairs in each of the Soviet Union's sixteen constituent republics.

Here again, the Soviet Union is in a position, all other things being equal, to attract small nations in a much more effective manner than was Germany. Of course, the activities of the Soviet Union toward such small nations as the Baltic States and Finland during the past five years have not been such as to attract the sympathies of many of the local people. But there is reason to believe that in both cases the Soviet Union was pressed for time in preparing for the war and was hampered by lack of experience.

The same thing has often been said about United States policy in

Latin America. It was not many decades ago that United States Marines were frequently present to 'observe' elections in the small Latin American countries. During more recent years, however, our Good Neighbor policy has been developed and our attitude and methods have become much more refined and much less objectionable to the Latin American peoples.

In January, 1944, Adolf Hitler, discoursing on European views of World War II, stated that 'Only one state will emerge as victor — Germany or Russia.' As usual, the hard-pressed Führer had taken a grain of truth and puffed it up to the size of his ambition or, in this case, his need.

The Soviet Union has emerged from World War II one of the world's three intercontinental powers and the leading power of Europe. If history repeats itself, one can expect that within three or four decades the Soviet Union will try to include, or at least control, all or most of Europe. This expansion might take place peacefully by a series of trade agreements, political alliances, exchanges of students and tourists, and commercial and social intercourse. If the small nations of western and central Europe resist this process, then force might be employed.

At this point several qualifications must be made. The first is that this expansion will certainly not come immediately. For the next decade or two, at least, the Soviet Union will be principally occupied in reconstruction and in raising its standard of living. These are primary considerations, for as long as the Russian standard of living remains as low as it has been during the last decade, Russia cannot meet the rest of the world on an even footing except in terms of sheer mass. Technical experts in Washington estimate that Russian economy will be back to its pre-war level in 1948-1950. To attain a 'Western' standard of living will take much longer.

The second qualification is that within the next twenty years, Stalin, already sixty-four, will almost certainly retire from active political leadership in the Soviet Union. If no other man equally strong and able appears, and so far none has been seen, Soviet leadership will devolve on a group — the Political Bureau of the Communist Party, perhaps. While the democratic processes which will almost certainly become increasingly important in the Soviet

Union will tend to throw to the top able men, it is still not at all certain that the Soviet Union will have the active and experienced leadership without which it will be unable to take and keep a dominant position in world affairs. On the other hand, it is possible that rivalry for power after Stalin's withdrawal or death might lead to a break-up of the Soviet Union. This happened in the case of the empires of Alexander and of Genghis Khan. It is not likely to happen in the Soviet Union because of its incomparably greater social and cultural homogeneity.

The third qualification is probably the most important. It is manifestly unfair to assume, *a priori,* that the Soviet Union will become aggressive simply because it is large and powerful. There are many important differences, geographic, economic, and social, between Russia under Stalin and Napoleonic France, the Germany of Wilhelm or the Spain of Philip II. I will try to deal with these differences later. Here we must limit ourselves to pointing out that in 1970 the Soviet Union will probably have the wherewithal to be an effective aggressor if it so desires. Americans cannot afford to overlook this fact.

Regardless of the three qualifications mentioned above, Russia overshadows Europe — a great menace in the minds of some, a great hope in the minds of others. A menace, because its future attempts to control Europe may lead to World War III; a hope, because for many the Soviet Union represents progress, economic and social democracy, and promises eventually to give Europe the federation or unification which may guarantee permanent peace and prosperity. As a consequence, an understanding of Russian plans for the future, so far as they can be determined, is vital to the formulation of a realistic, successful policy toward Europe.

Nearly ten years ago an American journalist, Roy Howard, asked Stalin in an interview what he considered the main cause of war. Stalin answered: 'Capitalism.'

Stalin's ideas on this subject have probably been modified, but it seems unlikely that he has found reason during recent years to forsake this belief completely. Stalin would like to believe, with many Americans, that peace can be secured by the planned, co-operative organization of nations. He wants peace because Russia needs peace. His previous experience with collective security, how-

RUSSIA — THE NEW MENACE OR THE NEW HOPE 211

ever, was of a kind to inspire caution. He must, therefore, plan for the future in such a way that if war does come, it will find Russia buttressed with allies and well-prepared. But the co-operation among the United Nations during the war, particularly among Britain, Russia, and the United States, has been generally good and certainly fruitful. It could be even more fruitful for Russia after the war. One Russian diplomat put it this way, 'After the war, we can reconstruct our country in ten years with help, or in thirty years with hunger.' Clearly, Stalin will do everything possible to ensure such co-operation and help.

Although a number of complicating factors and problems remain, great progress has already been made as a result of compromises. The Polish question, to take one of the most irksome, is on the road to solution, largely owing to several Russian compromises. For two years there simply was no Polish question as far as the Russians were concerned. There was simply a band of Polish *émigrés* in London who were making trouble. In the fall of 1944, however, after the British had taken the matter up seriously, the Soviet press published many lengthy erudite articles on 'The Polish Question.' From these, Soviet citizens learned that it had always been one of the great problems of eastern Europe, but that now it was, in collaboration with their British allies, in a fair way to being solved. This Russian acknowledgment of equal British participation was, in itself, a compromise of considerable dimensions. It has also been pointed out by some American officials, in contrast to the customary belief and attitude of press and commentators, that, in realistic terms, it was Russia that made all the concessions at Yalta on the subject of Poland. The Russians *had* Poland. Willingness to make it a subject of discussion was, again, evidence of Russian desire to maintain Allied co-operation and good-will at all costs.

There is a serious issue in the Middle East. In 1921, the Russians annulled their Persian treaty of 1907 under which northern Persia became Russia's exclusive sphere of interest. All property owned by Russian nationals in Persia was declared the property of the Persian people. Even the Russian-Persian Bank in Teheran became Persian property. Like other territorial withdrawals, from Finland and elsewhere, this was largely motivated by the weakness of Russia in 1921. Now that Russia has become strong, it would not be surprising if the old policy were to be resumed. The Russians may well develop interest in Persian oil as part of an attempt to become one of the great oil producers of the world. Among other things a substantial Russian oil export would help Russia over the difficulty of making payments during the post-war years.

For more than a decade now the center of Russian industrial activity has been moving eastward and Soviet Central-Asia has become an immense and rapidly growing industrial area for the safety of which Russia must be at least as much concerned as it has been previously for the Ukraine. In pursuing further policies calculated on increasing economic influence and strengthening security in the Middle East, London and Moscow will have a number of serious problems to settle. For one thing, millions of Moslems living in Iran, Iraq, Afghanistan, and eastern Turkey may in the very near future begin looking wistfully across the Soviet frontiers at kindred peoples, speaking the same languages, but living on an incomparably higher standard, both materially and culturally.

But this and other difficulties can and will be solved if the basic desire on the part of all three powers to continue in friendly collaboration remains steadfast. On the Soviet side, this desire is certainly present. This collaboration is an integral part of the ultimate aims of Soviet foreign policy. But what are these ultimate aims?

The Russians are, apparently, counting on a period of some twenty-five years, during which they regard it as a matter of vital import to maintain the most harmonious relations with the Anglo-Saxon powers and with all other nations. During this period their foreign policy will be to maintain security and stability, and to carry on extensive trade with all countries, if possible on long-term credit, direct or indirect. During these twenty-five years the major efforts of the Soviet people will be concentrated on reconstructing the Soviet economy and on raising the standard of living in the Soviet Union. This is absolutely fundamental and leaders in the Kremlin realize it. During the nineteen-thirties the Soviet population lived on standards well below those of almost all European countries. This was one reason why Hitler was able to unite so much of Europe in a campaign against the Soviet Union.

This is one reason why the Soviet Union will have to remain for some years rather isolationist. It is unlikely that the Soviet Union will encourage many foreign tourists in the post-war decade. People in Russia will still be terribly poor and to Anglo-Americans, for example, accustomed to very different standards, it looks bad, which hurts the Russian pride in themselves, their country, and their social system. In the same way the Russians have long been, and will for another decade continue to be, reluctant to permit their citizens to travel to foreign countries except on business. Most intelligent Russians regard this isolationism as undesirable and hope it will end soon, but all recognize that with the drastic difference of living standards it is virtually unavoidable.

Of course today a great change has been brought about by the fact that the standard of living in central Europe has been dragged down in many cases below that of the Soviet Union. But this does not alter or modify the overwhelming desire of the Russians to improve their own standard of living. And all the prerequisites for a great improvement are present. Natural resources are dispersed over the whole country, and, with a few trivial exceptions, are more than adequate to support the population in the country, or even a population twice as large, on a high standard of living. The people are intelligent, have learned to work well, farm scientifically, and to operate the most complicated modern machinery. Perhaps, most important of all, the Soviet Government is in a position to plan the economy of the country for years ahead, avoiding waste, bottlenecks, and regional disequilibrium.

If the Russians get their twenty-five years of peace and security, the national income will rise rapidly, while only a small portion of it will have to be spent on defense. The rest of it can go into capital investments and increased consumption. At the end of twenty-five years, the results of this will probably be startling. Experts estimate that in 1970 the Russians will have a population of some two hundred and fifty million. These people may well have a standard of living comparable to the American standard of living in the late nineteen-thirties. Furthermore, if their planned economy continues to function as effectively as it does now, they will be ensured against economic crises, unemployment, and insecurity.

During these same twenty-five years the Russian leaders believe the rest of the world may have some trouble. There may be trouble between Britain and America over the Latin-American market. There may be an economic crisis in the United States and elsewhere. The Negro question in the United States and throughout Africa, and hundreds of other social and economic problems, may result in serious conflicts. Besides all this, the Soviet leaders, still Marxists (or perhaps one should say Neo-Marxists, as there have been many changes in recent years), doubt whether capitalism can keep itself afloat, can beat off its own economic contradictions indefinitely, without undergoing fundamental changes. Unlike some of his more left-minded colleagues, Stalin himself is impressed with the possibility of a permanent survival of modified capitalism. He had a great deal of respect for the performance of capitalism in this war. He saw that America was able to double its national income (which, in all the years of Socialist planning, the Soviet Union had never been able to accomplish) and, at the same time, turn out better equipment than the Russians. The proof of capitalist staying power was running about all over Russia in the form of jeeps.

But as Stalin always kept alternative policies, the Russians probably hold alternative theories on the future of capitalism and will base their conduct on the way the facts turn out. The twenty-five-year period of post-war peace will enable them to submit both theories to a laboratory test, which they can watch in safety and consider objectively. In 1970, they might come to a more definite decision with regard to Russia's ever-changing relationship to the Great Collective Revolution of the twentieth century.

One thing does remain certain. If things go according to plan, by 1970, for all practical purposes, no possible combination of powers will be able to defeat the Soviet Union in war. The Russians could then afford to pursue a far more independent policy than they can at the present time.

XV

Rule Britannia — In a Way

DURING THE PAST TWO CENTURIES, in which several nations have attempted to dominate the Continent of Europe, Britain has been an isolated yet integral part of Europe. It was Britain which led the coalitions that defeated most of these attempts. In minor conflicts Britain tended to allow its allies to operate independently and to reap the rewards of initiative and effort, as long as these did not interfere too seriously with British plans. But Britain retained the political and economic balance of power.

For a long time the British held this enviable position because their natural resources, technical skill, and seamanship gave them a position of virtual monopoly in many industries as well as in the world's carrying trade. But during recent decades, Britain has been equaled and surpassed in industrial production, technical skill, and mass-production technique, by Germany, the United States, and, perhaps, the Soviet Union and Japan. Under such circumstances Britain might have been expected to yield the mantle of continental and world leadership to one of its competitors and retire to the position of a second-class power.

It is comparatively easy for a nation of two hundred million with great natural wealth, plenty of good agricultural land, balanced economy, the youth and vigor of a comparatively new social system, to pursue policies of initiative and leadership in world affairs. The United States, with its two oceans, its resources and population, naturally maintains a dominant position in this hemisphere and in the world.

But the British, a small island nation of under fifty million, with depleted resources, unproductive land, and a fatigued overstrained economy, have kept their status. Brain, brass, and tradition have helped them bring off this feat. For a long time, with their casual charm, their offhand assumption of superiority, the British have dominated many fields of international endeavor. The Germans needed all of Hitler's ranting and daily doses from the Goebbels propaganda machine to persuade them that they were better than other people. Englishmen simply take it for granted and rarely waste a syllable discussing it.

England has remained a formidable presence on the international scene, not only because of the toughness and tenacity of the average Briton, but because of the existence of a large group of Englishmen who, for generations, have received intensive training in the conduct of foreign affairs. For centuries, the system of primogeniture has forced thousands of the moneyless younger sons of aristocrats to seek their fortunes abroad. Winston Churchill as a young man served as correspondent and soldier in Africa, worked in India, and traveled many times over the Continent.

It is part of the education of thousands of young English boys to travel abroad. While they are popularly supposed never to learn foreign languages, I have been astonished at the number of Englishmen I have met scattered all over the globe who speak excellent Russian, who write Arabic for half an hour a day just to keep in practice, or who spend spare moments studying old Japanese scripts, and who converse idiomatically in the Continental languages.

In 1942, when Britain had lost two of her best capital ships and most of her Far Eastern Empire to the Japanese almost overnight, David Low had Colonel Blimp say, 'Gad, sir, what we have we will hold, if we can get it back,' and all of England laughed. This sense of humor, plus the British ability to avoid panic even under catastrophic circumstances, has made it possible for Englishmen to do things which seemed impossible and to keep on doing them under progressively less advantageous circumstances.

If England frequently presents an appearance that causes one to think it ridden by tradition and suffering from hardening of the arteries, the impression is apt to be quickly dispelled. A copy of such comparatively widely read, politically divergent periodicals as *The Economist, The New Statesman and Nation,* or *Manchester Guardian* will often surprise one by its modernity and alertness. They all boast a consistently excellent style, a steady pertinence, sobriety, and accuracy that seem beyond the reach of comparative American productions. Constantly, too, in England one is confronted by a susceptibility to new and daring ideas, a cool willingness to face hostile theories without blinking, in quarters where only the most ostrich-like complacency was expected. English brevity of expression and refusal to indulge in lengthy explanation strike many as insensitive. It is, however, connected with their talent for abrupt, effective action.

To mention a completely unimportant but amusing example of effective British casualness, I never ceased to wonder at the way in which Londoners broke engagements of all kinds with each other by telephoning and saying, 'A great rush of things came through, and there you are.' This formula spared them the dreary necessity of going into laborious details of private or business life. Many off-islanders consider things of this kind typically crude British evasiveness and hypocrisy. Actually they save a great deal of precious time and energy.

Nevertheless, whatever the national character, Britain's predicament at the end of the war was more grave than any in which it had been during its long history as a great power. A number of conflicting and complicated statements had been made by Englishmen on their basic policy. It had been outlined by Churchill in August, 1944, in his little publicized but extremely important seven points, phrased ingeniously in the interrogative:

1. Is there the right to free expression of opinion and of opposition and criticism of the Government of the day?

2. Have the people the right to turn out a Government of which they disapprove, and are constitutional means provided by which they can make their will apparent?

3. Are their courts of justice free from violence by the Executive and free of all threats of mob violence and all association with any particular political parties?

4. Will these courts administer open and well-established laws which are associated in the human mind with the broad principles of decency and justice?

5. Will there be fair play for poor as well as for rich, for private persons as well as Government officials?

6. Will the rights of the individual, subject to his duties to the State, be maintained and asserted and exalted?

7. Is the ordinary peasant or workman, earning a living by daily toil and striving to bring up a family, free from the fear that some grim police organization under the control of a single party, like the Gestapo, started by the Nazi and Fascist Parties, will tap him on the shoulder and pack him off without fair or open trial to bondage or ill-treatment?

Almost in the same breath with these high-sounding criteria, Churchill had reminded the nation that he had not become His Majesty's First Minister in order to preside over the liquidation of the British Empire, an Empire, which as everyone admitted, had been largely put together by methods that were in flagrant violation of the principles he had previously announced.

As Britain got closer and closer to victory in World War II, Churchill remarked that the war had become less and less ideological. This was clearly visible to anyone who examined the changes in British political policy during the war. First came the Atlantic Charter in August, 1941. Then Churchill signed the resounding Soviet-British alliance in 1942, committing Britain to full military, political, and economic collaboration with the Soviet Union for twenty years. Within a few months, Churchill proceeded to implement this by participating in the division of Europe into spheres of influence. On August 2, 1944, he remarked that Russia offered 'freedom, sovereignty, and independence to the Poles — they asked that there should be a Poland friendly to Russia. This seems to me very reasonable.' Turning southward, he said, 'Rumania, primarily must make her terms with Russia.' For Bulgaria, 'The moment of repentance has not passed.' A large British delegation of observers accompanied the Soviet Control Commission in Finland, thus stamping the Finnish-Russian peace with British approval. In December, 1944, the British gave their official approval to plans for the annexation by Poles of German territory, in compensation for western Ukraine and White Russia, which were to go to the Soviet Union.

Unfortunately, we do not yet know what was decided at Teheran, but it seems likely that at that time Churchill and Stalin drew a demarcation line between respective spheres of influence in the Balkans, leaving Greece to Britain, in return for which the British recognized and supported Marshal Tito and his left, Moscow-influenced coalition government in Yugoslavia.

In speaking of Germany and France, Churchill stated, 'The course of the war, the whole tide of events, show quite clearly that we shall once again have to deal with the problem of France and Germany along the Rhine.' This would seem to indicate British plans to balance a strong France against a moderately strong Germany.

Immediately after the last war, Britain encouraged a strong Germany in order to balance, first, what was considered a truculent France, and then what London thought of as the eventual menace of Russia. It is at least conceivable that this policy may again find a place in British plans. It conflicts, of course, with the spirit of the Soviet-British alliance, not to speak of the Atlantic Charter, but British policy has long been made up of a number of complicated and conflicting influences, the synthesis of which furthers the complex interests of the British Empire.

Thus, the Tory leadership of the British Government, with skill and determination, seems to be planning a post-war Europe based on the balance of power among small units and large. It is a precarious policy, but the only one which promises to maintain an economically puny England in the arena with the American and Russian colossi. One may like or dislike these expressions of British foreign policy, but one must face the fact that Churchill knows what he wants and he has ideas about how to achieve his ends. Furthermore, like Stalin, he is careful to leave an alternate road open whenever possible.

Domestically, the British Government has shown unexpected foresight and gone far to the left in proposed social legislation. The Beveridge Plan and its successor, the Woolton Plan, have been widely publicized and commented upon. They contain a social-security program which would have been considered shameless bolshevism by a Labor Government ten years ago. Yet now it is in the process of being planned and put into practice by Conservatives. After the war the British coal mines may well be nationalized; banks and assurance companies may be so restricted and controlled by Government that it will no longer be possible to consider them private enterprises. The Government is planning large-scale Socialist housing projects, modern communal facilities, a reorganized and democratized school system, and other social improvements which, a decade ago, would not even have been considered by any British Government.

By carrying out its policies, Britain has maintained a position of importance in spite of extreme economic weakness. In part, this has been the result of American help calculated on keeping Britain's head above water economically on the theory that excessive British economic weakness would be a catastrophe for the United States. To a greater degree, however, it is the result of the clear thinking of British economists, their realism and resourcefulness, backed by the stubborn industry of the island's population.

Britain has long been a trading and manufacturing nation. Export statistics are, therefore, an index to changes in its economic position from year to year. In October, 1944, export statistics for the years 1942 and 1943 were published in London. The published figures excluded shipments of munitions and were, therefore, comparable with the 1938 figures. These statistics showed that British export trade had been cut to ribbons. The volume of exports in 1943 was less than one-third of what it was in 1938, which was not a good year. The average price of British exports rose by two-thirds as the result of higher raw-material prices and manufacturing costs.

In spite of the rising prices, the total value of British exports had been cut in half from 1938 to 1943. In 1943, British exports were equal to only 2.8 per cent of the net national income instead of the 10.2 per cent of 1938.

Figures have been publicized indicating the disastrous decline in British overseas investments. Over one billion pounds of foreign investments were sold and nearly two and a half billion pounds of liabilities abroad incurred. To use a prosaic analogy, the British Empire sold its shirt and shoes in order to pay for the gun which it needed to keep its trousers from being stolen. The British merchant fleet has always been a great national asset. A very considerable proportion of this asset was sunk during World War II. In Great Britain itself, German bombs caused great economic havoc. One-fifth of the houses in England were destroyed or damaged.

Of course, some of these calamities may turn out to be blessings in disguise. If the British could replace their sunk tonnage by speedier, more modern vessels or transport airplanes; if London's damaged houses could be replaced by modern buildings that would bring fresh air and sunshine to the congested population, the British people would have benefited handsomely. But this economic reconstruction is expensive and must, at least in part, be financed by exports which, as we have seen, have fallen. There are additional difficulties in financing British reconstruction through its foreign trade.

During the war, British agriculture was tremendously overexpanded at great cost, in order to grow as much food as possible. I visited a farm in Buckinghamshire where they were growing wheat on land worth five hundred dollars an acre. After the war, this wheat cannot possibly hope to compete with grain from Canada, the United States, and other countries, grown on land worth one-hundredth as much and where climatic conditions for grain culture are more favorable. British agriculture will, therefore, have to be reorganized, which is expensive, and many agricultural products now home-produced will have to be imported, which again requires exports. Leading British businessmen and economists are, however, fully aware of the gravity of the situation.

Britain's entire economic position depends on a very simple factor — productivity. Some British industries have been notoriously slow in adopting new methods. For example, a cotton textile commission was sent to America in 1944 in order to find out whether the Manchester cotton industries had anything to learn from their American colleagues and competitors. On returning, they wrote a 581-page report which left no doubt that Britain had much to learn. Among other things the commission reported that in America 95 per cent of the looms were automatic — in Britain, 5 per cent. American productivity per man-hour was 18 to 49 per cent higher than British productivity in spinning, 80 to 85 per cent higher in winding, 79 to 89 per cent higher in beaming, and 56 to 67 per cent higher in weaving.

The average American textile worker was producing several times more than the average English textile worker. The main reason, the report stated, was that the Americans used more modern machinery. More astonishing still was the fact brought out by the report that the main advances in American textile machine technique were made as much as a quarter of a century ago and the British had simply not caught up with them. A main cause of this phenomenon was the innate conservatism and lack of foresight of British manufacturers, who preferred to take high profits each year rather than invest substantial sums on research and new equipment. These manufacturers were able to sell their goods because of the low standard of living of the British working classes compared to those of America and because, on a national scale, income from British investments abroad subsidized British exports.

★ 2. REORIENTATION ★

FORTUNATELY FOR BRITAIN, the response to this situation has been alert and comprehensive. The Platt Commission on textiles, the Bossom Commission on building and industrial methods, *The Economist* and a number of other British journals, have examined British economy from every angle. They have analyzed its weaknesses and have not only made specific recommendations, but suggested how to put them into effect. They have insisted that British economy must be planned on a more scientific basis and that the Government must use its powers to bring about increased capital investments in equipment and research.

This may involve a very considerable measure of socialism. But the owning and employing classes in Britain have had their ideas modified so much by bombs, an almost confiscatory tax rate, and the gradual infiltration into managerial positions throughout industry of salaried employees, that many of them are quite prepared to accept a considerable degree of socialism. Many of them even welcome the prospect.

Thus the British, in their domestic and foreign policy, are responding sharply to the world about them and making a concerted effort to keep their place in it. They may make mistakes. Their general policies are open to criticism and such aims as the maintenance of the Empire can be attacked as being downright reactionary, but the British know what they want. If intelligence, persistence, and willingness to try every feasible method can bring it about, they will succeed in realizing their desires.

The socialism in terms of which some people in England are beginning to think differs considerably from the socialism of Continental Marxists. Perhaps it should not be called socialism at all. Perhaps 'planned capitalism' or 'collective capitalism' would be better. Its principles have been formulated and the details of their application skillfully expounded in a series of articles that appeared in *The Economist,* entitled 'A Policy for Wealth.' The whole plan, with its distinctive features, is designed to cope with the difficulties created by the fact that the British community simply does not produce enough wealth to support its present population on a reasonable standard of living, even if all the productive facilities in the entire country were to be nationalized tomorrow. To quote some of the chief points in *The Economist's* summary of its own series of articles:

> For the British community, and for many years to come, the size of the cake of the national output is certainly as important as, and probably far more important than, any questions about the size of the various slices. Neither Full Employment nor Social Security will be accounted successes unless they can be combined with a rising standard of output.
>
> There is no good reason to suppose that the substitution of public for private ownership would, by itself, lead to any increased investment in productive equipment. But in a number of industries, of which coal and steel are examples, the present structure is an obstruction to rapid technical progress. The prescription is technical rationalization with the object of producing the maximum output at the minimum labor cost; ownership is a secondary matter.
>
> Both Labor and Capital should accept the historically demonstrable fact that good profits and high wages go together. Organized Labor should realize that it is in its interests to ensure a reasonable return on the productive capital employed in the industry —an aim which is entirely compatible with hostility to large incomes for individuals.

Included also in the program were the supplementary changes and policies that would have to be carried out in every sphere of national activity to make these major plans effective. It amounted to a thoroughgoing reorganization of society on the basis of private enterprise raised to a maximum of efficiency by planning and control. Government regulation was to be drastic and operative, not only over the total economy, but over such auxiliary fields as education, advertising, and science. Like the 'Full Employment Policy' to which the Government was already formally committed, the 'Policy for Wealth' would affect every branch of the administration and every ministry. *The Economist,* therefore, suggested that an 'Economic General Staff' was needed to prevent both policies from being brought to a halt by their sheer bulk.

I cite this program at such length because in it the program of post-war rehabilitation is so sharply defined. Too, it is not merely the result of theory, but the inescapable consequence of the condition of British economy, just as strikingly similar programs and plans were called forth in the Soviet Union of the nineteen-thirties.

The Russians, to be sure, were engaged in the process of creating a group of managers (men previously accustomed to thinking only in collective terms), who would be specifically interested in the production of their plants to a point where they would 'fight' for production; whose interests in the general national welfare would become secondary to their interest in their own enterprise. The British, on the other hand, were trying to create a group of managers (men previously accustomed to thinking only in terms of private competition) whose consciousness of the general welfare was so well developed that they would sacrifice their private interests for the collective good. Starting poles apart and moving in opposite directions, Russian and British industry were approaching the same point.

The Bolsheviks came to the conclusion that prosperity for society as a whole could be achieved only under a system of social ownership and operation of the means of production; and that this, in turn, could only be attained through class struggle and the dictatorship of one class — the proletariat. Marxists held this to be necessary because of their firm conviction that the owning and ruling classes were so selfish and blind that they would never relinquish their stranglehold on private property and their power to exploit it without a violent struggle. And yet, here in Britain, the traditional stronghold of capitalism, the center of the world's greatest Empire, a Conservative Government was being urged by an influential group of owners and managers to put into practice an economic policy involving a considerable degree of socialism, the nationalization of many resources and facilities, and strong state control over the management and operation of those industries remaining in nominally private hands.

The British have also been level-headed enough to realize that the mere act of initiating a plan does not solve the economic problems of a nation. The most skillful maneuvers of technical experts cannot circumvent the basic economic law that you have to pay for what you get. Economic plans are effective because they produce increased capital investments, whereas without a plan such investments are apt to be limited by the desires of individual owners for high immediate profits. The Russian Five-Year Plans were notable for their achievements in this direction.

Under them, capital was invested chiefly in heavy industry. Labor and materials were devoted to the construction of railroads, canals, factories, mines, on an extremely large scale. In 1932 and 1933, for example, in the Soviet Union the Russians reinvested roughly fifty-six per cent of their national income, mostly in heavy industry. In America, during the years of our greatest expansion at the end of the last century, we reinvested a maximum of some fourteen per cent. The Russians were able to carry on this massive reinvestment of capital because the Five-Year Plans were conceived for this purpose and the State had the necessary power to put them into effect.

To accomplish this, the State had to be able to organize the distribution of the limited amount of consumers' goods produced in such a way that all the members of the community could continue working effectively. In this respect the economic plan involved a calculated reduction of consumption for several years in the interests of accumulating capital equipment. At the end of the planning cycle, this increased capital equipment would turn itself into increased production of consumers' goods which would raise the consumption-level of the population far above what it had been at the start. Of course, what actually happened in the Soviet Union was that what should have been a steady improvement in the standard of living was checked by the preparation for operations in World

War II. Had it not been for the war, Soviet consumption would have gone up sharply during the late thirties and early forties.

But as a number of people of Britain have been saying and writing, economic planning, if it is to be effective, means temporary hardships for all concerned. These must be reckoned with and anticipated. The people who are talking and thinking in Britain in terms of some sort of socialism and economic planning are fully aware of the difficulties which it will involve. They realize that it will mean temporary reduction of consumption and many irksome restrictions, in some cases complete elimination of the freedom of individual manufacturers and employers to produce what they want and sell it for what they can get. They recognize further that only by making such sacrifices, only by such collectivist organization of their economy, can they raise British efficiency (therefore, British exports and eventually British consumption) to the level where Great Britain's position as one of the three great powers of the world can be maintained despite its present impoverished condition.

The British will have great trouble and many hardships in the course of putting this policy into operation. But the fact that so many people in England have seen the problem, analyzed it, and are in the process of devising means to solve it, is already, in my opinion, a good half of the struggle, a struggle in which America, though vastly more wealthy, populous, and strong, has not yet engaged — perhaps because it still is so comparatively strong and prosperous.

British thought has adjusted itself with equal flexibility to its new position in international affairs. The English know the problems that face them, and in some cases have taken steps to solve them which involve the reversal of century-long axioms. Early in 1945, in London, I had lunch with some people from the Foreign Office and heard a conversation about present-day policy. A younger man in the service said: 'All through the nineteenth century British foreign policy had three main purposes. We wanted to prevent any European power from becoming too much stronger than its neighbor. We wanted to maintain British supremacy at sea and protect the lines of Empire communications. Lastly, we wanted to keep the Russians or anyone else from getting across the Empire's vital Middle-Eastern artery or into India. Now in the middle of the twentieth century these three basic aims have become unattainable. Where does that leave British foreign policy?'

A senior colleague gave the answer: 'Today we are advocates of effective world organization from purest self-interest. We can no longer dominate. We must participate. We flee to worldism from self-interest plus a conveniently rediscovered idealism.'

London, however, also realizes that neither Moscow nor Washington is going to be very enthusiastic about a world organization — particularly one with its hub somewhere in West London. At every point in the vast network of the British Empire, there was apt to be trouble in the immediate future and apparently the men who ran it were preparing to cope with it.

In 1945, for example, Britain was in the unprecedented position of owing large sums of money to countries like Iraq. Specifically, most of it was owed to a few Iraqui businessmen who wanted payment in steam yachts, golf courses, race-horses, and similar frivolities. The British have always maintained their position in countries like Iraq through strong ties with the local aristocracy. However, within a few years, the Soviet Union will probably have succeeded in raising the standard of living among the Moslem peoples in Soviet Central Asia to a considerable degree above that of Iraq and the neighboring countries. These people will be threatened with disaffection from their kindred across the Soviet frontier. In a few years they may very well start drifting into the Soviet orbit.

The British experts know that the only answer is to invest money in capital equipment, increase the national income and thereby increase consumption in Iraq and the neighboring countries, entering, as it were, into competition with the Soviet Union to improve living standards in the Middle East. But holding back this scheme is the fact that the local Iraqui leaders do not recognize this state of affairs and would consider any move in this direction as bolshevism and indecent British interference in their internal affairs.

It is unlikely that specific decisions on this and similar fundamental problems have been reached in London. They are, however, very much on the minds and in the conversations of Foreign Office Middle-Eastern specialists. They seem to know most of the facts, recognize the difficulties, and approach them with characteristic realism and persistence.

America's Negative Foreign Policy Towards Europe

★   I.   CONFUSION   ★

PERHAPS IN NO SPHERE of American life is there greater confusion and lack of clarity than in our foreign policy, both in its official aspect and in the habits of mind of the great majority of Americans. To a great extent this may be due to the fact that in a certain sense America has led an independent existence, its needs and problems, its emotions and ideas, always differing somewhat from those of the rest of the world either in kind or degree. Thus, at present, where all of Europe and a great part of the rest of the world are thinking to a certain extent in terms of the class struggle and have assimilated socialist concepts, Americans still tend to analyze all world problems in purely nationalistic terms.

Thus, even so able a writer as Walter Lippmann in his *American Foreign Policy* considers nations as billiard balls. Each has a direction, mass, inertia, and velocity. If the forces can be calculated, then we should be able to predict what will happen when one billiard ball strikes another at a given angle. On the other hand, according to the standard Marxist analysis, the importance of a nation as such is reduced. We are to look for the meaning of events in the interaction of classes and economic forces that are hardly affected at all by national lines. At the stage of thought at which we are now, it is probable that neither theory should be accepted to the exclusion of the other, but that, like the corpuscular and wave theories of light, we should use whichever is the most serviceable to explain specific phenomena. Nations may be somewhat like billiard balls, but their internal structure is complex and heterogeneous. Inner forces and lopsided centers of gravity often make them behave in a very peculiar fashion for billiard balls, indeed. Moreover, contact between them is not only peripheral but interpenetrated. We have to take into account today the effect of such phenomena as the presence of millions of Russian prisoners in Germany and the constant contact during the last few years, not only of diplomats and officials, but of large numbers of soldiers and civilians of every nation.

During the early years of our nationhood, we were a revolutionary power. America was a republic in a world of monarchies and was confronted by many of the same difficulties that the Russians had to cope with in the early twenties and thirties. We were, however, farther away from the great conservative powers than Russia was one hundred and fifty years later, and, before any serious conflict could develop along ideological lines, monarchies had modified themselves to such an extent that we were no longer a revolutionary force in a conservative world.

During recent years, far from being a revolutionary power, we became the bulwark of free enterprise, the only country in the world, for example, where railroads are all privately owned and operated. We might notice parenthetically that, to the large modern state in which the democratic revolution was delayed the longest, the collective revolution came first, whereas in our country, which was the first to achieve the full democratic revolution, collectivism has penetrated least.

From the early days of the Republic, American foreign policy toward Europe has been negative. The United States Government avoided as far as possible all entangling alliances and commitments abroad. In 1823, Thomas Jefferson wrote to President Monroe that 'Our first and fundamental maxim should be never to entangle ourselves in the broils of Europe.' This principle was amplified and followed with fair consistency during the next one hundred and twenty years.

During most of the nineteenth century, the United States was expanding, and most of its foreign policy was devoted to the acquisition of the Mississippi Valley, Texas, California, the Northwest Territory, Alaska, and later some Caribbean and Pacific islands. By pioneering, by purchase, by war, we acquired our present territory and consolidated it. We knew what we wanted, we knew why we wanted it, and we realized our desires.

In Latin America, too, the United States had a policy, originally expressed in the Monroe Doctrine and recently rejuvenated and streamlined as the 'Good Neighbor' policy. If many of the actions of the United States in following out the implications of this policy were open to criticism, they at least made sense, and had some definite end in view. In the Far East, the United States for nearly half a century has pursued the 'Open-Door' policy. Its chief aims were military security and freedom of trade and opportunity for America in the Far East. This was likewise a positive policy, a definite set of ends to keep in mind, and a general line of action to follow in the conduct of our Far-Eastern relations.

But in Europe, the United States has always moved from one regional temporary measure to another without guiding principles. Often one measure nullified the previous one and was nullified by its successor. The Spanish-American War, though a European nation was involved, was essentially a Western Hemisphere affair, covered by the Monroe Doctrine and our policy of expansion. In general we were content to depend on a vague working agreement with Britain to look after our small interests in other nations.

The United States was dragged into World War I largely because of the stupidity of the Germans, although we should probably have entered eventually, in any case, to prevent a British defeat. For, ever since the beginning of the nineteenth century, America has depended on British naval power as a stabilizing force throughout the world and co-operated with it.

After World War I, the United States for the first time became deeply involved in Europe. Our capital investments in Great Britain and on the Continent became very large. During the twenties two major attempts were made by the United States to finance the shattered economy of the Weimar Republic and keep it from disintegrating. These two attempts — the Dawes Plan and the Young Plan — represented the undertaking by the United States of fairly extensive official commitments in Europe.

Thus, although America officially continued to avoid 'entangling alliances,' although the United States refused to join the infant

League of Nations created by the initiative of the President of the United States, while America was still, in short, officially following a policy of 'isolationism,' we had actually begun to make important commitments in Europe in the early twenties. But, as Mr. Lippmann has pointed out, these commitments were rubber checks, because the United States was not prepared or equipped, either in the early twenties or even in the early forties, to make them good by force of arms in case of necessity. Our foreign policy, to use Mr. Lippmann's phrase, was bankrupt. It was a sorry situation for which the United States paid heavily in 1941.

Americans were in general still suspicious about Europe. The man in the street was inclined to believe that all European diplomats were wily, unscrupulous knaves who invariably led American diplomats around by the nose. In spite of the fact that many Americans traveled in Europe during the twenties and thirties, in spite of the obvious difference between American and European standards of living, these popular illusions lingered, and are, in fact, still alive today. As World War II drew to a close, with American armies all over the Continent, American action in Europe seemed to be predicated on two contradictory attitudes: on the one hand, we were against any intervention in Europe; on the other, we would not tolerate certain kinds of governments in Europe. Out of this confusion, decisions had to be made.

At present, the old isolationism seems to be dead. The principal reason is probably the realization on the part of most Americans that our oceans are no longer guarantees against attack from either Europe or Asia. Flying bombs and rockets can now be directed with some accuracy across the ocean. The submarine and airplane have been developed to a point where an effective attack by a European nation on the United States is quite possible. In addition to this, Americans have had to cross the Atlantic twice in twenty-five years to participate in a European war which seemed vital to American interests. It seems logical to almost all Americans that, under these circumstances, the United States should not try to isolate itself from Europe politically.

It is generally agreed today in the United States that isolationism, which is a negative policy or the absence of policy, must not be allowed to continue. America must have a foreign policy in Europe.

It has long been fairly obvious that a course could be followed that would be in the best interests of the United States. America wants a stable Europe. Furthermore, like Great Britain, America does not want a Europe dominated by one power. If the Continent is controlled by one great power, then Britain becomes isolated and practically helpless. The United States, as twice in the past, would probably feel called upon to aid the British.

Our lack of formulated policy has often led us to actions that were inimical to our own best interests. When the Fascist bloc made a serious attempt to bring Europe under one power and one undemocratic ideology, it was in direct conflict with American interests. Yet America, like Britain, supported Spanish fascism during the civil war in Spain, under the guise of non-intervention, which amounted, in reality, to a blockade of the Spanish Republic.

Today many Americans are talking a great deal in terms of Theodore Roosevelt's famous dictum and want to 'Speak softly and carry a big stick.' Most of the men in the American Air Force in the European theater of operations with whom I talked want us to maintain a standing air force of some two million men which would be capable of keeping order in any part of the world. This is all very good, or very bad, but what kind of order do we want to keep?

Like everyone else, Americans desire peace and security, but there is a considerable distance between these general ends and the concrete means necessary to obtain them. First, we must make up our minds as to who is likely to help us realize our desires and with whom we want to deal. Our present uncertainty keeps getting us into awkward situations like the one that occurred in October, 1944, when Jefferson Caffery, new United States Ambassador to France, arrived in Paris and presented his credentials. The famous Parisian *Canard Enchaîné* made the most of our confusion in its account: 'The new American Ambassador today presented his credentials to General de Gaulle. Inasmuch as the United States Government has not yet recognized the Government of France, the letters of credence bore neither address nor signature. They were anonymous letters.'

The United States finally did get around to recognizing the French Government just before General de Gaulle boarded a plane for Moscow to sign a far-reaching alliance with the Russians who had recognized him months earlier without even bothering about the fact that he was a Catholic, an ex-Monarchist, and an acknowledged man of the Right.

In Africa and Italy, a policy of expediency was applied regionally at the discretion of the military authorities and under the general guidance of a number of individuals in policy-making positions in Washington who believed that the peace must be organized on pre-war lines and that the Catholic Church would be a suitable anchor to ensure European stability and a bulwark against social change. But social change in Europe cannot be prevented. It has already occurred. Americans must realize this and also that Europe has to work out adjustments to conditions that differ vastly from our own.

The United States must also understand the position of the Soviet Union as the strongest military power in Europe, a power that is definitely on the upcurve in population and technological development. It is also a nation which, thanks to its able foreign policy, still symbolizes to millions of Europeans the ideal of the common man struggling to liberate himself from economic chains. Dissenters may say, and with some reason, that the Soviet Union, though Socialist in name, actually grinds its people down much more ruthlessly than did many pre-war western European capitalist democracies. Other dissenters can perhaps prove that the social system in the Soviet Union has undergone changes which can only be characterized as the betrayal of the ideals of socialism. The fact still remains that its prestige among scores of millions of common people in Europe is very high.

Parenthetically, Russian prestige among eastern peoples is today higher than ever before, owing to an inexcusable American blunder at San Francisco. Having raised the issue of the ultimate independence of colonial peoples, the American delegation joined the British in voting for a sterile formula promising colonial peoples little, and allowing the Russians to stand before the world as champions of the hundreds of millions of dependent eastern peoples. This single action quite unnecessarily deprived America of its historic rôle as champion of liberty in the eyes of millions, and turned this invaluable asset over to the Russians.

Unfortunately, the same blunder has occurred repeatedly in Europe on less spectacular issues. We have given in to pressure from the British, and from our own reactionaries, and have identified ourselves with dusty little kings and equally dusty outmoded ideas from the nineteenth century, allowing the Russians to champion progress.

Without grasping two basic concepts, we can have no foreign policy in Europe worthy of a great nation like the United States. We must reconcile ourselves to social change in Europe and we must deal realistically with the Soviet Union.

★ 2. THE ANTI-SOVIET OFFENSIVE ★

R ECENTLY, a number of books and articles have appeared in the United States expressive of nothing but an unleashed hostility to the Soviet Union. Numerous articles and books, such as Mr. White's unfortunate account of what he saw and did not see in his rapid transit through Russia, are apparently indicative of a deep current of American opinion. It is worth while to investigate these opinions and attempt to follow out their implications.

One of the major contentions in this upsurge of hostility (which in some quarters seems to have gone the length of urging that we fight Russia) is that the Soviet Union is plotting and intriguing diabolically in Europe, stirring up revolutions, causing chaos and trouble for the American occupation authorities. It is impossible to prove, of course, that the Soviet Union is not intriguing and plotting in any country in Europe. It is only too easy to confuse the actions of local Communists, leading a struggle for left, popular, anti-Fascist governments, with the work of Moscow. But it is, I think, obvious to those disposed to be objective that revolutionary movements would inevitably occur in many parts of Europe after World War II even if Russia never existed, or even if the Tsar still sat firmly on his throne in the Kremlin.

There are revolutionary movements in defeated countries after every war. There were revolutions all over Europe in 1917 and 1918, many quite independent of anything that was going on at that time in Russia, which was completely isolated and blockaded. There was a revolution in Russia itself in 1905 after the country was defeated by the Japanese.

Revolutions follow defeats whether or not foreign powers intrigue or conspire. When Italy collapsed in 1943, there was a tremendous movement in which workers in the North Italian industrial towns began to take over factories. These were Socialist, revolutionary acts which the Nazis and 'republican' Italian forces suppressed only with the greatest difficulty. But they were most certainly not inspired by agitators from Moscow. It is very likely that mass seizure of German, Austrian, Czechoslovakian factories by their workers will occur during 1945. It would not be at all surprising inasmuch as many of these factories have no longer any legitimate owners, since they were taken over by the Nazis. These things would take place whether or not the Soviet Union existed.

So that if the American reader, prompted by many journalists and authors, blames Russia every time we have trouble with revolutionary movements in Europe, we shall certainly have plenty of opportunity to accuse Russian leaders of pursuing policies opposed to our principles and interests, and these accusations will often be without foundation. Such journalistic policy toward Russia might be derived from several motivations. It could simply be a relic from the muddled thinking of the Chamberlain era. On the other hand, people who write articles of this kind may reckon that if the United States has to fight Russia eventually, we might as well do it now while Russia is relatively weak and we are strong. Polls taken among American troops overseas revealed that many of them believe that we should have to fight Russia almost as soon as we get through with Germany.

Let us examine this trend of thought and try to follow it through to its logical conclusion. The argument runs something like this: (a) Russia today is exhausted, economically depleted, and has suffered great losses in manpower: we are at the peak of our military and economic power; (b) we will have to fight Russia eventually, anyhow, because of the threat of communism, the threat of Soviet imperialism, and the simple fact that we cannot afford to let any one nation get as strong as Russia is going to get; (c) we must fight Russia sooner or later, and if it would be easier to fight now, the obvious answer is — fight now.

Let us assume that these arguments are valid. Let us assume that policy-makers in the United States decide to fight Russia now. What would the results be? If we are going to fight Russia now, we are going to have to do the attacking. Russia has virtually no navy and a relatively small bombing air force, and, furthermore, has no frontiers over which she could attack the United States or Britain. Besides this, it is quite obvious that Russia now, and even for several years to come, has no conceivable reason to attack either Great Britain or the United States.

Agreed — we must attack Russia. The minute we do this, the Soviet Union might make common cause with Japan. Japan and Russia, between the two of them, could almost certainly settle the Chinese war by a combination of political and military pressure. Japan would retire from China. The Russians would guarantee the integrity of the Chinese Republic and at the same time many millions of Chinese Communists, whose political orientation has so far been enigmatic, would probably spring to the head of a Left, popular Chinese Government which the Soviet Union would support.

Thus, during the first few days of the war the Soviet Union would weld together a military bloc running from the South Pacific to the North Cape, from Bering Strait to the Adriatic, with a population of some 800,000,000, with untold natural resources. This area, furthermore, with the exception of several large Japanese cities, would have very few practicable bomb targets. There would be few concentrations of population like those in Germany or England. It is highly doubtful whether the United States and Great Britain could defeat such a combination.

No, it would seem advisable then to wait for the attack on the Soviet Union until Japan has been defeated.

Let us assume that this occurs in 1945 or 1946. As soon as Japan is defeated, an attack on the Soviet Union starts. Who does the attacking? It would be inadvisable for the United States to undertake such an operation alone. Russia is too big, both in area and population. Perhaps Britain would help us in this colossal venture?

But the Conservative Government of Great Britain has a twenty-year alliance with the Soviet Union and the people of Great Britain are in no mood at all to fight against the Soviet Union.

In cinema theaters in several parts of England in 1943, when pictures of Roosevelt, Churchill, and Stalin were flashed on the screen, in almost every case the applause for Stalin was greater than for the other two combined. The British people are extremely grateful to the Russians for having absorbed German strength at a time when England was unable to defend itself from German bombing. Of course, people forget, and by 1946 the British people will have changed somewhat, but I do not believe that even in 1946 the British people, without the greatest difficulty, could be sold the idea of invading Russia. But let us assume that the difficulties are overcome and the British put up an army of two million men to join our army of perhaps five million, in an attack on the Soviet Union. It is still not enough. The Germans made the attempt with a larger army and lost. Since then the Russians have learned much, and have received much valuable equipment from us.

What other allies could we find? Germany is in no condition to enter any war for at least several years. Besides, are we going to create another strong Germany as a bulwark against Russia the way we did a decade or two ago, only to have our cities bombed and our ships sunk again by the Germans?

The French? De Gaulle has signed an alliance with Moscow. The French population is in no mood to attack Russia. French antagonism is at present concentrated squarely on Britain and many Frenchmen are fed-up with the Anglo-Saxon powers and their democracy. Furthermore, from the standpoint of French national interests, what have they to gain from a war against Russia? The Finns, Rumanians, Turks, and the Poles might conceivably be persuaded to fight the Russians, but at the present time these areas are either occupied by Red armies, or are so thoroughly controlled by the Russians that no such move would be possible.

The Chinese? I do not know the Far East, but it seems highly doubtful to me that the Chinese could be induced to attack Russia or, if they did, that they would be able to send an effective military force over areas where there are neither railroads nor roads, and where distances are measured in thousands of miles. Who else is there? The Greeks, the Yugoslavs, the Czechs, and the Italians would hardly participate in an expeditionary force against the Soviet Union. The Spaniards, if General Franco were still in control, might send another Blue Division. In short, it seems that the job would have to be done by the United States, with possible British aid.

Of course, if we were to wait a little while — say ten years — new allies might be prepared for an attack against the Soviet Union. The most likely country would be Germany. But the effects of this policy in the past have been so disastrous that it seems unlikely that any government in Britain or the United States would attempt a repetition unless it was composed of outright Fascists.

So, we are forced to the conclusion that fighting the Soviet Union immediately is impossible; after the defeat of Japan, possible but extremely difficult; even in ten years doubtful, dangerous, and almost necessarily resulting in great domestic difficulties. Organized labor would resist a war of aggression against the Soviet Union and so would millions of ordinary unorganized Americans, who would feel that it was pointless. It would mean that a small group of men would have to force upon the country a policy with which most of the community would disagree, a policy which would involve the loss of millions of American lives. It would require drastic coercion, perhaps something very like Fascism. Given our national temperament, and the notorious warmth which usually accompanies such occasions as football games and election campaigns, Fascism in America would be an extremely bloody affair.

But let us assume we pursue our chosen policies despite all internal difficulties. We invade the Soviet Union. The war is a bitter one. The Russians defend their lands fanatically. Not only that, they stir up trouble in our rear. The Greeks who felt badly because of British intervention in 1944 overthrow the sound conservative government they had been given and join a large force of South Slavs under Marshal Tito which interferes with communications, harries patrols, and raises a hornet's nest of feeling in the Balkans against the Anglo-American crusading forces. The French remain stubbornly neutral and Paris becomes a hotbed of political intrigue. Agents, Russian, Serb, and French, stir up trouble, organize sabotage, and instigate labor disputes throughout the Continent.

It is a difficult war, but we are indefatigable. We move forward gradually from base to base. We make supreme sacrifices, we hold Europe in a grip of iron and force the Europeans to make sacrifices too. After several years of bloody campaigning, after enormous losses, after sacrificing our freedom, our democracy, and our standard of living at home, after burying several million American boys under the icy wastes of Russia, we succeed. We invade the country to the Urals from both directions; Stalin is shot, the Soviet régime dissolved, and Tsar Nicholas III, or Kerensky II, or perhaps some Republican, is placed at the head of some new Russian State. The country is split up into small units; the Finns get Karelia, the Rumanians the Ukraine, the Turks Armenia. Then what?

As we have seen, the Soviet Union has two great assets: a large and rapidly increasing population and tremendous natural resources. Neither of these can be taken from the Soviet Union effectively without continued large-scale occupation. If everybody agrees that Germany should be kept weak, all you have to do is cut the country off from its supplies of high-grade iron ore and a few other necessities and effectively control imports. But the Soviet Union cannot be cut off from natural resources. It has all it needs. The only way you can take away its natural resources from Russia is to send an army of workers, protected by an army of soldiers, into the country and mine the manganese, the petroleum, the bauxite, and the coal, and take them away and dump them on the world market, where, perish the thought! they will compete with the products of the Standard Oil Company, the Aluminum Company of America, and other interested parties.

This is so highly unsatisfactory that the victorious nations would almost certainly abandon such a long-term economic occupation and leave some sort of independent Russia under some kind of control.

Under these circumstances, even supposing that no conflicting interests between the victorious powers made it possible for the Russians to get aid and encouragement from one as opposed to another, even supposing that the anti-Soviet forces remained solid and solved their own internal problems satisfactorily, even then in twenty-five years the Soviet Union would still have an extremely large population and great natural resources.

In addition to this, it is almost certain that the victors would squabble and argue, that the class struggle would raise its ugly head in every city in the world, and that, in the end, Britain and the United States, the presumable leaders of the coalition, would be confronted by insurmountable difficulties.

We have pursued the argument to its logical conclusion and I am sure that most readers, during the course of it, have several times asked themselves, 'But is it really necessary for us to fight the Soviet Union?'

It is perfectly obvious that if even a part of this policy is put into effect, it will eventually spoil relations between the Soviet Union and the Anglo-Saxon powers. If, for example, at the peace conference, Germany is given colonies, resources, and in other ways encouraged to become strong, the Russians can hardly fail to conclude that Germany is being groomed for an attack on the Soviet Union and they will promptly begin taking counter-measures. These would probably take the form of internal interference in Germany which would be a very fertile field and perhaps interference in other parts of Europe.

No, this basic policy — and if we adopted it, this would be a 'foreign policy' — must be pursued either fully or not at all. And herein lies the great danger.

There is little danger, I think, that we will actually attack the Soviet Union. But there is great danger that we will allow ourselves to become involved in a series of petty incidents, leading to bad relations with the Soviet Union. In London I heard one American junior officer in uniform say in a restaurant: 'We must stop killing Germans as soon as possible, because we are going to need every German available to use in our war against the Soviet Union within a very short time.' This remark is overheard by many and is reported to the Russians, who cable it to Moscow. In the Kremlin, the younger left group in the Politburo — Zhdanov, Malenkov, Shcherbakov — go to Stalin and say: 'You see. We told you so. We can't trust these Anglo-Saxons. They are plotting against us already. We must undertake counter-measures. We must have bases in western Germany [for example] to forestall such plans.'

Of course, as soon as the Russians reach out for bases in western Germany there is a howl from Anglo-Saxon military men and others who demand bases in eastern Europe to forestall Russian aggression. And so the vicious circle has begun.

We must assume that the Russians read articles and editorials in the American press with great attention; that they have wondered on many occasions whether the group of people who want to see the Anglo-Saxon powers fight the Soviet Union is really as weak and ineffective as the Governments in London and Washington would like Moscow to believe. Like us, the Russians examine the possibilities logically, and Stalin rubs his chin meditatively, and says characteristically, '*Pochemu nyet?*' — Why not? The chances of the Anglo-Saxon powers adopting a policy directed toward making war on the Soviet Union are small — perhaps minute — but Stalin cannot afford not to take precautionary measures against even minute possibilities.

As quietly and inconspicuously as he can — for Stalin wants to avoid friction and war with the Anglo-Saxon powers more than anything in the world — he tries to prevent the formation of federations or blocs which might be directed against the Soviet Union. He pays great attention to France and Italy, tries to make lasting friends there, both on the left and on the right. He insists on exerting an influence in the affairs of western Europe, and only with reluctance permits his allies to have any in eastern Europe. In a word, he does all the things that he has been doing for the past twelve months, and which have aroused suspicion and resentment in London and Washington.

Suspicion breeds suspicion, distrust distrust. An atmosphere of tension and hostility is created. Maneuvers, intrigues, are begun and precautions taken which are expensive and wasteful for all. How much of this is necessary?

XVII

Getting Along With Russia

ALTHOUGH the best possible American foreign policy would be to promote a world federation, and although many detailed and feasible schemes have been worked out for such an organization, we have seen that at the present it is unlikely to come into existence and is even somewhat utopian. We have also seen that an American policy based on an aggressive or preventive war against the Soviet Union or the preparation of one is difficult, dangerous, expensive, and to be avoided at all costs.

The sole remaining workable policy is one based on a long-term working friendship among the great powers with each acting as the center of a galaxy of small nations. Blueprints have already been drawn up for such a post-war world at Dumbarton Oaks, Teheran, and in the Anglo-Soviet and Franco-Soviet alliances. They were further elaborated at Yalta and at San Francisco. Though many important questions remain to be threshed out, it offers the only chance for a realistic solution of our problems and it is in this direction that we must turn our efforts.

In spite of many differences and irksome disputes, good Anglo-American relations have been maintained for a long period and the continuation of these relations for some years can, I think, be taken for granted. Continued good relations with Russia are far more problematic. Russian need for reconstruction and internal development, however, makes it almost certain that in the immediate future the Soviet Union will not follow a policy of active aggression against either Britain or the United States. There will, of course, be many serious disagreements during the next twenty years, just as there have been recently on the subject of Poland. But such disputes are certainly no more serious than those which occur constantly between Washington and London over the Argentine market, Middle-Eastern commercial policy, and a number of other matters.

The Soviet Union does not have to pursue a policy of aggressive expansion to become powerful and wealthy. Germany did. That made Germany a more immediately dangerous competitor and potential enemy. The Soviet Union will be content for years to import large quantities of all sorts of manufactured goods from the United States and Great Britain and continue the present political and economic collaboration, *provided* Britain and the United States do not pursue policies hostile to the Soviet Union. Obviously, the dangerous period for this collaboration (this the advocates of war against the Soviet Union point out at every opportunity) comes in a generation when the Soviet Union has become wealthy and strong, raised its standard of living to a high point, built a navy and a large air force, and perfected its economy and political technique.

Suppose we pursue friendly policies toward Russia now, could not the danger in 1970 be avoided? I believe it could. I believe that the century-long cycle of a series of wars among imperial competitors can be broken. I think that essentially the Russians want permanent peace. I believe, furthermore, that there are so many psychological and historical similarities between the Russian and American people, so many compelling reasons for maintaining good relations, that a solid, enduring friendship between the two countries can continue to exist and develop.

Let us assume that we are going to try to get along with Russia, to try sincerely to avoid policies which will be provocative to the Russians; to meet them halfway and thereby attempt to lay a firm basis for the prevention of the war which might threaten in 1970. In order to do this, we must understand the Russians better than we do.

Considerable progress has already been made in this direction. It is a cause for satisfaction, for example, that the newly appointed assistant to the Secretary of State, Charles Bohlen, is one of very few Americans who are both eminently well-informed and objective on the Soviet Union. It is likewise a cause for satisfaction that during recent months several statements have been made by men in authoritative positions in Washington expressive of a sincere desire to understand the Russians and meet them halfway, or even a little more. One such was Mr. Edward Stettinius who, on November 7, 1944, said:

'The friendship between our two countries is a cherished heritage of our people. Our relations have grown close in the ordeal of this world-wide war in which we have joined our efforts in a joint cause.

'In a spirit of friendly collaboration and of mutual confidence and faith in each other we have taken the first necessary steps to establish an international organization to maintain peace and security. In that same spirit we shall take further steps. We shall continue to act together and to work in fullest co-operation.

'As we, the United States and the U.S.S.R. have fought and worked together, we have come to know each other better and we have found that the cordiality of our relations has grown. Differences in points of view and method of work shrink as there is mutual knowledge and understanding of each other's ways of thinking and of living. I am certain that we shall work out whatever problems confront us in full realization that the greatest goals of each of us must be the common goals of both of us.'

Of course, all this does not and should not mean that we should give in to Russian desires and wishes on all points where our interests diverge. On the contrary. Our conduct toward the Russians must show good-will and a desire to reach a mutual accord, but it must also be firm and determined on matters of importance.

During recent months the United States press has tended to see our relations with the Soviet Union either as pure black or pure white. Some want us to give the Russians the benefit of every doubt, accept their every whim and condone their every error; to sign over to the Soviet Union all the interests which we formerly had in countries which border on the Soviet Union, like Finland. Others urge that we heckle and harass the Russians wherever and whenever we can, secure bases against them, and use the economic aid we are giving them under lend-lease — an aid amply paid for in advance by Russian blood — as an instrument of political pressure against the Soviet Union.

We should, of course, attempt to steer away from both reefs. Recently, there has been some trouble in Rumania. We have accused the Russians of moving oil equipment, which belonged to American firms before the war, from Ploesti into Russia. The Russians made counter-accusations. According to the Soviet-Rumania armistice terms, which we countersigned, there was a proviso authorizing the Russians to do almost anything if it was necessary to the war effort. Perhaps the removal of this oil equipment was necessary. This is a question for investigation. But on one point there is a question of principle. The Russians did not permit American engineers to go to Ploesti and see what was happening. Now it may be that for some reason the men involved were not personally acceptable to the Russians. In that case we should send men there who are acceptable. But we should insist that American observers be permitted entry into the Ploesti oil fields. We should insist on the highest levels, and we should implement our insistence by whatever reciprocal measures on the same level seem necessary to make the Russians understand that we consider this a question of importance. But we should not, in this connection, either in our press or in conversations, raise the issue of bolshevism, of Communist agitators, of Soviet imperialism, of the authoritarian or dictatorial character of the Soviet State. It complicates issues and makes trouble. It is quite possible to hammer on tables about observers in oil fields without calling into question the sociological structure, the ideology or the sincerity of the countries involved.

We should be firm with the Russians on many such issues. We can challenge them on many specific points without attacking Russian policy as a whole and Russian good faith. Thus, Anglo-American correspondents are not at present permitted access to such eastern European countries as Rumania, Poland, Hungary, and Bulgaria. The State Department and Whitehall could demand an immediate improvement in this situation. If this request is refused, they could take the step of placing restrictions on Russian correspondents in Italy, the Low Countries, and Greece, where they have at present free access.

In order to get along well with the Russians over a long period of time, we must try to analyze possible causes for conflict. There are many things about us which the Russians like — our informality, our technical competence, our energy, our efficiency. There are many Russian characteristics which most Americans approve —

their courage, the open-hearted simplicity and generosity of their common man; we like their music, their ballet, their literature.

What is it that Americans tend not to like about the Russians? Many Americans do not like their N.K.V.D., or G.P.U. as it was formerly called — their secret police. We think their language difficult, disapprove of their behavior toward Finland, Poland, and the Baltic countries. Many Americans do not like the Soviet attitude toward the Church. Most Americans deplore the failure of the Soviet Government to allow its citizens to express disagreement with its politics in writing or by word of mouth. Many Americans fear 'communism.'

Some Russians, on the other hand, think we are romantic sentimentalists in insisting on the right of fair open trial even for a traitor, in insisting on the right of the isolationist press to continue functioning. If many Americans think Stalin crude and brutal, many Russians thought Franklin D. Roosevelt had no center of gravity.

Recently in Stockholm I had dinner with a friend of mine, a captain in the United States Air Force. He told me of a large formal diplomatic luncheon he had attended, where he sat across the table from the Soviet Air Attaché and his two assistants. 'You know it was extraordinary,' the captain said, 'those fellows did not speak a word of English or Swedish. They just sat there eating all through the lunch and all they said was "skål." They were three very able-looking boys and they held their heads right up. It even seemed to me that there might have been some wood under those epaulettes on their shoulders. Their attitude seemed to be, "If you want to talk to me, Buddy, you learn Russian." Now, damn it all, I want to get along with the Russians. They have done a wonderful job and they are good boys, but when they go around with a provocative attitude like that, it is going to lead to misunderstandings. I want to get along with the Russians, sure, but if they think I am going to learn Russian, that's going too far. If they want to speak to me, they can learn English.'

Here, in a nutshell, are the difficulties created by the difference in language. Most Russians do not speak foreign languages. Few Anglo-Saxons speak Russian. This creates a national barrier. It seemed to my captain friend that the Russians had a chip on their shoulders and were demanding that everybody else speak Russian. The Russians probably thought the same thing of Americans. Actually the teaching of the English language has been made compulsory throughout the Soviet school system. In America and Britain some graduate university students and a few amateurs study Russian. Few others.

Many Americans don't like the G.P.U., collectivization, Soviet imperialism, communism. I believe most of these dislikes are the results of misunderstandings. The Russians have a secret police, a very ruthless and effective organization which operates both in peace and in wartime on the general assumption that a suspect is guilty until he proves himself innocent, and on the theory that it is less dangerous to the State to have an innocent person suffer than to have a guilty one go free. This secret police has partly been necessitated by the ring of actual and potential enemies which have surrounded the Soviet Union. It has in part been the result of historic tradition and habits rooted in the nation. Russia has always been run with the aid of a secret police.

Owing to these differences in basic concepts and in historic background, the Russians have developed a high degree of very dictatorial discipline in civilian life and in their armies. The acceptance of this discipline has been facilitated by the fact that the entire Russian people have been drawn into the war by the German invasion and are therefore much more willing to endure restrictions than are, for example, the American people.

The results of this high degree of discipline are often unfortunate. For example, a friend of mine was in Iran. One night he went for a drink to a bar frequented by both Russian and American troops. During the course of the evening, one Russian junior officer got extremely drunk and began waving his revolver around. The Americans, pleased to have met at least one Russian they could outdrink, persuaded the young Red Army officer to put his revolver away and quieted him down. Later, two M.P.s escorted the man to his quarters. The Americans forgot the incident. But the next morning the Russian Commander paid a formal visit to the American Commander, apologized gravely for the intolerable misbehavior of the night before by a member of the Red Army garrison, and expressed his hopes that the incident had not inconvenienced the Americans. He regretted that the Red Army officer in question could not present his excuses in person as he unfortunately had died during the night.

This created a very bad impression among the Americans, who concluded that the Red Army was a barbarous army. It produced an equally bad impression on the Russian troops, who noted that when an American soldier got drunk, which occasionally occurred, all that happened to him was that he was put to bed by M.P.s, perhaps demoted. This double misunderstanding resulted from failure on both sides to understand the traditions and background of the other side. Such misunderstandings can only be eliminated by more contacts, more thorough study by the Americans of the Russians, and *vice versa*. With good-will on both sides it will come in time.

Many Americans bristle at Russian policy in Finland and Iran and other expressions of what is sometimes referred to as Soviet imperialism. That many of the Russian actions are morally and politically indefensible is beyond dispute. It must also be realized that the power politics of every large nation also falls very much into the same category. I am not suggesting that we condone any of these acts, but that we at least classify them properly. Granting a few regional differences and the more secure and invulnerable position of America in the Western Hemisphere, Russian policy in the countries that surround it has not been so vastly different from our own good-neighbor policy. Both are based on real situations which require solutions. By dwelling on the similarity between Russian and American viewpoints, we might have been able to influence them to modify some of their actions in Finland, for example, toward greater moderation. By insisting and dwelling on the differences between Russian and American behavior, we can only increase and exaggerate them.

On my way back from Europe in February, 1945, I stopped at Puerto Rico and spent the evening at the house of Rexford Tugwell, American Governor of Puerto Rico, talking with him and the local leaders. I was told, during this and several other discussions, that if a plebiscite were to be held, Puerto Rico would undoubtedly become independent of the United States. However, although the majority of the Puerto Ricans wanted independence, the acquisition of this boon would undoubtedly wreck the economy of the island, since Puerto Rico would find itself outside American tariff barriers. To make certain that this would not occur, the leader of the Puerto Rican independence movement had been provided with a comfortable lodging in an American jail for the last few years. We had taken it upon ourselves to decide what was good for the Puerto Ricans without paying much heed to their desires, except for the purpose of thwarting them. The American public, however, rarely thinks about Puerto Rico and prefers to concentrate on events in far-off Estonia or Latvia.

Many Americans do not like Russia's attitude toward religion. The old Church in Russia before the Revolution was the Greek Orthodox Church, an institution far from perfect in its organization, its ideas, and personnel, as those familiar with the story of Rasputin must agree. When the Revolution occurred, the Greek Orthodox Church, realizing that it was threatened, did its best to thwart and oust the new régime. The Bolsheviks, on the other hand, regarded the Church as a powerful enemy, and in accordance with their theories, proceeded to confiscate church property and to destroy the organization of the Greek Orthodox Church. Several years after the Revolution, the Bolsheviks decided that administrative anti-religious measures did not pay and limited themselves to intensive anti-religious propaganda while relaxing the legal restrictions on the Church.

For twenty years the Soviet youth was told in school, in the cinema, from the lecture platform, over the radio, that religion was a racket; that the way to live well was to work hard, earn more money, and spend it on good living, rather than to invest in a dubious life after death. In Moscow before the Revolution there were sixteen hundred churches; in 1941, when I left Moscow, there were twenty-one churches in operation. I went to church myself several times and some of my Russian acquaintances went regularly. They suffered no punishment or penalty. But I noticed that most of the church-goers in Moscow were men and women (particularly the latter) over forty-five years of age.

When the war started, there were still many millions of Russians, especially in rural areas, who believed in God and wanted to worship. The Soviet Government, therefore, assisted in the reorganization of the hierarchy of the Greek Orthodox Church, facilitated the establishment of the Holy Synod, and created what was in fact a new State Church — a Soviet State Church, whose many activities were directed toward strengthening the Soviet war effort. The Moslem Church was also resurrected.

This resuscitation of religion in the Soviet Union was basically a tactical move in the Russian war effort. But it was also, I believe, the beginning of a new period of religious tolerance in the Soviet Union. Twenty-five years ago, the Church in Russia was a dangerous threat to the Soviet régime, and its implacable enemy. Today the new Church is neither threatening nor inimical. I believe the Russian leaders will continue to allow it to exist, although I am convinced that it will never have the same hold on the Russian people that it had before the Revolution.

I believe, however, that the Russians will in time have a new religion. I do not know what it will be called. Indeed it matters little. Europe has many churches. In the sixteenth century in central Europe, the Catholic Church had reached a point where it no longer satisfied the interests of the great masses of people. The Reformation took place and a new Church was formed. This process took a long time and while it was going on few understood what was happening.

So today it is still unclear whether or not the Church in Russia will revive anew. But a flat assertion, such as is often heard in America, that there is no freedom of religion in Russia, is simply inaccurate.

Many Americans have been upset about the fate of the Baltic States. There are some two million Lithuanians, Latvians, and Estonians living in the United States, and there are at the present time some thirty thousand Baltic refugees in Stockholm. Many of these are vicious in their condemnation of the Russians. That the Russians were overbearing and arbitrary when they entered the Baltic States in 1940, few question. But there is a historic background which few realize. Until July, 1922, the United States Government withheld recognition of the newly formed Baltic States, then granted it reluctantly in the belief that their independence would not be of long duration. Though the American Government sympathized with their national aspirations, the American High Commissioner, Mr. Evan Young, who recommended recognition, stated at the time: 'It is entirely possible, or even probable, that some time in the indefinite future these states may once again become an integral part of Russia — however, until that time comes, they will be able to maintain their political stability, and with that their independence. . . . Admitting that from our point of view, a strong Russia is greatly to be desired, it is still difficult for an observer here to suggest any course of action other than the immediate recognition of these States.'

In 1940, the Russians were hastening their preparations for war against Germany which they were sure was coming soon. In their haste they stepped on many Baltic toes. Officially they have not admitted this, though I have heard several responsible Soviet diplomats admit, in private, that 'Many mistakes were made — *mnogo peregibi dopushcheni.*' But I think that official recognition will come, and that if and when the Russians feel secure against attacks from the west, the lot of the Baltic peoples will be greatly improved.

All these remarks do not represent attempts to condone Soviet policy, or pardon Russian *peregibov.* I have been merely trying to indicate that there is a Soviet point of view on these questions, an explanation. And we should try to see their point of view, and understand, though we may disagree and argue with, their explanations.

It is undoubtedly going to be a strain on the nerves of many Anglo-Saxon diplomats and businessmen to handle current diplomatic and commercial relations with the Soviet Union because of major difficulties of language, tradition, and background. The Russians are simple people who know what they want and are not hampered by any elaborate inhibitions.

A friend of mine accompanied Secretary Hull to the Moscow Conference. He describes amusingly how, on several occasions, British representatives said something which was not quite consistent with something which they had said before. When the Russians pointed this out, the British would turn red, fidget, and withdraw. On several other occasions the Russians said things which were completely incompatible with other things they had just said. When this was pointed out to them, they would look at the Anglo-Saxon delegates blankly and say: 'Why, of course we want this, and we want this too.'

As people today, the Russians are still poor, hard-working, and tough. They do not feel at ease in Western drawing rooms, because most of them have spent a great part of their lives in overalls. Of the five Tass representatives in Stockholm, for example, four had been in overalls ten years before. The same thing is true of many Russian diplomats. Most present-day Russians do not speak foreign languages and are traditionally suspicious of foreigners. In particular, many of the Russians still have a chip on their shoulder because they feel their country is not accepted as an equal by other nations and the Russian representatives and officials feel that they have not yet been admitted into the club, so to speak.

Another great difficulty is caused by Soviet pride. Russians today are tremendously proud of themselves, their government, their army, their country. Every article, every speech, contains the proud ringing note of a people who were on the brink of unmitigated disaster and by their own heroic efforts saved themselves and half the world and marched into the enemy camp to make the final kill. The Russians are also proud of the fact that the Red Army in the latter stages of the war became an army of liberation. To quote Stalin: 'Now that the Fatherland war is approaching its end, the historic rôle of the Soviet people appears in its full grandeur. Today all recognize that the Soviet people with their heroic struggle have saved the civilization of Europe from the Fascist subjugation. In this lies the great contribution of the Soviet people to the human race.'

On July 17, 1944, 57,600 German prisoners were led on foot through Moscow. The parade was watched by virtually every man, woman, and child in the city. The officers were on foot, wearing their military flashes and shoulder tabs, and many of them with decorations. The proud invaders had been defeated and Moscow knew it. Every Russian stopped his work for long enough to swell his chest in pride.

This pride is frequently the pride of youth, and sometimes leads the Russians to an arrogant attitude which complicates even simple intercourse. The Soviet Government, of course, has tried to stimulate this because it was useful and necessary in strengthening the Soviet war effort. For example, in describing the advance of the Red Army through Rumania, driving out the Germans, reports in the Soviet press rarely mentioned the fact that the Rumanian Army was helping the Russians in considerable strength. Thus, sometimes the Russians tend to be more proud of their feats than circumstances justify, although in general their pride is certainly as well-founded as that of any people in history. Some Russians tend to feel that they have beaten one western European power and it is 'a pushover, once you get the hang of it.'

But at present there are many signs that this attitude is being modified. I have been told that at Yalta, for instance, the Russians were relaxed and genial as they had never been before, ready to sit back and engage in informal conversation with British and American leaders, to banter and be bantered, to criticize and to listen to criticism. The attitude of Stalin, in particular, was one of great cordiality. My informant was also impressed by the way in which Stalin made what seemed to many snap judgments which were binding. For example, one morning a point was brought to Stalin's attention. It was a point on which Molotov had fought like a tiger the previous evening for several hours. It was an American question to which Molotov had made a categorical objection. Stalin looked it through, then said, 'All right, I withdraw our objection.'

The Russians were not arrogant regarding their military achievements. They were quite willing to admit that in the beginning of the war the Red Army was inadequate in many respects. At one point Stalin said to Roosevelt, in a rather humorous vein, 'Of course, your intelligence service with regard to Russia prior to 1941 was not quite perfect. But it must be said that our performance in Finland in 1939 and 1940 and against the Germans in 1941 was far from brilliant. The basic factor which you misjudged, however, was our ability to make a new army during the course of the war.'

Throughout the conference Stalin very seldom used the word 'soviet' as an adjective, almost always the word 'Russian.' He frequently used the words 'We Russians' as a preface to giving the Soviet outlook on some question.

There are fair signs that many of these minor sources of friction will be eliminated, but the fundamental question still remains. Most Americans and most Russians are worried chiefly about whether capitalism and socialism can continue to exist in the same world and whether the countries based on these systems can remain friendly and at peace with each other.

Many Russians, bred on orthodox Marxist-Leninism, still feel that peace and prosperity in the world can only be achieved after capitalism has been overthrown, although Soviet diplomats and journalists have, for the last two or three years, been extremely careful not to express these opinions to their American allies. The issue has not been mentioned in the Soviet press and has even been slurred over in courses at the Marx-Engels Institute in Moscow.

Many Americans, on the other hand, feel that we can only get along with Russia on a permanent basis when the Russians have given up their bolshevism and gone back to the sound principles of free enterprise, democracy, and capitalism. American correspondents and diplomats, and indeed a large section of the American press, have been avoiding this point for the last two or three years in the interests of co-operation with the Soviet Union. But millions of Americans still feel that the basic contradictions between socialism and capitalism form a formidable crevasse between the Soviet Union and the rest of the world.

A century or two ago a very major question in Europe was: Can monarchies and republics get along together? After the great French Revolution, thousands of French aristocrats swarmed for a generation in London, urging the British to destroy, or at least ignore, the impertinent republican rabble which had taken control of France. The young American Republic too had much difficulty with some monarchs. And yet now, after only three or four generations, the question has become a purely academic one. No one thinks of it any more. The passage of time and events have erased the question. Why? Very simply because both republics and monarchies were modified in such a way that their similarities became more numerous and more important than their differences.

The British monarchy became far more democratic than the Chinese Republic. As we have seen, the ruling classes of Britain were far-sighted and clear-headed enough to perceive that the British monarchy was going to have to change, to improve and to develop if it was to compete with the young republics across the Channel and across the Atlantic.

On the other hand, in the case of France at least, the more extreme revolutionary ideas introduced by the early republicans at the time of the Commune were modified, softened, and changed. In other words, monarchy and republicanism had made a compromise. Intelligent monarchs accepted many of the more progressive ideas of the republicans. The republicans accepted the benefit of the greater administrative and technical experience of the monarchies, in order to make their republics work more efficiently and repudiated those of their ideas which were most obnoxious to people elsewhere in the world.

The same process is now going on with regard to capitalism and socialism. As I have tried to make clear, Europe is undergoing a revolution in the direction of some form of collectivism, some degree of governmental interference and control of private enterprise, some minimum standard of social legislation — in a word, to some sort of socialism. Even England, led by a Conservative Government, has made significant steps in this direction.

In the case of the Soviet Union, this revolution took the form of bloody insurrection, dictatorship, and civil war, at the end of which they achieved an extreme socialism characterized by poverty and inexperience. From this extreme they have since been modifying up. In England, the change took the form of modification down (the words up and down are obviously relative, one might as well say down and up) from the position she formerly held as the stronghold *par excellence* of *laisser-faire,* free enterprise, capitalism. The terminology has stuck in people's minds, just as in some parts of the United States the terms 'Confederate' and 'Union' have remained as verbal monuments to an era long past; but in a sense, one can no longer speak of socialism and capitalism as black and white, extreme and mutually exclusive competitors in the social development of our Western world.

The Soviet leaders so far have not pointed out these developments to the people of the Soviet Union, although I am sure they are well aware of them. They are not doing so primarily because they are busy with the war; and because they fear that those influences in America and Britain and elsewhere which desire to attack the Soviet Union may possibly win out. In this case, Russia may face a war against an Anglo-American coalition. If this occurs, it will be much simpler for the Soviet leaders to explain things to their people in terms of capitalism, or neo-fascism versus socialism.

But if things go well between the Anglo-Saxon powers and Russia in the immediate post-war period, I am convinced that the Russians, who have studied these social developments more closely than most others, will come out officially with a new supplementation of Marxist-Leninism along lines suggested above. They may call it the 'theory of the growing together of capitalism and socialism,' and explain it by the 'acceptance by the great capitalist democracies of the socialist ideas long advocated by the Soviet Union.'

Of course, this synthesizing process, which has already been going on for more than a quarter of a century, can be expected to continue for a long time, perhaps for another quarter-century, before the question becomes as academic as that of monarchy versus republic. But as soon as we realize that it is going on, it gives us a great advantage in analyzing contemporary events, particularly in Europe, which at the moment is the football field on which the game is being played.

Under examination we find that none of our reasons for disliking the Russians seems important enough to warrant a major dispute. Many of them, indeed, are questions of misunderstanding. With study and effort these misunderstandings can be ironed out and lasting friendly relations with the Soviet Union established.

In working for this understanding, it is important that a maximum of freedom of criticism be established. Americans must be free to criticize the foreign policy (or its absence) of the American Government. We cannot insist that the Russian people criticize their own Government, as that would border on interference in the internal affairs of the Soviet Union, but we can insist on our right of criticizing Soviet policies in the American and British press.

One of the most awkward factors in the frequent misunderstandings with the Russians on matters relating to the press is the Russian failure to understand our diversity of opinion on foreign affairs. On one occasion in Moscow an official of the Soviet Foreign Office, irritated by what the American newsmen had written and the American press printed on the Reubens case, told our Chargé d'Affaires, Loy Henderson, that he considered it up to the American authorities to control the American press. Henderson told him quite honestly that he could not control the American correspondents, while the authorities in Washington could not censor the press on such stories (this was before the war). The Russian did not believe him, and left with the impression that the American Embassy was planting a story or angling a story in a way undesirable to the Russians.

The Russians get furious at the small reactionary Polish-language press in Britain. They are irritated and confused by the polemics in the Anglo-Saxon press on vital current issues even during the war. It is absolutely essential that the Russians be helped to understand the character of Anglo-Saxon journalism; that Moscow recognize the right of the press in London and the New York journals to criticize the policies of the Kremlin just as the Anglo-American press criticizes the policies of their own governments. If this is not done, a sizable body of 'anti-Soviet' public opinion will crystallize in Britain and America, only a small portion of which will be against the Soviet policies themselves, and the preponderant weight of which will be irate over the right in principle to criticize Soviet policy. A good beginning might be made if half a dozen prominent American newspapers and magazines should invite a Soviet journalist, to be chosen by the Soviet Government, to come and work for a year in editorial offices in New York. They would learn our point of view, to everyone's benefit.

Many of the younger Soviet foreign correspondents with whom I have talked in Stockholm and London and elsewhere understand this quite well. But apparently many functionaries in Moscow still look for a Machiavellian governmental plot against the Soviet Union every time anyone attacks some phase of Soviet policy in the Anglo-Saxon press. This is most unfortunate, and makes the task of British and American diplomats in their relations with the Russians even more complex and delicate than it already is.

XVIII

A Policy for the Future

SIMPLY GETTING ALONG with Russia could hardly be called a foreign policy. What should our foreign policy be? Granted that it should be based on broad collaboration with Russia and Britain, but toward what ends?

The foreign policy of a nation cannot be detached from its domestic policy and its internal conditions and needs. The policy of expansion which has been Britain's since the eighteenth century developed out of the fact that British industries required markets and British surplus capital an outlet for investment. Until the second World War, most of the products of American farms and factories were sold to American consumers. Exports were a relatively unimportant item in our national income.

After this war, we will be confronted by serious alterations in our economic situation. The capacity of our production in many fields has been increased to such an extent that the domestic market will not be able to absorb our output. The most seriously affected will be the machine tool, aviation construction, and allied industries. Latin American markets will be able to take something of the surplus, but it must be left to our foreign policy to open up imperatively needed new markets for American industry and enterprise.

Two obvious opportunities will be afforded by the reconstruction of Europe and the reconstruction and further industrialization of Soviet Russia. The Russians will be anxious to buy everything from ships to electric fans. If our relations with Russia remain cordial, the Russians will also do their best to stimulate the purchase by its smaller neighbors of American capital equipment. However, to become substantial markets, the nations of Europe must get on their feet as soon as possible and have the opportunity to develop their economy as their people wish. The economy of a country functions best under a popular government, because it works with the consent of the people and does not have to devote most of its energy to staying in power.

Our policy, then, should obviously be to allow and encourage the peoples of Europe to choose their own governments. So far we have been able to do this more successfully than the British, perhaps because they are hampered by imperial commitments while we are not. A pointed example in Greece made this apparent. We have in general been more fortunate, though conditions in Italy are certainly far from ideal. If we keep on insisting that all liberated countries have the right to select their own governments, then we shall, in the long run, be acting in the best interests of the United States.

No matter how tempting it may be, to support certain governments simply because we like them or have been favored by them is ultimately disastrous. Unpopular governments are unstable and injurious to the economy of a country. It is to our interest to put our weight in the balance on the side for free elections, even in countries which were not involved directly in the war. This applies, of course, particularly to Spain, the last stronghold of fascism in Europe.

Our greatest problems will arise in working out a viable attitude on countries which lie in the Russian sphere of influence, such as, conspicuously, Poland. We undoubtedly want Poland to have free elections and I think we should bring whatever influence we have to get Russia to consent to hold them. This does not mean that a serious breach has to be created or antagonism provoked. We should attempt to make it a point of pride with them, indicate the essential unsoundness of any other approach, and in a spirit of informal, friendly counsel demonstrate that it is necessary to the maintenance of the spirit of unity and co-operation between Russia and the Anglo-Saxon democracies. In doing this, we should avoid any action which could be interpreted by either Russians or Poles as an attempt at misplaced intervention in Polish affairs.

There are two great pitfalls into which American foreign policy is liable to blunder in the next few decades. One lies in the temptation to allow ourselves to go to war or to become involved in situations leading to wars in order to solve our domestic problems. The other is constituted by the temptation to allow wars to develop in other parts of the world in order to do business with one or both sides. Besides the moral reprehensibility and monstrousness of such a policy, it cannot even be recommended on the ground of success. Many people favored appeasement of Japan because it was good for business. We were selling to both Japan and China. In the first month after Pearl Harbor, however, we lost more than everything we had gained from all our Far-Eastern trade during the previous decade. At the same time that we attempt to promote democracy in Europe, it is to our own advantage to do our best to disarm potential aggressors and look forward to the day when objective conditions will favor the formation of the European or world federation which is the only guarantee of a permanent peace.

It must also be realized that the basic concern of Europe today is the conflict between capitalism and collectivism. We cannot take an attitude toward this wholly predicated on our likes and dislikes, but must understand the conditions in Europe which determine the evolutions of its economy. To attempt arbitrarily to corral that economy into the direction we desire will be calamitous. It will be equally calamitous to transfer our own fear of internal change and domestic difficulty to Russia or the European Revolution. We cannot escape the necessity for solving our own problems by making a devil image out of Russia or any other country that develops along somewhat different lines from our own.

I have tried to demonstrate that the Russians anticipate a period of about twenty-five years during which they will try to reconstruct their economy, build up their country, and test their fundamental concepts. It is very probable, too, that during this period there will be a gradual increase of personal liberty and democracy in the Soviet Union — the process is, indeed, already noticeable now. As they experiment and strive to improve themselves and their institutions, the Russians will keep a careful watch on developments in America and Britain, with the desire to learn and with equal willingness to accept or reject our institutions as they prove their efficiency and value.

Many Russians expected capitalism to fall in the early twenties through its own weakness and many believed the Western democracies would not be able to withstand the onslaught of the Nazis. They were wrong both times and they were quick to change their opinion. The British pulled their island together in a gigantic effort, the heroism of which won the admiration, and the efficiency of which earned the respect, of every Russian who witnessed it and millions who read and heard about it. The United States performed a feat which caused the Russians to gape in open-mouthed surprise. A capitalist country, in which private enterprise, compared to the control of the Russian State, was allowed to run wild, hammered its economy into a maximum efficiency within the broad objective of the war effort and in doing so doubled its national income within three years. From $80,000,000,000 in 1939, American income soared to $220,000,000,000 in 1943. (Prices increased some thirty-five per cent.) The Russians, with an economy completely controlled by the State, never achieved any increase of similar size, speed, or significance.

If capitalism in America could accomplish this prodigious feat, doubling its national income, winning a war for which it was not prepared, aiding Russia, England, and all of Europe, without cutting, and in some cases even increasing, consumption, then, as the leaders of the Soviet Union know, it is far from moribund and they can learn much from its methods.

I do not believe that the Russians will reinstate a capitalism, as such, in Russia, merely because it works well in the United States in certain circumstances. But the fact that some Russians at the present time are living on income derived from interest payments on state bonds and deposits in state savings banks is an indication of how far-reaching the modifications are that the Russians are permitting and introducing into their system.

The fact that money derived from such sources is not called 'unearned income' in Russia does not change its character any more than the fact that the new swank Russian private schools, in which officials, stakhanovites, and highly paid technicians can give their children the benefit of a superior education for substantial tuition fees, are called 'Gymnazia' instead of 'public schools,' as they are in England, eliminates the resemblance between them.

Thus, neither Russia nor Europe is a wholly closed corporation.

If we believe in our institutions and wish to see them spread, the best thing we can do is to make them work well, and this is the first, the primary necessity without which whatever foreign policy we develop will be ineffectual. The greatest propaganda for the American system abroad will be our own domestic prosperity and tranquillity.

Many Americans believe that we are outside the sphere of the collectivist revolution and are completely unaffected by it. This is not true. Collectivism was developed as a remedy for the defects of the system of private enterprise, and although whether as a whole it is a successful one remains to be seen, we have nevertheless already adopted many elements of it which have demonstrated their value and efficiency. Countries which are not willing to change with the times lapse into the same decay that afflicted Russia when it lagged behind the rest of the world during the nineteenth century.

There are many in the United States who think they can turn back history and restore the *laisser-faire* economy of capitalism as it was before the first World War, if only the Soviet Union and the menace of bolshevism can be removed. They are just as wrong as those who a century ago believed that Europe could return to domination by hereditary absolute monarchs if only Napoleon and republican France could be destroyed. Napoleon was destroyed, and so, for a time, was republican France, but Europe went right along the road of progress, away from absolute monarchy and toward the institutions of democracy and individual liberty. Analogously, even if the Soviet Union, by some miracle, were to fall tomorrow into the Arctic Sea, the collectivist revolution of the twentieth century would not stop; indeed, many think it might even go faster. If anything, the Russian desire for a twenty-five-year period of peace and stability tends to act as a brake on revolutionary change throughout the world.

I hope and believe that such a period will actually follow the defeat of Germany and Japan. During it a sort of peaceful competition between the modified socialism in the Soviet Union and the modified capitalism of Britain and the United States will probably develop.

If during these crucial years Anglo-Saxon capitalism works efficiently; if during this period the national income continues to rise; if equitable distribution ensures everyone reasonable material welfare and social and economic and racial disorders are prevented by wise leadership and planning, then the modified capitalism of the Anglo-Saxon countries will have justified its continued existence.

If during the same period Soviet economy flourishes, the standard of living rises, unity and peace prevail within the federation of Soviet republics, the socialism of the Soviet Union will likewise have justified its continued existence. In this eventuality the two nations will probably continue to develop peacefully side by side, growing closer generation by generation and benefiting by increased contact, mutual intercourse and understanding.

But if either of these two systems gets into serious difficulties; if, for example, we in the United States undergo another economic crisis similar to that of 1929; if we become involved in wars with other modified capitalist nations; if our racial antagonisms become sharpened instead of eliminated, while concurrently the Soviet Union is having none of these difficulties, then our system will probably become modified in the direction of the Russian system, and the modifying will probably be done, not by Russian agitators, but by the people of the United States. If, on the other hand, the Soviet Union breaks up, or fails to raise its standard of living, or suffers other setbacks, while we in the West prosper, then we can expect to see the return of private economy to the Soviet Union, and this will probably be done, not by American armies, but by the Soviet people.

Thus, the way in which we solve or fail to solve our problems during the next two decades is of tremendous historical import. It means much more than the welfare of a hundred and thirty million Americans. It is a test case for the world. The greatest single problem we face is our own economy. Can we retain enough of personal liberty to remain a democracy and at the same time restrict ourselves sufficiently, using the processes and machinery of democracy, to be able to plan effectively and wisely?

During the last three years we have doubled production and most of the increase of roughly $110,000,000,000 has disappeared in the smoke and flame of war. After the war, we must cut production back to what it was or else increase consumption. If, and preferably, our national income remains at its 1943 level, then we must double consumption. Everyone who has one car must have two cars; those who went on vacation in Florida for two weeks must go for one month. It sounds simple enough, after all. The goods and services are being or can be produced. The only further requirement is to make sure that those who produced these goods and services get a chance to consume them. It sounds simple, but it requires production for consumption instead of for profit, which means planning.

In 1939, there were forty-five million wage-earners in the United States, of whom ten million were women. In 1943, there were sixty-seven million wage-earners, of whom twenty-two million were women. (Of the sixty-seven million, eleven million are in the Armed Forces; of these, three million are women.) The average working week in the United States increased from thirty-five hours in 1939 to forty-seven hours in 1943. If the working week is reduced again to thirty-five hours and if the twelve million women go back to housework, and if consumption is increased by, say fifty per cent, a crisis can be avoided. But if consumption is not increased, then we shall have a crisis of overproduction. There is no valid reason why this problem cannot be solved. The ingenuity and adaptability of the American people have made it possible for us to overcome greater obstacles in the past, specifically during the Civil War and World War II. But never have we been confronted with a more important problem, or one with more far-reaching consequences.

For there is more involved than an economic competition between modified Socialist Russia and modified capitalist United States. It is also a competition between two different systems of thought. America represents, among other things, a measure of personal political liberty which the Soviet Union has not attained, and does not at present even aspire to. I have in mind not the economic liberty of the individual; in this respect the Soviet Union is working toward the same things we are, and at more or less the same level. I mean the liberty to disagree.

Even in times of crisis, America has permitted its dissenters great freedom. Conscientious objectors, for example, have been treated well in the United States. Opposition newspapers of all shades have been published all through the war. Only those publications of unquestionable and violent Fascist character have been suppressed.

I have asked a number of Soviet Russians whether they thought that after the war opposition parties, or organized groups with political opinions that differed from those of the Government, would be permitted in Russia. In every case the answer was 'No.' Not only that, these Russians see no reason to encourage dissension. They see nothing desirable in opposition. They seem satisfied with the present arrangement under which opposition is considered first cousin to treason, and dealt with as such.

There are many reasons for this difference of viewpoint. Perhaps if we had been invaded up to the Mississippi, and lost millions of men reconquering our own country, we should feel differently. But this did not happen to us. It did happen to the Russians.

Explain it as you will, America does stand for a certain freedom of the individual, not only to ourselves, but to millions of people in the world outside America. In solving our problems wisely and well, we shall be defending the freedom of the individual everywhere. In untangling the knotty contradictions between freedom and organization, we shall strike a blow for the rights of all men. In making our economic system work, not by compulsion, but by making all see that planning is necessary and benefits all, we shall blaze a trail for others to follow.

But if, for any reason, we fail in this undertaking, if we allow our economy to crash, or if we sacrifice our liberties, then it will be a dark day for those who, like myself, want to be free to disagree, and still have a decent, well-ordered life.

THE END

Index